THE

PUNJAB AND DELHI IN 1857

THE

PUNJAB AND DELHI

IN 1857

BEING A NARRATIVE OF THE MEASURES BY WHICH THE PUNJAB WAS SAVED AND DELHI RECOVERED DURING THE INDIAN MUTINY

BY THE

REV. J. CAVE-BROWNE

IN TWO VOLUMES
VOL. II.

GYAN

Published by

Gyan Publishing House
5, Ansari Road
Daryaganj, New Delhi-110002
Phone: 011-47034999, 9811692060
E-mail: books@gyanbooks.com

Distribution Network
gyanbooks.com
India, USA, Canada, UK, Australia

ISBN: 978-93-6433-476-1 (Set
978-93-6433-001-5 (HB)
First Published, 1861

2nd Impression 2024

Printed at: Gyan Press, Delhi.

THE PUNJAB AND DELHI IN 1857, (VOL. II.)
Author: J. CAVE-BROWNE

THE

PUNJAB AND DELHI

IN 1857

THE

PUNJAB AND DELHI

IN 1857

BEING A NARRATIVE OF THE MEASURES BY WHICH THE PUNJAB WAS SAVED AND DELHI RECOVERED DURING THE INDIAN MUTINY

BY THE

REV. J. CAVE-BROWNE, M. A.

ASSISTANT-CHAPLAIN, BENGAL PRESIDENCY

CHAPLAIN OF THE PUNJAB MOVEABLE COLUMN IN 1857

VOL. II.

WILLIAM BLACKWOOD AND SONS

EDINBURGH AND LONDON

MDCCCLXI

CONTENTS OF THE SECOND VOLUME.

CHAPTER XI.

[JULY.—PART I.]

CHAPTER XII.

[JULY.—PART II.]

CHAPTER XIII.

[July.—Part III.]

CHAPTER XIV.

[August.—Part I.]

CHAPTER XV.

[August.—Part II.]

CHAPTER XVI.

[August.—Part III.]

CHAPTER XVII.

CHAPTER XVIII.

CHAPTER XIX.

CHAPTER XX.

CHAPTER XXI.

CHAPTER XXII.

APPENDIX.

ILLUSTRATIONS IN THE SECOND VOLUME.

THE PUNJAB AND DELHI IN 1857.

CHAPTER XI.

[JULY 1857. — PART I.]

THE CAMP—ITS REAL DIFFICULTIES—ITS POSITION, AND NUMBERS AS COMPARED WITH THE REBELS—ANOTHER ASSAULT PLANNED AND ABANDONED — POORBEAH TRAITORS IN CAMP — ARRIVAL OF H. M. 61ST AND COKE'S RIFLES, AND OF ROHILCUND BRIGADE IN THE CITY — ALIPORE ATTACKED AND RECOVERED —BRIDGES IN REAR DESTROYED—GENERAL BARNARD'S DEATH —GENERAL REED ASSUMES COMMAND—THREE IRREGULAR CAVALRY REGIMENTS WITHDRAWN—ATTACK ON SUBZEE MUNDEE—CHANGES IN THE STAFF—GENERAL REED RETIRES—BRIGADIER A. WILSON COMMANDS—GREAT IMPROVEMENTS INTRODUCED — NEWS FROM BELOW — THE STATE OF THE CITY — THE KING'S OFFER TO TREAT FOR TERMS — THE QUESTION CONSIDERED — THE ABANDONMENT OF SIEGE THREATENED, AND CONDEMNED BY SIR J. LAWRENCE — THE WITHDRAWAL FROM PESHAWUR DISCUSSED.

A MERE spectator of the momentous drama which was being enacted before Delhi, might have been tempted to regard the scene on which the curtain rose with the month of July as one of improvement everywhere, or at least of increased hopefulness, as compared with that which had been presented a month before.

The army, then struggling onwards for Delhi, was now not only planted on the ridge commanding the city, but apparently strengthened at every point. Not an inch of ground, once gained, had been lost; not a single position once taken had been abandoned; every attack, from whatever quarter, or however formidable, had been repulsed, and that with some advantage gained. Before the retreating rebels one point after another had fallen into our hands, to be thenceforth held by strong picquets or advanced batteries; while the loss of the enemy was reported to be almost fabulously severe. Moreover, reinforcements had come in during the end of June, and more were reported to be on the way. Thus the little handful of English were boldly holding their own, and seeming to gain ground. Ever and anon would float up whispered rumours of a coming assault. All this tended to raise hope in the camp itself, as well as in the Punjab.

But men the while forgot, or perhaps willingly kept out of mind, at how great sacrifice this position was being held; they would not reflect that every advance made, every sortie repulsed, had cost the little band men they could ill spare, and perhaps never replace; that one hundred lost on our side were not to be compensated for the loss of a thousand on theirs. Little was said of the pyrrhic character of the triumphs we were gaining, or of the fact—for such it was—that all the reinforcements so joyously hailed in camp, and so loudly proclaimed back to the Punjab, did little more than fill up the gaps which fatal disease, sunstroke, and fatigue, even more than the bullets and round-shot of the enemy, had made in our ranks. Occasionally, indeed, a complaint would be heard of want of order in the camp; no system of relief to save and husband the men's strength; the advice of youthful members of the staff listened to, and the counsels of older war-trained officers disregarded; attacks planned and abandoned; orders and counter-orders following each other with bewildering rapidity. But when the wish was father to the thought that all was steady progress; where men hoped all was well, they would not believe it could be otherwise; they would seize the daily bulletins (so wisely issued by the Judicial Commissioner from Lahore to give confidence), and seeing there no mention of these *desagremens,* would at once set down the authors of such complaints as croakers or disappointed men, and condemn them as lacking proper *esprit de corps,* and every sort of spirit that became a soldier. So the best was caught at, and believed.

Yet under this surface, so smooth and bright and hopeful, there *would* flow an under-current of doubt and misgiving, even among men who did not know the whole truth. What then thought they who were behind the scenes, who did know all? They found it, if truth be told, far easier to impart to others, who were in hopeful ignorance, a confidence which they hoped might after all be justified by the result, than to quiet their own fears and doubts as to the possible issue.

July was, with all its little glimpses of breaking light, the darkest month during the whole siege.

Let the reader transplant himself in imagination to the camp, and take a brief survey of our position. We hold the old cantonment as our camping-ground, with the ridge, about two miles in length, the only high ground for miles around, along our front. On the left flows the Jumna, which, with picquets run out at Metcalfe House and stables to the very edge of the sands, effectually secures that flank; along the rear runs a deep canal, only to be crossed by one bridge, which is strongly held by picquets of horse and foot and a couple of guns; while to the right-rear of the camp, commanding the open ground between the canal and the ridge, is a small mound, held by picquets of all arms, with two batteries of heavy and light guns; but on the right flank itself, where the ridge is abruptly broken, stand three batteries and a massive breastwork, held by strong picquets of Rifles and Goorkhas; and in the Subzee Mundee suburb the Sammy House and Serai, held in force, to protect this our weakest and most exposed point.

Such was the position of the camp, with a force of all arms, native and European, under 5800 effective,* to hold it. Now, this force, distributed as it was to the best advantage, could scarcely cover a sixth part of the city walls. Our guns could only command two of the seven gates on the land side—the Cashmere and

* Of non-effectives there were already in camp nearly 1000, including sick and wounded.

Cabul gates—leaving the other five, and among them *the Lahoree Durwaza*, the main entrance of the city, wholly undisputed; while on the river side all was their own, the Jumna flowing up to the walls, and the bridge of boats, about 2500 yards from our nearest guns, giving them undisturbed command of the whole Doab for supplies and reinforcements. Then as for ammunition, the magazine, with its inexhaustible store, was in their hands, while every rebel detachment that joined them brought in more. Their resources in this branch were constantly shown; a gun silenced and perhaps knocked over at night, would be always replaced by a new one before daylight.

In short, it was a struggle between a mere handful of men along the open ridge, and *a host* behind massive and well-fortified walls. To settle down for a systematic siege, according to the prescribed rules of warfare, was out of the question: instead of the besiegers being three to one of the besieged, we could scarce have brought into the field one armed man to their ten. So the abandonment of the siege was gravely spoken of, and but for the firm resolve of Sir John Lawrence it would have been carried out. General Barnard, in command of the force, found himself in a position he would never willingly have taken up. Mr Greathed,* the Commissioner, as belonging to the North-west Province, was not very cordial in acknowledging the authority of the Punjab government, and was ever looking to Agra for his instructions, and ready to second the withdrawal from

* GREATHED'S *Letters, passim.*

Delhi, on the ground that it was more important to restore authority in the Doab, and to reopen communication between Meerut and its seat of government, Agra. However, the remonstrances of Sir John Lawrence prevailed, and for the time the idea of retreat was put off. Still the progress was slow and wearying; and some of the bolder and more daring spirits in camp revived the old project of *an assault*. The best that could be said of it was that it was only a forlorn hope; and the worst, that it was a little better than "a defeated gamester's throw."

It was decided on; the whole plan was concocted, those only who were to take part in it were admitted to the secret. One column was to effect an entrance by blowing in the iron grating of the canal near the Cabul Gate, another column to enter the Cashmere Gate after it had been blown in, a third column to escalade the Cashmere Bastion, and a detachment, creeping round by the river-side, to endeavour to effect an entrance in that direction.* And all was ready for the venture—when all was suddenly abandoned. The secret, so well kept in camp that even some of the General's staff were sleeping soundly that night in blissful ignorance of what was in contemplation, was no secret in the city. The rebels, who knew every movement and every plan, were on the alert; a large body had been moved down by a circuitous route into a large walled garden, about two miles to our rear; and while the storming party, allowed to make their way in silence up to the palace

* NORMAN'S *Narrative*.

gateway, would there have found the guard waiting for them, the ambuscade on our rear would have rushed into camp, mastered the guards, and all have been lost. It was this intelligence, opportunely brought to the General's tent, that saved the camp — and thus ended the second and last attempt at carrying the city *by coup-de-main.*

It was clear that there must be traitors in camp, even among the choice few that composed our native force. Yet where could they be? There were the noble little Sirmooree Goorkhas, under Reid, holding on fearlessly and resolutely at their post of honour and of danger, at Hindoo Rao's house; there were Rothney's Sikhs, never flinching nor flagging; the Guides everywhere covering themselves with glory; Hodson's Horse, with their intrepid leader, winning golden opinions; and Coke's Rifles, who had more recently joined, giving promise of good and faithful service: still there was something wrong; desertions would occur; every plan and movement seemed known to the enemy—even that most secretly concocted assault. Then another circumstance aroused suspicion; the loss of European officers in some of these corps had been beyond all proportion to the men who had fallen. In the Guides, Quintin Battye had been killed; Daly, the commandant, Kennedy the adjutant, Hawes, Shebbeare, De Brett (57th N. I. doing duty), Chalmers (3d N.I.), Murray (42d N.I.), all wounded—some twice, and and even three times: twice had the complement been replenished, and twice knocked over. In the 4th Sikhs, too, who had only lately arrived, already had Yorke (of the 3d N. I.) been killed, and Packe (4th N.I.) and Pullan (36th N. I.) been wounded. Now, even the gallantry and rash daring of young blood could scarcely account for such a list of casualties: moreover, some had been noticed to fall unaccountably at moments when the enemy were not firing! This had led men to wonder: when the whole was discovered and disclosed. In the Guide corps, as a part of its very constitution, was a Poorbeah company, and the 4th Sikhs and other Punjab corps, though mainly composed of Punjabees, contained some Poorbeahs. Here were the traitors; many of the officers had been shot down, not by the enemy at all, but by the Poorbeahs of their own corps! Then came further disclosures, not only of spies and traitors, but of emissaries of treason from the King; some of the leading Poorbeahs were systematically tampering with the loyalty of the Sikhs and Punjabees, with offers of high pay in the King's service. All this was brought to light on the 2d of July.* One of these traitors was shot down on the spot by a faithful Sikh while attempting to tamper with him, and three more were given up and hanged the same evening; and before nightfall the entire lot of Poorbeahs in the several corps were cleared out; and the whole camp experienced a feeling of relief.

Allusion has been made to the arrival of Coke's Rifles, who, after their little exploit at Loodiana, had pushed on for Delhi. The camp had the day before

* GREATHED'S *Letters, &c.*, p. 90.

received another valuable reinforcement. The right wing and headquarters of H. M. 61st had been moved down from Ferozepore under Colonel W. Jones, C.B., who, on hearing of the losses sustained at Badlee Serai, and being set free by the dispersion of the mutineers of the 45th and 57th N. I. at Ferozepore, had written to offer half his regiment. On the morning of the 1st they marched into camp to the thrilling notes of "Cheer, boys, Cheer!"*

But as if to qualify the joy caused by their arrival, at the very time they were being welcomed to the ridge, 450 strong, a force about ten times as strong was encamping on the opposite bank of the Jumna. The Bareilly, or more properly Rohilcund, brigade, which had been for many days threatening to advance on Meerut, and filling that garrison with consternation by its unwelcome proximity, had at length, to their great relief, moved off and marched for Delhi; and here they arrived in full force, the 8th Irregular Cavalry, the 18th, 20th, 29th, and 68th Regiments of Native Infantry, with 6 guns of Captain Gravenor Kirby's battery under Mahomed Bukht Khan, whilome a subahdar of artillery, and now General of the Brigade. The river had been rising rapidly during the end of June, and had broken the bridge, so that this force had to resort to the more tedious process of crossing in boats; but even this they were able to accomplish without any opposition. Not one of our guns could

* It was the first regimental band which had been brought to Delhi, and was all the more welcome.

touch them—there were no *Armstrongs* on the ridge—and two days after the bridge was repaired, when a long line of above 400 carts laden with treasure, elephants, camels, and horses almost without number, might be seen filing over and up the causeway into the Calcutta Gate. On the same day came 35 Sikhs, of the regiment of Loodiana,* from Benares, bringing the cheering assurance that mutiny had triumphed even to the borders of Bengal.

The arrival of this strong force foreboded more immediate danger to the camp than was anticipated. From their spies the rebels had been duly apprised of the expected arrival of a convoy from Umballa, and also of a large number of sick being sent off to the hills; so instead of carrying out their original design (for which our spies had prepared us) of a desperate attack in full force on our right flank, the Rohilcund and Nusserabad brigades moved out of the Lahore Gate and bore away in a westerly direction. A strong force was at once sent out from camp to follow them up, and, if possible, cut them off; but the country had been so flooded by the heavy rains, that when our party did come in sight, they found themselves hopelessly separated from the rebels by a wide jheel, and were compelled to retire *re infecta*.

The object of the rebels remained a mystery until next morning, when it was found that Aleepore, the first station on our rear along the Kurnal road, which had always been friendly to us, and was held by a small

* They had mutinied at Benares on the 4th of June.

detachment, was the point of attack. Here they thought to intercept our convoy of—so city report said—11 lakhs of treasure, besides other desirables from Ferozepore, and to kill all our sick. However, the sick had passed on the day before, and the convoy had been delayed one day on the road, so the rebels were doubly disappointed, and could only vent their fury on the poor Sikh guard, and punish the loyalty of the villagers by plundering and then burning their houses to the ground. But they were soon avenged. The next morning brought in tidings of the attack, and off started a second column, consisting of the wing of H. M. 61st, with Coke's Rifles and the Guide Cavalry, all under Major Coke. They came upon the rebels while leisurely retiring to the city, had a severe encounter, killed about 200 with trifling loss to themselves, and, having recovered and regarrisoned Aleepore, returned that night to camp. Before daybreak on the morning of the 6th, a small force of some 300 men, under Captain Brookes of H. M. 75th, went out to meet the convoy, and escorted in in safety the treasure and ammunition which had had so narrow an escape of falling into the hands of the rebels.

This attack on Aleepore, while it showed that the rebels, finding themselves unable to make any impression on our front, were beginning to turn their thoughts again towards our rear, made the authorities realise more fully the danger which threatened us from that quarter. The whole road, above 70 miles in length, which connected our camp with Kurnal, and was in reality the main artery of our military system before Delhi, was only protected by a few Sikhs, some Jheend Horse, some newly-raised police, and a few guns, distributed in small detachments at the several camping-grounds along the line of road. During the latter part of June the constant passage of troops had kept the road comparatively safe; but now that the stream of reinforcements had wellnigh spent itself, the danger was becoming imminent. Had the rebels once gained a footing at any point, our communication with the Punjab would have been at an end, our supplies would have been cut off, the besiegers have become in reality besieged, and the army starved out. That the rebels did not at this time organise such an attack can only be accounted for by a recognition of the intervention of that Providence which had favoured us throughout. No such attack was made in this our time of weakness; and when it was attempted, in the month of August, we were happily in a position to avert the danger. However, the only precautions we now could take were taken, if not to prevent, at any rate to render the attempt less easy. The canal from the Nujjufghur Jheel, running nearly parallel with the main road for many miles, presented itself as our natural ally, which we might call in to our aid. It was crossed at various points by bridges of massive stonework, and by blowing up these the canal would present an almost impassable barrier; so a strong engineering party was sent out to destroy all these bridges for some miles, only retaining the one at the rear of the camp for our own use.

The most important of these was the one called the Bussaye Bridge ; this was destroyed on the 8th of July. "This," said one of the party, "was the most fatiguing day's work we had yet had." A strong force of all arms, comprising twelve guns, two squadrons of cavalry, detachments of H. M. 8th and 61st, the 2d battalion of Fusiliers, and Coke's Rifles, in all above 1500 strong, under Brigadier Longfeild of H. M. 8th regiment, went out as escort to the engineering party. After marching for two miles along the road, they crossed the canal and turned off to the left ; and then began the labour. The rain had fallen very heavily for some days, and the waters were out on all sides ; for five miles did the force drag itself along over those flooded ploughed fields, the infantry ankle-deep in mud, the cavalry up to the saddle-girths in water, and the guns perpetually brought to a stand-still in the furrows. However, on they pushed in spite of water below and a scorching sun overhead, and accomplished their task without seeing a single enemy.

On returning to camp in the afternoon, they learned how it was they had met with no opposition. The rebels had been otherwise engaged. The departure of so large a body from camp could not fail to be observed or reported by the spies in the city ; and under the belief that nearly our whole force had gone out, and that all our guards and batteries had been greatly weakened, Pandy thought to make easy work of the few that remained ; so they poured out in full strength, and made a desperate attack on the Subzee Mundee picquet. However, a steadier resistance awaited them than they anticipated. From its extremely exposed position, this picquet was always strongly held, and four companies of the 2d Fusiliers turned out to receive them. Supports of the 60th Rifles and of 1st Fusiliers soon came down to their help, and a hard fight ensued. The rebels had been deluded into coming too near, and they paid dearly for their rashness by leaving some 400 on the field. One party, about 160 in number, thought to take shelter in a serai, but soon found out their mistake. The Europeans forced the gate, rushed in, and not a man escaped; while the loss on the part of our troops was comparatively slight.

Another piece of engineering work was achieved about the same time. One of the greatest monuments of a bygone Mohammedan period is a gigantic aqueduct, by which water was brought a distance of many miles into the heart of the city. It crosses the canal by a bridge known as the *Pool-Chuddur*, by which horsemen were enabled to pass to our rear. This was also blown up, and a double end thereby gained; the passage of the horsemen obstructed, and the water cut off from the city; though the latter was a matter of less importance, from the city being on the banks of a river, and also abounding in wells.*

An event, however, had in the meanwhile occurred in camp, which demands especial notice. It has been mentioned that from the very first, cholera, that scourge of India, had made its appearance among the troops. It

* NORMAN'S *Narrative.*

had been committing its ravages with more or less severity ever since the advance from Umballa. One of its earliest victims had been General Anson, who died at Kurnal while marching down to Delhi; and now General Sir H. Barnard, who had succeeded to the command of the force, was destined to add another to the long list of its victims. On the morning of Sunday the 5th July, the first symptoms of the disease manifested themselves, and by three o'clock in the afternoon he had succumbed to its violence. Rarely has a general been followed to his grave with deeper feelings of personal respect than was Sir H. Barnard. "Brave, kind-hearted, and hospitable, it is doubtful if he had an enemy; he was regretted by the whole force, and most by those who knew him best." So wrote one who, from his office, and from the ready zeal and judgment with which he throughout performed its duties, was among those who knew him best.* "He was a high-minded excellent officer," wrote the leading civilian in camp, "and on European ground, and in a European war, would have done the State good service."† But in that camp it was felt by all, and perhaps by none more so than by the General himself, that he was in a false position. His whole military experience had been confined to the few months of the Crimean war.‡ Of even ordinary service in India,

* Lieut. Norman, in his *Narrative.*

† GREATHED'S *Letters*, p. 94.

‡ "A Crimean education is not the best for this service. Having the sea close at hand, there was no care about communications; and

with an army so differently constituted, he had had no experience at all; and now, within a few weeks after his arrival in the country, he found himself at the head of a force, on a service that was without parallel or precedent even in Indian warfare. General affability and hearty courtesy, stamped him the English gentleman, and won for him the personal regard of the whole force. The brave old man never spared himself when duty called; he never shrank from work nor shunned danger; but palpable inexperience and consequent want of firmness lost him confidence as the head; men regarded him as a friend, but could not look up to him as a general. At length the sense of responsibility weighed him down, anxiety of mind and constant exposure to sun and rain had been for some days telling upon him, and predisposed him to the disease; and, his frame already too severely taxed to bear up under it, he sank after a short six hours of suffering. "Tell them I die happy," was his solemn parting charge to his heart-broken son, who lovingly watched his dying bed.*

General Reed, as the senior officer in the Punjab, and hence provisional Commander-in-Chief, now assumed the personal command of the Delhi field-force.

Allusion has been made to the discovery of treachery among the Poorbeah sepoys in the Irregular Infantry

in estimating the amount of resistance to be expected within the walls, the General is disposed to treat the Pandies as Russians."—GREATHED'S *Letters*, p. 92.

* ROTTON'S *Narrative of the Siege*, p. 117.

corps; the camp was now to be startled into a conviction that the presence of the Irregular Cavalry regiments was no less fraught with danger. There were a wing of the 9th Irregular Cavalry, under Captain A. B. Fenwick, from Hosheyarpore; a wing of the 17th Irregular Cavalry, under Captain P. R. Hockin, from Shumshabad; and a wing of the 1st Punjab Cavalry, under Captain W. T. Hughes, so gallantly brought in from Asnee. All three had more or less a Poorbeah leaven: the 9th, though most strongly vouched for, really lay under the greatest suspicion, while the 1st Punjab Cavalry stood the highest in favour.

All doubt, however, was removed on the morning of the 9th of July. The account of this day's adventure is so lucidly and graphically given by Captain Norman in his official report of the siege, that the reader shall have it *in extenso*:—

"About ten o'clock," he says, "the insurgents appeared to be increasing in numbers in the suburbs on our right, when suddenly a body of cavalry emerged from cover on the extreme right of our right flank, and charged into camp.

"There was a mound on our right on which was placed a battery of three 18-pounders, with an infantry picquet, all facing the Subzee Mundee suburb. To the right of the mound, on the low ground, was a picquet of two horse-artillery guns and a troop of dragoons, the guns being this day furnished by Major Tombs' troop, and commanded by Lieutenant Hills; the cavalry from the Carabineers, and commanded by Lieutenant Stillman. Still further to the right, at a faqueer's inclosure, was a native officer's picquet of the 9th Irregulars, from which two videttes were thrown forward some 200 yards on the trunk-road. These videttes could see down the road towards Delhi as far as our picquet at the Serai—perhaps 700 or 800 yards, and up the road to the canal-cut, about 200 yards. Across the road were rather dense gardens.

"The place at which the videttes were posted was not visible from camp; and some horsemen in white advancing attracted but little notice, their dress being the same as that of the 9th Irregulars, from which corps the faqueer's picquet was taken.

"Some alarm, however, arose, and the two horse-artillery guns at the picquet were got ready; but the leading cavalry insurgents, beckoning men in their rear, dashed on at speed, and the troop of Carabineers, all very young, most of them untrained soldiers, and only thirty-two in number of all ranks, turned and broke, save the officer and two or three men, who nobly stood. Lieutenant Hills, commanding the guns, seeing the cavalry come on unopposed, alone charged the head of their horsemen, to give his guns time to unlimber, and cut down one or two of the sowars, while the main body of horsemen, riding over and past the guns, followed up the Carabineers, and a confused mass of horsemen came streaming in at the right of camp.

"Major Tombs, whose tent was on the right, had heard the first alarm, and, calling for his horse to be brought after him, walked towards the picquet just as the cavalry came on. He was just in time to see his gallant subaltern down on the ground, with one of the enemy's sowars ready to kill him. From a distance of thirty yards he fired with his revolver, and dropped Hills' opponent.* Hills got up and engaged a man

* Lieutenant Hills appears to be as capable of wielding his pen as his sword. His account of the adventure, written in all the freedom of friendship to an old chum, and published in the *Times* newspaper, is too good to be lost:—"The alarm went, and off I started with my two guns to a position laid down for them, when, to my astonishment, through an opening on my right, only fifty yards off, dashed a body of cavalry. Now I tried to get my guns into action, but only got one unlimbered when they were upon me. I thought that by charging

on foot, who was cut down by Tombs,* after Hills had received a severe sabre-cut on the head.

"Meanwhile great confusion had been caused by the inroad of the sowars, most of whom made for the guns of the native

them I might make a commotion, and give the gun time to load; so in I went at the front rank, cut down the first fellow, slashed the next across the face as hard as I could, when two sowars charged me. Both their horses crashed into mine at the same moment, and of course both horse and myself were sent flying. We went down at such a pace that I escaped the cuts made at me, one of them giving my jacket an awful slice just below the left arm—it only, however, cut the jacket. Well, I lay quite snug until all had passed over me, and then got up and looked about for my sword. I found it full ten yards off. I had hardly got hold of it when three fellows returned—two on horseback. The first I wounded, and dropt him from his horse; the second charged me with a lance—I put it aside, and caught him an awful gash on the head and face. I thought I had killed him; apparently he must have clung to his horse, for he disappeared. The wounded man then came up, but got his skull split. Then came on the third man—a young, active fellow. I found myself getting very weak from want of breath, the fall from my horse having pumped me considerably, and my cloak somehow or other had got tightly fixed round my throat, and was kindly choking me. I went, however, at the fellow, and cut him on the shoulder; but some 'kupra' (cloth) on it apparently turned the blow. He managed to seize the hilt of my sword, and twisted it out of my hand; and then we had a hand-to-hand fight, I punching his head with my fists, and he trying to cut me, but I was too close to him. Somehow or other I fell, and then was the time, fortunately for me, that Tombs came up and shot the fellow. I was so choked by my cloak that move I could not until I got it loosened. By the by, I forgot to say that I fired at this chap twice, but the pistol snapped, and I was so enraged I drove it at the fellow's head, missing him, however. Then, when I got up, Tombs was so eager to get up to a mound near us, that I only picked up my sword and followed him. After being there some time, we came down again to look after the unlimbered gun which was left behind. When we got down I saw the very man Tombs had saved me from, moving off with my pistol (he had only been wounded, and shammed dead). I told Tombs, and we went at him. After a little slashing and guarding at both sides, I rushed in at him and thrust; he

* "Tombs' account of the affair of the 9th, when the enemy's horse rode through our camp, was torn up by Colonel Mackenzie. He had omitted to say a word about himself, so Mackenzie gave the General the true version."—GREATHED's *Letters*, p. 119.

troop horse-artillery, which was on the right of camp, calling on the men to join them. The native horse-artillerymen, however, behaved admirably, and called to Major Olpherts' European troop, which was then unlimbered close by, to fire *through them* at the mutineers. The latter, however, managed to secure and carry off some horses, and several followers were cut down in camp. Captain Fagan,* of Artillery, rushing out of his tent, got together a few men, and followed up some of the sowars, who were then endeavouring to get away, and killed fifteen of them. More were killed by some men of the 1st brigade, and all were driven out of camp, some escaping by a bridge over the canal-cut in our rear. It is not estimated that more than one hundred sowars were engaged in this en-

cleverly jumped aside and cut me on the head, knocking me down—not, however, stunning me, for I warded his next cut when down. Tombs, following him up, made him a pass, and up I jumped and had a slash at him, cutting him on the left wrist, nearly severing it. This made him turn round, and then Tombs ran him through. He very nearly knocked over Tombs, for he cut through his cap and pagrie, but, fortunately, did not even cut the skin. I fancy I am indebted again to Tombs for my life, for although I might have got up and fought, still I was bleeding like a pig, and, of course, would have had a bad chance. One thing, however, if Tombs had not been there the second time, I should have fought more carefully. It was the wish to polish off the fellow before Tombs could get up to him, that made me rush at him in the way I did. I wanted awfully to bone the swords of the men I killed as trophies, but I was getting very faint, and had to come into my tent as fast as I could; but before I got the wound bound up the swords had been looted off. I lost an awful lot of blood, as two veins were cut through; but I fancy it did me good, keeping off inflammation. The wound was a beautiful one, just as if it had been done by a razor. It was four inches long, and down to the skull, a line being left on it; so I had a narrow escape. However, if I live to see the end of these mutinies, I shall have good reason to thank the 'Sowars' for their charge, Tombs's name and mine having been sent up to the Governor-General by the Commander-in-Chief, the latter recommending us 'worthy of the highest honour for distinguished bravery and gallantry.'" *Both received Victoria Crosses.*

* "Fagan was writing at the time, and had only a pen in his hand when he started; but he came back with a sword and minié carbine, of which he had relieved a ressaldar of the 8th Cavalry."—GREATHED'S *Letters*, p. 105.

terprise, and about thirty-five were killed, including a native officer.

"All this time the cannonade from the city and from many field-guns outside raged fast and furious, and a heavy fire of musketry was kept up upon our batteries and on the Subzee Mundee picquets from the enclosures and gardens of the suburbs.

"A column was therefore formed to dislodge them, consisting of Major Scott's horse-battery, the available men of the wing, 8th and 61st Foot and 4th Sikh infantry—in all, about 700 infantry and six guns, reinforced *en route* by the headquarters and two companies of the 60th Rifles under Lieutenant-Colonel J. Jones; the infantry brigade being commanded by Brigadier W. Jones, C.B., and Brigadier-General Chamberlain directing the whole. As this column swept up through the Subzee Mundee, Major Reid was instructed to move down and co-operate with such infantry as could be spared from the main picquet. The insurgents were cleared out of the gardens without difficulty, though the denseness of the vegetation rendered the mere operation of passing through them a work of time. At some of the serais, however, a very obstinate resistance was made, and the insurgents were not dislodged without considerable loss. Eventually everything was effected that was desired, our success being greatly aided by the admirable and steady practice of Major Scott's battery under a heavy fire, eleven men being put *hors de combat* out of its small complement.

"By sunset the engagement was over, and the troops returned to camp drenched through with rain, which for several hours had fallen at intervals with great violence.

"Our loss this day was one officer and forty men killed; eight officers and one hundred and sixty-three men wounded; eleven men missing.*

* The casualties on this memorable day were as follows:—Lieutenant Mountsteven, H. M. 8th, killed; Captain Daniell, H. M. 8th; Captain Burnside, H. M. 61st; Lieutenant Griffith, do.; Ensign Andros, do.;

"The enemy must have lost near five hundred men, most of whom were killed on the spot.

"The exact circumstances of the inroad of the cavalry into camp were never correctly ascertained;* but there seems little reason to doubt there was some treachery on the part of the picquet of the 9th Irregulars; and the insurgent cavalry evidently reckoned upon assistance in our camp, particularly from the native troop of horse-artillery, who, however, behaved nobly."

Thus the danger was averted; but the adventure taught two lessons: the first was, that it was not wise to leave guns and a picquet on the most exposed point of our position in the charge of native guards alone; and the second, that it was not safe to keep in camp any corps containing so strong a Hindostanee element as the Irregular Cavalry. The result of a first lesson was, that H. M. 75th were moved out to the right to supply guards for the guns and picquets on the Subzee Mundee flank; while the second had been as promptly acted upon. Doubts had been often and strongly expressed of the fidelity of these corps, but they had powerful friends in camp, foremost among them Brigadier Neville Chamberlain, whose former connection with the 9th, and the loyal protestations of his old friends among the native officers, not unnaturally made him their champion. However, that there

Lieutenant Hills, Bengal Artillery; Captain Kemp (5th N. I.), with 2d Fusiliers; Lieutenant Eckford (69th N. I.), with Goorkhas; and Pullan (36th N. I.), with 4th Sikhs, wounded.

* It was openly said *in the city*, according to our spies, that the attack was preconcerted between the rebels of the 8th Irregular Cavalry and the picquet of the 9th.

had been treachery on the 9th no one doubted; and a peremptory order came down from Sir John Lawrence for the immediate removal of all three corps from camp; the 9th and 17th * were sent back into the Punjab, and the 1st found occupation in the neighbourhood of Umballa.

In the beginning of the month there had been a comparative lull, which was broken by the attack on the 8th and the adventure of the 9th; then came another lull of four days, but on the morning of the 14th it was clear that the rebels meant to give us a day's work. Out they streamed from the Lahore Gate through the Kissengunge suburb, and advanced upon our Subzee Mundee picquet. This flank, however, had been within the last few days considerably strengthened. A guard of the 75th had taken possession; a strong breastwork had been run up on the crest of the ridge; while a fresh battery had been mounted to command the approach from this point. On came the rebels, as usual, under cover of the gardens and the

* Proof was soon given that the 9th was not the only corps that contained traitors. The night before the order was given for the withdrawal of these corps from camp, a trusty native officer of the 17th reported to Captain Hockin that there were several men, all in one squadron of the left wing, who were resolved to desert and make for the city as the regiment marched out; this they could the more easily effect from that troop being in the rear in the line of march. The only notice Captain Hockin took of this information was to insert, in the regimental orders for the line of march, "Left in front." By this arrangement the would-be deserters found themselves in front, with the whole regiment at their backs! Thus outmanœuvred, they marched on in sullen silence, and Captain Hockin brought away his men intact, and on arrival at Ferozepore quietly made over the traitors to the authorities.

ruined houses; but our men now had shelter also, and orders had been given that not a man should move from under cover of the breastworks. Here, strengthened by another body of the 75th and some of Coke's Rifles, they maintained the defensive, and at the same time did considerable execution whenever any Pandies came from under cover and ventured too near. The fighting had gone on for some hours in this manner; the men were beginning to fret at the restraint; they panted for the order to be "up and at them," when about 4 o'clock in the afternoon, to their great joy, permission was given to clear the Subzee Mundee. A column was formed, consisting of detachments of H. M. 75th, the 1st Europeans, Coke's Rifles, and six guns from Scott's battery, the whole under Brigadier Chamberlain. The order once given to advance, first over the breastwork sprang Chamberlain himself, and the day's work began in earnest. At the sight of our advancing column, the rebels, as usual, took to their heels; a pursuit ensued down the main street, through the by-lanes, over garden-walls—wherever a Pandy skulked our fellows followed; and, if a truthful one, the list of casualties sent into the King that day must have been a more than usually heavy one. A thorough clearance of Subzee Mundee was made.

Well had it been had the pursuit ceased here; but as the rebels scampered on in hundreds for the Lahore Gate, our men pressed on in full career, until unhappily they were carried away, and never stopped until they came within musketry-range of the city walls. Here they began to fall fast, and a retreat was ordered. No sooner did they retire than the rebels poured out again, though prudently keeping within cover of their own guns. At this moment Hodson, "who always turns up in moments of difficulty,"* arrived with some of his horse; a dashing charge sent the rebels again flying, and our column was drawn off without further loss. Yet dearly did we pay for the over-daring advance, a return of 15 killed and 150 wounded made a sad gap in our little body of effectives. The loss most heavily felt in camp was that of Brigadier Chamberlain himself, who had the bone of his left arm splintered by a grape-shot; for as Adjutant-General of the army, men had already learned to look to him as the life of the force.

A great change had gradually been taking place in the staff of the army. Major Laughton, who, being the chief engineer officer of that division, had accompanied the force from Umballa, had, in the end of June, been recalled into the Punjab; and Colonel Baird Smith, an officer of some distinction in that corps, had been summoned down from Roorkee to succeed him, and joined the force on the 13th, Lieutenant Alexander Taylor holding the post during the interval; Brigadier Graves had also been obliged to go to the hills for change of air, and Colonel W. Jones of 61st succeeded him. Then General Reed, who had been from the first so great an invalid as to be utterly incapable of taking any active part, and whose debility and disease increased under the discomforts of camp life,

* GREATHED'S *Letters*, p. 122.

had resolved upon retiring; the question of a successor greatly occupied men's minds, for all felt how much depended upon the choice. But for his recent wound, it is more than probable that Brigadier Chamberlain, a man in whom the whole force had confidence, would have been selected.* Next to him in public esteem came Brigadier Archdale Wilson, whose successes on the Hindon, followed by his masterly arrangements at Budlee-Serai, had already given good proof of generalship, and therefore the army was well prepared to receive him as its new general.† Colonel G. Congreve, C.B., of H. M. 29th, Quartermaster-General of Queen's troops, being the senior officer with the force, entered a protest against what he considered a supercession of his own claims, and retired to Simla. Colonel T. Seaton, C.B., was appointed to officiate for Brigadier Chamberlain as Adjutant-General; while the more laborious duties of that office were, throughout the siege, performed with a rare combination of courage, energy, judgment, and courtesy, by Lieut. H. W. Norman.

Scarcely had Brigadier Wilson assumed the command, when the rebels inaugurated his promotion by another desperate attack on our right flank on the 18th; it had been promised the day before, so our spies said, for a large accession from Jhansi had arrived in the city on the 16th, consisting of the 14th Irregular Cavalry, the 12th N. I., and a light field-battery.

According to custom, the new-comers were to try their hand on our batteries in all the freshness of their

* ROTTON'S *Siege of Delhi*, p. 143.

† See Appendix K.

mutinous zeal; however, a day's rest was given them, and on the morning of the 18th they turned out in force. The camp had been put on its guard the day before, and the friendly Rujjub Ali repeated his warning, that a force of some 12,000 infantry were to occupy Aleepore, and when the British went out to the rescue, a rush would be made upon the camp. "So take care and be warned in time." The warning was not thrown away. The rebels, however, only carried out one-half of their plan, and that but feebly. From some cause or other,* the attempt upon Aleepore was abandoned altogether, and the day's work confined to the attack on our position. Directly the alarm sounded, the main picquet at Hindoo Raos' was strengthened by an additional 100 of the 60th Rifles, and after some hours of desultory interchange of shots between the rebels skulking about under shelter of the Subzee Mundee walls and gardens, and our men under cover of the breastworks, an order was given to form a column for the clearance of the suburb, composed of detachments of H. M. 8th, 61st, and 75th, and of the 2d Bengal Fusiliers, with two companies of Coke's Rifles, and some of Hodson's Horse, and four guns, under Colonel J. Jones of the 60th Rifles. As on the 14th, at the first signs of our advance the rebels began to retreat; then followed the

* They had intelligence that a large convoy of stores was expected in camp, and thought to cut it off; and, no doubt, subsequent intelligence reached them that General Reed, on leaving camp on the 17th, had been escorted by a squadron of Dragoons, some Punjab Cavalry, and 200 of the Guides, which opportunity served as a return escort for the convoy; and the rebels had no fancy for contesting it with such a force.

usual rat-hunting process; the streets, lanes, and serais were all cleared out, and the retreat became a scamper for the Lahore Gate. But the affair of the 14th had taught a lesson by which Colonel Jones benefited. Having cleared the village and remained in position for some time, he was ordered to retire, for the object of the day was accomplished. The generalship displayed by Colonel Jones in withdrawing his men was the subject of general praise; it was effected so gradually, the guns being worked all the while, that the rebels made no attempt at rallying, and the loss on our side was comparatively trifling; the only casualties of the day among the officers being Lieutenant Crozier of H. M. 75th killed, and Lieutenant Walker (45th N. I.) doing duty with the 2d Fusiliers, who was struck down by *coup de soleil,* and died almost immediately; though there were nearly 60 rank and file killed and wounded; while the loss on the part of the enemy was evidently very severe. The enemy gave out they would repeat the attack four days consecutively; however, the 19th passed over quietly, so did the 20th; till late in the afternoon, when a feeble demonstration was made by the enemy, but it ended in nothing.

That evening, a gloom was thrown over the camp by the death of Captain Greensill of H. M. 24th, an officer of considerable engineering talent, who had volunteered to join the force in that department. He had been sent out with a small party to reconnoitre; separating from his party to make one round while they made another, he came up to join them at the picquet, but was not recognised from the darkness of the night; he was challenged, and his answer, if given, was not heard, and the sentry fired. He fell mortally wounded, and after lingering for some hours in great agony, died early on the following morning.

On the 21st and 22d the alarm sounded, but both days passed over without any fighting. This was almost regarded as a disappointment on the 21st, for this had been promised as a day of great things. The old King boasted of that appendage to royalty, an horologer, Pundit Hurree Chunder, who claimed to read the heavens, and had declared this year that the sepoys would rule over India. The stars had pointed out to him the 21st day of July as the great day which was to witness the triumph of the Emperor of Hindostan. His announcement was duly proclaimed throughout the city. "The horses' hoofs will be steeped in blood, and the action will rival the great conflict of the Mahabharat." So the 21st of July was looked for with impatient hope by the rebel troops, who professed themselves ready to dare anything at the *hookum* of their seer, and with hope too, and perhaps some little anxiety, in the British camp. However, the worthy Pundit must have been out in his calculations, or the stars must have played him false, or some more mundane influence must have been in the ascendant, which he had not taken in the account; for the 21st dawned in peace, and although a false alarm did sound about noon, it was one of the most peaceful days of the whole siege.

The 23d, however, was a stormy one. Early in the

morning, the movement of the troops at the Cashmere Gate attracted attention. It seemed that, in despair of carrying our position on the right, they were determined to try what could be done on our left flank. They brought out some guns and put them in position at Ludlow Castle, and began shelling into Metcalfe House and stable picquet. A column was formed under Brigadier Showers, made up from H. M. 8th and 61st, Coke's Rifles, and 4th Sikhs, with some guns. The ground on this side was much more open; the advance was made in splendid style in one grand skirmishing line, with the guns in the centre; they swept all before them; however, the rebels worked their guns with grape so effectually that our loss was heavy, and they were enabled to carry off their guns in safety. Here, as on the 14th, the temptation to follow up was too strong; in the endeavour to overtake and seize the guns, our men, who had now closed up, were drawn too near the city walls. Brigadier Showers was himself wounded and disabled, and Colonel Jones of the 60th Rifles took his place. The troops now fell back out of range, and the firing, chiefly confined to the artillery, continued all the afternoon until about four o'clock, when the troops were withdrawn. Though the rebels had succeeded in carrying off their guns, they had learnt that a battery was not to be established at Ludlow with impunity. But the little force had to deplore the loss of Captain W. G. Law (10th N.I.), attached to Coke's Rifles; and, in addition to Brigadier Showers, Colonel T. Seaton (35th N. I.), a few days before appointed to officiate as

Adjutant-General for Brigadier Chamberlain, Lieutenant-Colonel R. Drought, 60th N. I., Major Turner, and Captain Money of the artillery, among the wounded. Thus ended our twenty-fourth actual engagement with the rebels since the 8th of June.

After a storm comes a calm. The few remaining days of July were allowed to pass over almost in uninterrupted quiet, the only exception being the advance of a body of rebels from the Cashmere Gate, with the vain endeavour of again luring us out within range from the walls. However, experience had taught one or two lessons, of which this was one, that it was a fatal policy to follow up the retreating rebels. Many valuable lives had been needlessly sacrificed in this headstrong zeal; it was a system in which we gained nothing, and lost very much; and it was one of General Wilson's first measures summarily to put a stop to it. He ordered that in future our position should, as far as possible, be purely defensive. It was enough to repel any attack, no attempt was to be made to follow it up. The conduct of the rebels themselves offers the best comment on this change of system. When they began to find that they could not lure out a soldier beyond cover of his breastwork, they, too, changed their tactics; and instead of almost ceaseless harass, days would now pass without any attack. The boom of the heavy guns of the Moree and Cashmere bastions continued with more or less regularity, but the shot chiefly spent itself on the breastworks, or buried itself in the hill-side; now and again one would ricochet over the crest of the hill, and even lob over into the camp beyond; some times a shell would drop into a battery, or find its way into that heroic garrison at Hindoo Rao's, and many a fine brave fellow thus fell a victim. But now for days together, beyond an occasional random shot at an advanced picquet, the rattle of musketry would scarcely be heard; and all this time our gallant little force was recruiting its strength and gaining heart.

Other great and vital changes, too, were introduced in the latter part of this month. At first the whole ridge had remained unprotected by any sort of breastwork; all communication between the batteries and picquets along the road which traversed the length of the ridge had been effected at imminent peril; the relieving guards, the officers on duty, the orderlies, the native servants, all had, as it were, to run the gauntlet of the enemy's fire between point and point; and of course casualties had been frequent. Now this evil had been greatly remedied. An almost unbroken line of breastwork had been run up from the Flagstaff Tower on the left to our extreme batteries on the right. Materials for the purpose abounded; the hill-side was covered with vast blocks of stone; these, piled up breast-high, having the intervals filled in with sand-bags and fascines, formed a covered-way under which men could pass from point to point in comparative safety.* Another grand reform marked Brigadier

* Mr Greathed gives the following admirable anecdote (page 150): "Sir E. Campbell of the Rifles has always got some new story; his last is of a rifleman telling him he didn't half like the new breastworks, as men now only get hit in the head!"

Wilson's accession to command. It cannot be denied that a very sad deterioration of discipline and tone had taken place in camp; the absence of a master-mind, or of wise counsels at the head, had begun to tell on the whole body. There was no regular system of reliefs; when the "alarm" sounded, the whole force turned out, perhaps twice or three times a-day, and would be kept under arms for hours together at the slightest signs of advance from the city on whatever quarter. The consequence was, that certain, undisturbed rest was unknown; the men were worn out with ceaseless fatigue and exposure; a spirit of recklessness was making way among them, amounting sometimes to desperation: at the sound of the "alarm" men have been heard to say they hoped they might be knocked over—"a speedy death was better than that slow one;" indeed, instances did occur of soldiers blowing their own brains out, so utterly had they lost heart! But one of the first steps taken by Brigadier Wilson was to establish a system of reliefs; only those on duty, or warned for support, were to turn out at the "alarm," and then all were to sleep accoutred, to be ready at a moment's notice. And with this system of reliefs came a greater strictness of order; to guard against sentries or videttes sleeping at their post, they were to be visited more frequently and regularly by the officer on duty. Another sign of remissness in discipline he strongly reprobated: the soldiers had been accustomed to turn out in their shirt-sleeves; this he at once put a stop to by requiring that all should appear in uniform, and properly armed.

The effects of these various changes were soon apparent. With regular rest and food—for both had suffered—the soldier had begun to recover heart as well as strength. Sanitary measures also kept pace with this improved organisation, and the General was soon repaid for this judicious husbanding of his men by witnessing their speedy improvement in health and tone.

As the month advanced, the news from below assumed a more definite and a more cheering character. In the beginning of July, all that reached the camp was vague rumour, and that frequently obtained from the city itself through our spies;—that Wheeler and Lawrence were still holding out at Cawnpore and Lucknow;—then that Wheeler had been relieved, and was moving up a large European force to our succour. These rumours, in their vagueness and apparent impossibility, had little effect in camp beyond making all feel more keenly their own utter isolation. It seemed as if a vast gulf separated the Punjab from the rest of Hindostan, and was ever growing deeper and wider. From Delhi to Allahabad spread a seething sea of rebellion, in which not even a *Cossid* could live. The only communication with Calcutta, and that at best tedious and very precarious, was by Mooltan and Bombay. Letters and papers which came by this circuitous route only showed that in Calcutta an utter ignorance prevailed of all that was passing in the North-west and the Punjab. There came reports of the arrival of troops from Madras and the Mauritius, some retained for the safety of Calcutta, others pushed up; but as they passed Benares these disappeared; they seemed to enter an ocean of rebellion, the waves of which closed in behind them, and all trace of them was lost.

Again, the non-arrival at Delhi of the many native regiments which were known to be in a state of mutiny in Hindostan looked very suspicious: there were the Agra, Cawnpore, and Lucknow brigades; scarcely a man had made his appearance at Delhi. Where had they gone? The inference was that there must be some other *rendezvous*—some other focus of rebellion. Delhi was not the only battle-field in which the death-struggle for empire was being maintained. This was so far comforting, in the hope it held out that the already overwhelming rebel force in Delhi was not likely to receive further accession of numbers from below; but it brought also the saddening conviction that whatever troops might pour into Calcutta would find ample work in their hands elsewhere; and that if Delhi was to fall, its fall must be effected by the troops in the Punjab. In the middle of the month came a painful confirmation of the state of Hindostan, in the too authentic intelligence of the Agra disaster, of the advance of the Neemuch brigade, the treachery of the Kotah contingent, the consequent discomfiture of the Europeans, and their hasty retreat into the fort, having on their list of casualties the name of one that made many a heart sad in camp, that of Captain Edward D'Oyly, of the Bengal Artillery; and before the close of the month the bloody tale was told of the Cawnpore massacre.

With this last, however, came the welcome tidings of

Neil's advance, of the recovery of Cawnpore—though all too late to save the poor women and children—and the condign retribution he inflicted on their murderers. This was like a little gleam of sunshine finding its way into camp ; it helped to sustain and give vigour to the new life which had been infused there.

The reader must now pass from the ridge into the city. Here, too, the month of July had its lights and shades. The hereditary death-strife of the two races could with difficulty be restrained ; daily it was in danger of breaking out : one day there was a riot because some Mohammedans had killed a cow ; another day the whole city was in commotion because the Hindoo Pundits declared a day to be unfortunate on which the Mohammedans had planned an attack upon our rear. In this disunion, this perpetual liability to a rupture, this conflict of interests, rivalry of claims, this mutual suspicion, the absence of any one leading mind, lay our chief safeguard. In vain did the old King and the princes resort to conciliation—concession—in order to preserve peace, or to restore confidence. In vain did they announce each outbreak in the Punjab as a gain to Delhi ; in vain did they point to the death of two Commanders-in-Chief, who, they said, had poisoned themselves in despair. The rumours of the advancing troops from below (which always got into the city before it reached camp) made their hearts quail, and strengthened the growing conviction that their mutiny was a failure, and that a day of retribution for them was at hand.

The news from Agra was proclaimed by a royal

salute from Selimghur, and the walls of the city of Shah Jehan* resounded with the notes of "God save the Queen," in honour of the announced capture of the fort of Akhbar! Yet in vain did the generals taunt their men that the Neemuch force had taken Agra, while they had not taken a single battery on the ridge.†

As for the old King, amid all this division and strife it fared but ill with him. Those few weeks of seeming success had sufficed to show the "Emperor of Hindostan" how perilous a course he had chosen; better to have remained in pensioned pomp a king only in name, and have ended his days in peace, than in evil hour have listened to the voice of ambition, and have made a struggle for independence, to become the mere puppet of a horde of soldiery, among whom he had aroused a spirit he could not control. Milo had rent the oak, and already felt the rebound.

"The sepoys, and not the King, rule in Delhi; all is confusion and riot," was the terse report of Rujjub Ali.

The old man himself, indulging in an imagined gift of poesy, describes his forlorn condition about this time in the following pathetic strain, roughly translated from the Persian:—

> "The army surrounds me; I have no peace nor quiet.
> My life alone remains, and that they will soon destroy."‡

---

* Shajehanabad is the Mohammedan name of the present city of Delhi, so called from its founder.

† GREATHED'S *Letters*, p. 118.

‡ One other from the piles of poetic fragments with which the royal

His difficulties seemed daily to increase; the very accession of strength in the Bareilly brigade brought with it a fresh trouble. The clever and ambitious Mohamed Bukht Khan, as the head of such a "following," claimed to thrust his obese form even into high places: backed by his brigade, he dared to beard the old King in his own palace, and to dictate terms for himself in the council chamber, as an equal in power with the royal princes, who now commanded the army. This claim was first of all met by a compromise, and General Mohamed Bukht Khan was appointed Commandant of the Magazine, and Commissary-General of Ordnance, and Commander-in-Chief; and for a time peace was restored in the council. Still the King's position was far from comfortable—feuds and jealousies of his own sons, insolence of the upstart generals, clamours of a hungry army, loud remonstrances of the merchants and bankers of the city at the insatiable demands on their wealth, were incessantly dinning in his ears. Even in the female apartments, to which he fled for shelter from the turbulent scenes which were being daily enacted in the Hall of Audience, he looked in vain for peace—they had become a perfect hotbed of intrigue.

At length his life was rendered so miserable, that, to the amazement of the few admitted into the secret,

bard used to solace his weary hours, deserves to be rescued from oblivion: it runs as follows:—

"The Persian hosts and Russian armies could not prevail against the British;
But an impure cartridge has sapped the foundations of their power."

at the very time when the rebel force seemed the strongest, and our position the most perilous, *Shah Bahadoor Shah, Emperor of Hindostan, sent in to camp to treat for terms!* His proposal was to open the gate of Selimghur at the bridge, let in our troops into the palace, and place all in our hands, on condition that he was restored to his former condition of titular king, and his former pension of twelve lakhs a-year. Was it a *ruse* to gain time by negotiation, and to ward off the threatened assault, or to test our own position by the mode in which we should receive the proposal? This was the first question. Then, could he fulfil his part of the agreement? Was he in a position to open the Selimghur Gate to us? Or, after all, was it not a mere piece of Asiatic treachery—a trap to catch us in?

The proposition was immediately telegraphed to the Chief Commissioner, whose reply was, that the King should first prove that he was guiltless of the blood of any Christian, and then satisfy the authorities that he has the power of placing the palace in their hands. "Treat, but beware of treachery;" and he stipulated peremptorily, that at all events the King should quit the city. Mr Montgomery was less disposed than Sir John Lawrence to treat at all with the King, and strongly urged that it became us to take the highest ground with such a traitor. However, whether there was treachery or not would never be told. It soon appeared the King had not the power of making good his promise —he was not master even of his own palace; and so the negotiation came to nothing. Yet this transaction has been so grievously misrepresented, that a few words of comment are necessary, if only to vindicate the character of those concerned.

This is one of the acts of Sir John Lawrence which have been, in high places, dwelt on in depreciation of the policy of his administration. "Even Sir John Lawrence," said Lord Granville in the House of Peers, "was willing to make terms with the King; but Lord Canning, a civilian, had the courage to take upon himself the responsibility of absolutely refusing these propositions." Now let us mark the facts of the case. It was on the 5th of July Sir John Lawrence received first intimation of the King's proposal. The same day took back to camp his brief telegraphic reply, and a letter stating at length his opinions, and the reasons on which he based them; and on the following day he communicated to Calcutta a full account of the whole transaction. When, if ever, this communication reached the Council does not appear, for it was never answered. But two months after, on the 4th September, an official letter was received by Mr Greathed,* the Commissioner with the force, of which the following is an extract: "Rumours have more than once reached this Government, that overtures have been made by the King of Delhi to the officer commanding the troops there, and that these overtures may be possibly renewed upon the basis of the restoration of the King to the position which he held before the mutiny of Meerut and Delhi.

* GREATHED'S *Letters*, p. 252.

The Governor-General wishes it to be understood, that any concession to the King, of which the King's restoration to his former position should be the basis, is one to which the Government, as at present advised, cannot for a moment give its consent. Should any negotiation of this sort be contemplated, a full report of all the circumstances must be submitted to the Governor-General in Council before the Government is committed to anything." Yet it is on this expression of opinion, received two months after, that Lord Granville bases his statement; whereas the whole affair had, so to say, settled itself within *two days*.

It is in such cases as these that the full benefits which the sepoys conferred on India, in cutting the telegraph wire, may be estimated. They enabled Sir John Lawrence to act independently, and to escape the fatal delay of perpetual references, which, had it been possible, must have been made to Government—references which, even under the existing circumstances, the Governor-General seemed to insist on, forgetting that it must take some three months before an answer could be received, and that probably on a point on which the fate of the Punjab might turn within as many days. Nor, indeed, with due respect be it said, was the Council at Calcutta in a condition to form a fair and sound judgment on such momentous events as were daily occurring in the Punjab. Lord Canning himself had only landed in India a few months, and scarcely been twenty miles north of Calcutta, and only one of his immediate advisers had ever had official acquaintance with that province;* much less could they in Calcutta, in the month of August (when the letter under consideration was written),—with European troops flowing in, and the river crowded with ships, ready for an escape in the event of emergency, with an Indian trained general, Hearsey, at Barrackpore, and Sir Colin Campbell, the hope of England, sent out to their rescue,—realise the position of the Punjab during that most critical month of July, when it was a struggle for existence—when to fail would have been to perish.

Another point there was of momentous importance, which about the same time pressed on the Chief Commissioner's mind, and on which the line he was prepared, if driven to extremities, to adopt, has been misunderstood. It was the abandonment of all our *trans*-Indus territory. Now, what were the facts of the case? He was being constantly reminded that the advance on Delhi had been originally made solely at his instigation, that the personal advisers of General Anson had, as has been already stated, nearly all opposed it. Sir H. Barnard, then commanding the Sirhind Division, had strongly condemned it,† and now that circumstances had placed him in command of the force, he seemed to maintain the siege under protest; and hints were constantly thrown out, that unless more reinforcements could be sent down from the Punjab, the siege must

* Mr G. F. Edmonstone, then Secretary to the Government of India in the Foreign Department, had been Commissioner of the Cis-Sutlej States, and, for a few months, Financial Commissioner of the Punjab.

† GREATHED'S *Letters*, p. 94.

be abandoned, and the force withdrawn until succours could arrive from below. Frequently did Sir John Lawrence remonstrate against so fatal a step; the siege must be maintained at all hazard, even though the Punjab could not spare another man. Even now, in moments of calm security, one's heart sinks at the thought of all that a retreat might, and most probably would, have involved—the certain loss of the Punjab, and the almost certain sacrifice of every man, woman, and child still left in the country. Retreat is the one trial an English soldier cannot endure; it is fatal to subordination—fatal to the *morale* of an army: both subordination and *morale* were already shaken, and a retreat would have ruined all. Corunna, of chivalrous yet bloody memories, speaks to us of the effects of a retreat on English troops, even under a Sir John Moore. We may point, indeed to Busaco, where Arthur Wellesley, with his retreating columns, repelled the pressing foe, and rallied around him in redoubled force his wavering allies; or to Torres Vedras, where, during long weeks of firm discipline, he restored order and tone to a disorganised and disheartened army. Why not re-enact a Busaco at Kurnaul, and a Torres Vedras at Umballa? For one reason, among others: perhaps in nothing does Asiatic warfare differ more widely from European than in this, that in the one a retreat may be acknowledged as masterly strategy, in the other it is sure to be regarded as an admission of defeat. At the first sight of a retrograde move, our native allies, who were still so nobly fighting for us, would have *gone*—it would have snapped the last link of the chain of loyalty, or of interest, which held them to our side. Jheend could no longer have breasted the tide of rebellion which surged around; Puttiala even could not have stood, and with him would have gone Nabha and every Sikh chief. And how would our army have fared? Had we once given up the vantage-ground on that ridge—had we moved one single march from camp, our native troops would doubtless have turned against us *en masse;* our irregular cavalry would have harassed the rear, and cut up all the sick and stragglers; the city would have poured out its 50,000 armed men, and its multitude of budmashes; the whole country around would have risen; the villagers would have mobbed and clubbed the worn-out famished soldiers; the sun of Hindostan would have proved as deadly as the snows of Cabul, and the banks of the Jumna have witnessed the annihilation of an English army stronger than that which perished in the Khyber.

Nor was this all; with Delhi abandoned, there would be little hope of saving the Punjab. Between the Sutlej and the Indus were only four European regiments—one with Nicholson's column, and the other three weak in numbers, and weaker still by being broken up into detachments over seven stations; with three more beyond shut up in the Peshawur valley; while above 10,000 women and children had to be cared for and protected. At Lahore itself above 3000 had been concentrated from the neighbouring stations;

as many more were at Umballa and the hills; at Murree were above 1500, and quite that number at Peshawur, and how was their safety or their escape to be provided for?

All this the Chief Commissioner saw, and when the subject was again revived by General Wilson, with the possibility of the retreat from Delhi being attempted, his only hope lay in bringing into use the three regiments at Peshawur. He was prepared, if the exigency arose, to make a present of the valley to Dost Mohammed, to give back to the Douranee empire its long-lost, long-mourned province, if at such a price he might save the rest. It was a desperate step; one only to be attempted when all else should fail. Cotton, Edwardes, Barnes, and other of his most trusted friends, to whom he had most confidentially broached the subject, strongly opposed it; abandon Delhi, but don't give up Peshawur. Still Sir John remained unchanged in his opinion, that in this step might lie the only chance of saving the thousands of women and children, by bringing them down under strong escort, and then, that achieved, the three regiments, if only mustering 1000 bayonets among them, would have been above all value at Delhi. Nor, despite the strongly-expressed opinions to the contrary, did the Chief Commissioner, in calmly reviewing the struggle of that time, modify his own opinion. "In that extremity," he wrote in May 1858, "the only chance for the British of even preserving existence, would have been to collect the European troops into one solid mass,"* though he still admitted that, at best, it was but *a doubtful chance.*

Providentially the extremity never arose. Changes already alluded to were taking place in camp, and events to be described in the next chapter were occurring in the Punjab, which combined to avert it.

General Wilson wrote thus to Mr Colvin on the last day of July :—

"MY DEAR SIR,—It is my firm determination to hold my present position, and to resist any attack to the last. The enemy are very numerous, and may possibly break through our intrenchments and overwhelm us, but the force will die at their post. Luckily the enemy have no head and no method, and we hear dissensions are breaking out among them. Reinforcements are coming up under Nicholson. If we can hold on till they arrive, we shall be secure. I am making every possible arrangement to secure the safe defence of our position."

The siege still held on, and Peshawur remained untouched.

* *Chief Commissioner's Punjab Mutiny Report,* par. 39.

CHAPTER XII.

[JULY 1857.—PART II.]

THE PUNJAB—FAVOURABLE APPEARANCE VERY DECEPTIVE—MANY POORBEAH REGIMENTS STILL ARMED—COLUMN MOVING UP FROM JULLUNDHUR TO UMRITSUR—58TH DISARMED AT RAWUL PINDEE—A DAY AT JHELUM—THE SEALKOTE OUTBREAK—NICHOLSON DISARMS THE 59TH AT UMRITSUR AND THE WING OF THE 9TH CAVALRY, AND CATCHES THE SEALKOTE MUTINEERS AT TRIMMOO GHAT—KANGRA, THE 4TH N. I. GIVE UP THEIR ARMS—FEROZEPORE, THE 10TH IRREGULAR CAVALRY DEPRIVED OF THEIR HORSES—THE COLUMN MOVES DOWN AGAIN.

IN the Punjab, as before Delhi, there was the same deceptive appearance of improvement. All *seemed* favourable. That little slip of printed paper, the official bulletin, which day by day announced the state of the body politic, and was circulated through the Punjab, brought each day the welcome announcement "The Punjab perfectly quiet"—"All well in the Punjab." And so far it told truly. But it told only half the truth ; and perhaps less. The Punjab *was quiet ;* but from the Indus to the Sutlej were mines of treason, ready charged, which might explode at any moment.

It was with little confidence or comfort that Sir John Lawrence, and those admitted to his counsels, saw five regiments of native infantry and two of cavalry scattered over the Punjab, still retaining their arms, with in reality only two European regiments and a few guns available to overawe or punish them.* At Rawul Pindee were the 58th N. I., at Jhelum the 14th N. I., at Sealkote the 46th N. I., with a wing of the 9th Light Cavalry, and the other wing in the Moveable Column; while the 59th N. I. were at Umritsur, the 4th N. I. at Kangra and Noorpoor, the 2d Irregular Cavalry at Goordaspore, *all armed.* Against these were only H. M. 24th Foot at Rawul Pindee, with a battery, and H. M. 52d L. I. with the Column, with a troop and a battery, besides a few newly-raised Punjab levies. Thus it was clear that the train of treason fired at any point, the whole would be in a blaze; and little could be done towards extinguishing it.

Such was the real state of the Punjab at the end of June. Of all these native corps the 14th had always been regarded with the greatest suspicion and anxiety;† and unfortunately their position, the farthest up except the 58th, added to the danger. For the ball of rebellion once set rolling here, what was there to stop

* H. M. 81st at Lahore are, of course, not included, as they were tied down watching the disarmed corps at that station. The troops at Peshawur, too, are left out, as having their hands full. It may here be noticed that, from their separate position and duties, the latter are never included in any general review of the European force in the Punjab, but are treated of separately.

† When the author was leaving Rawul Pindee, *in the middle of May*, to join the Moveable Column, he was told by one in all the state secrets, "If you get safely through Jhelum, you are all right." The hint was taken, and the author, after a delightful day in the camp of the 4th (Rothney's) Sikhs, took advantage of the wing of the 17th Irregulars, then pushing on to join the Column, to enter Jhelum, with his friend Captain P. Hockin, at the head of that corps.

it? At Jhelum itself there was not a European soldier, nor at Sealkote, or Kangra, or Goordaspore. It would have rolled on, gathering force as it came, and carrying all along with it. Sir John Lawrence had heard (and his secret-intelligence department was perfect) that the spirit of mutiny was becoming very active in this corps. So it was resolved, in the Rawul Pindee councils, to avert, if possible, the impending danger by disarming them, and also the 58th at Rawul Pindee, of whom, despite the loud protestations of their commandant, Colonel Barstow, no very favourable opinion was entertained. The first step was to weaken the traitors of the 14th by bringing up two companies to Rawul Pindee on some detachment duty; the next was to arrange for a simultaneous disarming of the two regiments at the two stations. Another failure, like that a month before at Jullundhur, and the Punjab would be shaken to its centre, perhaps lost after all.

In former chapters the narrative of events has of necessity been somewhat disconnected. Each station having in most cases been compelled to act independently of its neighbour, the reader has been frequently carried from one station to another without any connecting links between the different points of action. But the case is now different. The events about to be recorded all formed parts of one plan, or rather were a series of contingencies, hanging one upon the other, which were all taken into account and provided for by the one controlling head.

To understand them aright the reader must have a

good map of the Punjab before him. He must remember that we left the Moveable Column at Philour, nearly 200 miles from Rawul Pindee. At the end of June a *hint* had come down from Sir John Lawrence to Nicholson to move the Column upwards. He started on the 28th, taking with him the two corps, the 33d N. I. and 35th L. I., disarmed by that master-stroke at Philour. At Jullundhur he left the 33d under the eye of the 21st Punjab Infantry, a new corps just raised there by Captain Tulloh, and some Kuppoorthulla men; and taking the 35th L. I. across the Beas, he dropped them at Jundhiala, one march from Umritsur, and then brought the Column on to Umritsur. Bitter were the regrets and unsparing the censures which this move called forth in the Column. The hope of "Delhi," which had cheered them on a few days before, now disappeared as they set their faces once more upwards. The move was simply incomprehensible: its object no one could imagine, and therefore every one condemned it. But a few days sufficed to show its object and to prove its wisdom.

In the meanwhile a corresponding move was being made from above. On the morning of the 1st of July a little force, consisting of three companies of H. M. 24th (260 strong) under Lieutenant-Colonel Ellice, 3 horse-artillery guns under Captain Cookes, and 150 of Miller's Police Battalion, were proceeding downwards from Rawul Pindee *with sealed orders.* On the 3d the Mooltanee levies under Lieutenant Lind (already mentioned as being at Nowshera when the 10th Irregulars were disbanded) came in, mustering some 460 cavalry and 250 infantry, and were pushed on to overtake Colonel Ellice's force, and to place themselves under his orders.

On the morning of the 7th, Rawul Pindee was on the *qui vive;* there was a brigade of all arms—four companies of H. M. 24th, the three remaining guns of the Horse-Artillery, some of Capt. Miller's Mounted Police, and the 58th N. I., with the two companies of the 14th N. I., all drawn up in the open space between the European barracks and the church. It was avowedly to hear a general order read;* nor did even the officers of the native corps suspect that anything else was contemplated. The civilians had gathered around in some numbers, and anxiety might be traced on every face. The general order was read. The Brigadier (Colonel Campbell of the Artillery) gave the word for the infantry and artillery to wheel to the left. Round went the 24th, round thundered the guns, down crashed the trails of the limbers—and off broke the sepoys! They saw what was meant, and made for their lines. Their officers, at the risk of their own lives, accompanied them, manfully endeavouring to allay the panic, and to persuade the men to lay down their arms quietly. With the 58th they prevailed; and on arriving at their lines the sepoys gave up their arms. Not so the two companies of the 14th N. I. They had been the first to fly, and were now seen making for the city, musket in hand. Miller's Mounted Police were after them and

* That all heirs of soldiers killed in action should receive pensions.

cut up several. Some got away for a time; but a price was set on them, and the next morning their heads were soon brought in by the villagers. Thus was the object gained, though for a time the issue seemed rather doubtful. The only European wounded was Captain Miller himself, who, in gallant pursuit of the fugitives, had his arm broken by a musket-ball. Thus ended the affair on the Rawul Pindee parade-ground.* The city remained perfectly quiet.

At Jhelum a similar scene, but unfortunately with far different results, was also taking place. To prevent the possibility of one station being put on its guard by the fate of the other, it was arranged, as has been stated, to effect the disarming at both *simultaneously*.

On the morning of the 6th, Colonel Ellice's little force, now strengthened by Lind's Mooltanees, had reached Deenah, one march from Jhelum. Here the sealed orders were opened, and the object of the expedition was no longer a mystery. Colonel Ellice at once detached half of the Mooltanee Horse and sent them off in advance, with orders to proceed through cantonments and cross the river, so as to allay suspicion—and also to guard the opposite bank. He himself rode into Jhelum, and made arrangements with Colonel Gerard, who commanded the 14th N. I., for carrying out his orders on the following morning.

Before gun-fire on the 7th, the horse-artillery guns,

* Mutiny, however, still lurked in the ranks. A week after, some of the 14th and also of the 58th were arrested and tried; some were blown away from guns, and others hanged.

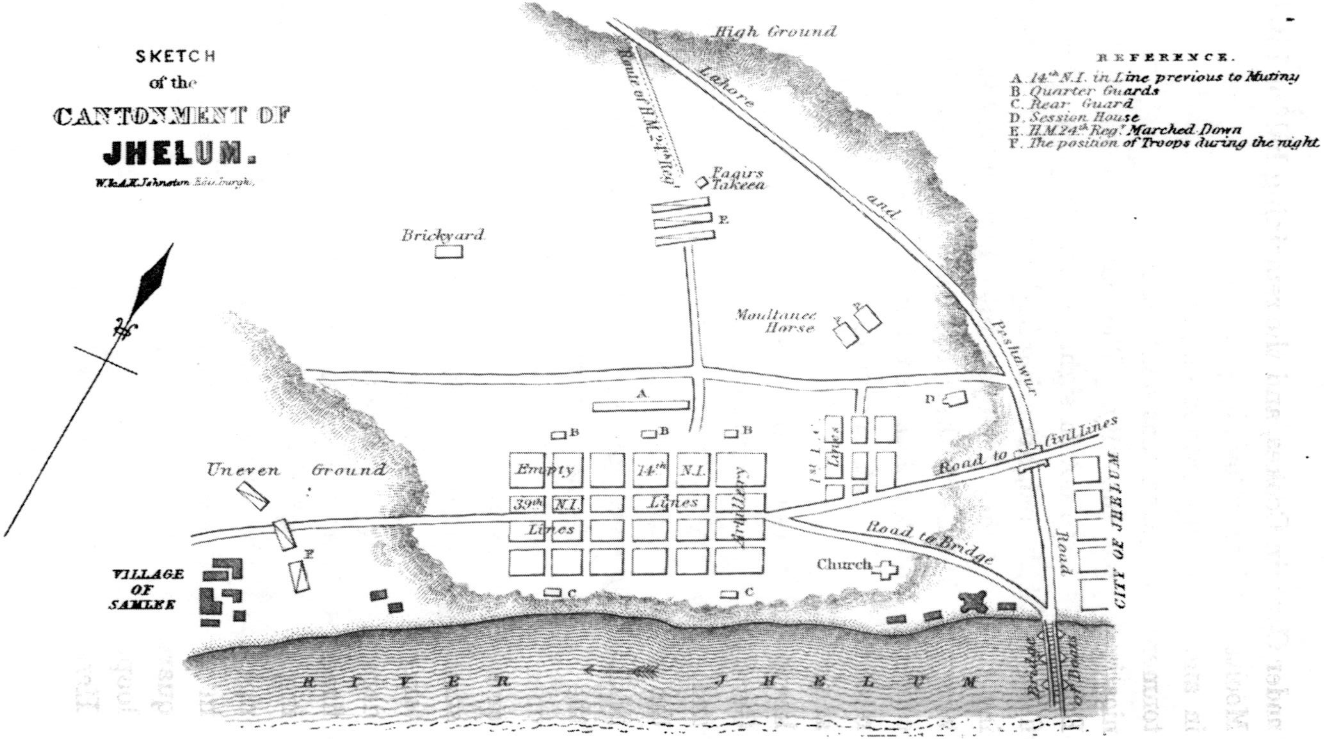
SKETCH
of the
CANTONMENT OF
JHELUM.
W. & A. K. Johnston, Edinburgh.
REFERENCE.
A. 14th N.I. in Line previous to Mutiny
B. Quarter Guards
C. Rear Guard
D. Session House
E. H.M. 24th Regt. Marched Down
F. The position of Troops during the night
High Ground
Lahore and Peshawur Road
Route of H.M. 24th Regt.
Faqirs Takeea
Brickyard
Moultanee Horse
Empty
14th N.I.
39th N.I.
Lines
Artillery
1st I. C. Lines
Road to Civil Lines
Road to Bridge
Church
Uneven Ground
VILLAGE OF SAMLEE
CITY OF JHELUM
Bridge of Boats
RIVER JHELUM

under Captain Cookes, and the remaining half of Lind's Mooltanee Horse, had, by previous arrangement, moved in and taken up ground on the extreme right of cantonments to guard that flank, and cut off any communication with the city. The day dawned; but the Europeans were not in sight: at length they appeared, filing down the neighbouring high ground; and on reaching the level they deployed into line. The 14th N. I. were at the time on their own parade-ground, in open column; about a hundred Sikhs had just been separated from the rest, and were standing apart. As soon as the sepoys saw the European force advancing, they knew what was meant, and began loading. Colonel Gerard and the other officers remonstrated, but in vain; and, perceiving their own danger, rushed forward from the regiment towards the Europeans (as also did the Sikhs), and were followed by several stray shots from the sepoys, but no one was touched. The sepoys at once broke and fell back on their lines, making the quarter-guard their advanced position, and placing a small body across the road leading to it. The Mooltanee Horse, though five hundred yards off, were ordered to charge. Down they came; not a shot was fired till they were within thirty yards, when a withering volley met them. On they went, cutting down right and left; but the sepoys were soon under shelter in the verandahs, and on the battlemented top of the quarter-guard, and in their own huts, which they had loopholed, as if preparatory to such an emergency. Here they defied the cavalry. Unfortunately, the infantry had not yet come up in support. Lieutenant Lind's charger was shot dead; and his men seeing him fall, wavered and fell back—not, however, before they had done good execution among the mutineers, though with heavy loss to themselves. In that short ten minutes' encounter, of the two hundred and forty who had charged into the lines, nine had fallen, and twenty-eight were brought off wounded, and some sixty horses killed and wounded. The Mooltanee Infantry and the police now came up, and went in bravely; but they were mere recruits, some raised scarcely a fortnight, and armed only with matchlocks; and they could not stand before the superior numbers, arms, and discipline of the sepoys. The guns, too, now came to the front, and were soon in full play; but the sepoys had so much shelter that the grape could scarcely touch them. For some time they held their lines, and especially the quarter-guard,* and were in comparative security. At length, the 24th came up in grand style, and some fifty of them, with Colonel Ellice at their head, made a gallant dash, and carried the quarter-guard, but with the loss of their leader, who fell dangerously wounded in the neck and thigh. The sepoys were now driven from their own lines, and made for those of the 39th N. I. adjoining. Here, however, they did not stay long; a well-directed shell blew up the regimental magazine, and they were quickly in retreat on the

* One of the improvements in station architecture has been the giving battlemented tops to quarter-guards for defence; the battlements now answered a purpose little contemplated by the engineer.

village of Saemlee, still mustering some three hundred strong.

Now came a short respite. It was just one o'clock in the day; the men of H.M. 24th, after a long march, and about seven hours' fighting, were spent and faint; and, unfortunately, finding out the 39th N. I. mess-house, and Major Knatchbull's far-famed stores, they helped themselves, perhaps too freely; so that for a time all order was lost. The Mooltanees and the artillery alone remained watching the village. However, at 5 P.M., Colonel Gerard, who had assumed command on Colonel Ellice being wounded, resolved on an attack. A desperate struggle ensued. The Mooltanee Horse and police troopers were again placed on the left flank, to prevent the rebels escaping. The artillery were brought to the front, but too near, notwithstanding Captain Cookes's remonstrance; the sepoys, safe behind the walls and houses, picking off the gunners with fatal precision, while the grape spent itself on mud walls, or passed harmless over their heads. Had a rush been now made, like that under Colonel Ellice at the quarter-guard, the village must have been carried at the bayonet's point. But it was not attempted in any force. Captain M'Pherson of the 24th, with five or six men, made a gallant dash, and effected a lodgment on the wall; but not being supported, he gave it up, and drew off his brave little band, *fortuna favet fortibus,* without the loss of a man. The ammunition began to fail, and the infantry were ordered to retire. The artillery were losing horses and men fast, and were compelled to follow; the howitzer, which had been unhorsed and wellnigh unmanned, they could not bring off, and were obliged to leave behind. The whole force now fell back beyond musket-range, Captain Spring being borne off mortally wounded. The rebels made a sally, seized the disabled howitzer, dragged it in, limber and all, into the village; the howitzer they tumbled into the river, but preserved all the ammunition, as likely to be useful.

It was now sunset. All hope of taking the village that night was abandoned. The men, wearied with the day's work, threw themselves down on the ground in front of the village, and there bivouacked for the night.

The telegraph had reported all that was passing to Rawul Pindee. Colonel Browne of H.M. 24th was sent off express to take command, and a further detachment of the regiment followed under Lieutenant Holland.* When the day dawned, however, and the Europeans were preparing to renew the attack, it was found that the rebels had saved them the trouble—they had slipped off during the night, and the village was empty! However, the 14th had still to learn that, though they got off for a time, resistance and mutiny were, in the long-run, a losing game. The arrangements of Major Clement Browne, the Deputy Commissioner, were far too good to give them a chance to escape; the bridge

* This detachment had only reached Goojur Khan, just half way, when a counter-order overtook them, and they returned to Rawul Pindee, all need for them at Jhelum having ceased.

of boats across the river, which ran along the rear of cantonments, had been secured the first thing in the morning by some Punjabee police, who relieved the usual sepoy guard. All the ferry-boats on this and all the Punjab rivers had been long before seized by the authorities. Some private boats were found moored alongside the cantonment gardens, for in the palmy and peaceful days of Jhelum, boating was one of the chief amusements of the station,—a luxury indeed in India. Some of the Pandies seized these boats, and pushed off; one boatload was brought by the current under the opposite bank, where a party of Lind's Mooltanees were down upon them, and only three or four escaped to tell the tale. One party had a longer respite, only to endure greater sufferings, and after all not to escape the death they merited. They had started twelve in number, and after drifting for four days down the river, they reached Jhung, where they were stranded and taken prisoners; one had died of starvation, and another killed himself in despair; the remainder, a native officer and nine sepoys, too famished and weak to offer any resistance, were seized, tried, and executed.

The 14th N. I. had paraded on the morning of the 7th some 600 strong; of these, 100 Sikhs had been at once separated, of the remaining 500 only about one-tenth eventually escaped.* A great number were captured in the district, and brought in by the villagers; and

* 150 were killed in the encounter, 180 captured afterwards, and 120 given up by the Cashmere authorities, leaving only an odd 50 not "accounted for." The Sikhs did excellent service during the whole day.

those who did contrive to escape by the Munglas Ford, some miles up the Jhelum, into the Cashmere territory, were subsequently given up. But there had been heavy loss on our side. The 24th lost one Captain (Spring) killed, and had its Colonel (Ellice) and two subalterns, Lieutenants Streatfield and Chichester, dangerously wounded; and a young civil engineer named Scott, who had gallantly volunteered and done good service, was also wounded.*

Thus closed the Jhelum affair in the final defeat and destruction of the mutineers of the 14th N. I. But, as will be seen, the temporary success of their resistance was a shock which vibrated through the Punjab.

SEALKOTE, only thirty miles off, was the first station to feel it.

The position of this station had from the first been most precarious. The withdrawal of the European force in the end of May had left it wholly unprotected. About a dozen officers belonging to the wing of the 9th Cavalry and the 46th N. I., who remained, the Brigadier and his Staff, with a few soldiers left to guard a small number of sick of H. M. 52d and artillery, who were too ill to be moved — not forty

* The total loss on that day was as follows:—

	Killed.	Wounded.
Officers,	1	4
H. M. 24th, rank and file,	22	48
Artillery,	1	8
Mooltanees,	9	32
Sikhs,	3	1
Police,	8	16
	44	109

Besides 53 horses killed, and some 40 wounded.

able-bodied men in all — constituted the European strength of the station ; while there were several ladies with their families, who had disregarded the advice to move down to Lahore. All these were in the power and at the caprice of some 250 mounted troopers, and above 700 armed sepoys. For six weeks, it may truly be said, every man's life was in his hand ; they were all living, and they felt it too, on the edge of a mine of treason, which might be sprung at any moment, and destroy them all, while they were utterly powerless to avert it. The policy of Brigadier F. Brind, who commanded the station, was throughout to *appear* to place the fullest confidence in the native troops, for every effective European soldier had been withdrawn for the Column.* To have acted otherwise would only have hastened the catastrophe. To the wisdom of that policy, those six weeks of unbroken quiet are the best testimony. That it at length failed, under irresistible pressure from without, can hardly reflect on his judgment or his courage.

In the course of the 8th, private intelligence reached Mr Monckton, the Deputy-Commissioner, of the attempt to disarm the 14th at Jhelum, and their desperate resistance. It was communicated confidentially to the Brigadier ; he felt that probably the fate of the station was now sealed ; and no effort they could make would at all avail to ward it off.

The news from Jhelum had also found its way into the lines, probably in an exaggerated report of the

* See vol. i., p. 229, *note.*

success of the mutineers. By an unhappy coincidence, a trooper of the 9th Cavalry had that day come in on leave from the left wing, and reported that the Column was moving up, had reached Umritsur, and was probably coming on to disarm the Sealkote troops; moreover—which perhaps settled all—a foot-messenger arrived with *a letter from the King of Delhi.** Thus did the clouds gather and close in on the night of the 8th of July; and while the residents, ignorant that a more than ordinary danger was at hand, resigned themselves to rest, the traitorous troopers of the 9th Cavalry were planning with the utmost deliberation for their morning work of bloodshed, even to the placing picquets, mounted and armed, on every road by which escape was likely to be attempted, especially the one leading to the fort.

At gun-fire the outbreak commenced. The main picquet, which the Brigadier had originally established on the south-west of cantonments (and always retained, as if to impress upon the sepoys his belief that any danger that might befall Sealkote would come from without), marched off without orders to their own lines.

* An officer of the 46th N. I., on galloping down to the lines, met his pay-havildar, and asked him what the disturbance all meant; the havildar replied that four troopers of the 9th Cavalry had just been through the lines, and said that "the *chhuppa* (printed letter or circular) had come, and," added the havildar, "what can we do?" Another officer, in his flight, at the village of Tulwundee, was told by a villager that a *king's messenger had passed through the day before for Sealkote.* One of the sepoys who saved the life of Colonel Farquharson and escorted him to the fort, declared that the names of the 35th L. I. and 46th N. I. were down in the King of Delhi's book as pledged to join in the mutiny *so long ago as last January.* The *chhuppa* was doubtless a call on them to fulfil their pledge.

Shouts and yells were soon heard on the 46th parade-ground. The officers, roused from their sleep, were quickly mounted and among their men, whom they found in open mutiny. Brigadier Brind (in whose house Captain Chambers, the cantonment magistrate, and Captain Balmain of the 9th Cavalry, had passed the night for many weeks, keeping alternate watch) soon learned that the crisis had come. Capt. Balmain, relieved of his guard by Capt. Chambers, had just before gun-fire gone to his own house close by, and thrown himself on his bed to snatch a short sleep, when a faithful trooper of the 9th Cavalry rushed in in undress, and told him the men were mounting and "mischief would come." Rousing the Brigadier as he passed, he hastened down to his lines; here he found it hopeless to attempt to restore order; the men were already mounted, and one troop had galloped off to force the jail. Escape was the only course; some of his troopers offered to protect him in the lines, but this he would not hear of. He galloped back to the Brigadier, and urged him to mount and fly to the fort. As if reluctant to leave his post, even when all was over, the Brigadier delayed over some final arrangements; and that delay was fatal. On turning out of his compound-gate, a body of troopers were seen bearing down along the road which led to the fort, pistol in hand; as they passed, all, except three, fired, but without effect; neither the Brigadier nor any of the officers who were with him were touched. The three troopers who had reserved their fire wheeled round sharp as they passed, and shot at the Brigadier from behind; a ball entered his back; repeated attempts were now made to cut him down as he rode off; and it was mainly through Captain Balmain, and the other officers who had rallied round him in his retreat, that he was able to reach the fort at all.

On the parade-ground of the 46th, the officers, warned* and entreated by the better disposed of the sepoys, had galloped off in the opposite direction, the road to the fort being no longer open, and reached Goojranwalla; a few stray shots followed them as they passed the lines and one of the guards, but they escaped untouched. Dr Graham, the superintending surgeon, a man whose kindliness of heart towards all classes should have been his safeguard, endeavoured to escape in his buggy across cantonments to the fort, accompanied by his daughter, but some troopers, apparently on the watch for him, cut him off, and shot him down in his carriage. His poor daughter was allowed to proceed unmolested, and escaped into a garden; here she was subsequently discovered by a trooper, who carried her off to the cavalry quarter-guard, where she found Colonel and Mrs Lorn Campbell (the colonel commanding the cavalry), and with them was protected during the day. Dr J. Graham, of the medical depot, was also attacked while driving his carriage towards the fort, and shot down; but Mrs Graham and Mrs Gray, the wife of Lieutenant Gray,

* "Jao, Sahib, jao, runj ootha hai" (Go, sir, go, grief has come; or, We are come to grief), said a havildar to the Adjutant Le Gallais. Lieutenant Smith's horse's bridle was seized by a sepoy, who led him off the parade-ground, and implored him to fly.

adjutant of the artillery division, were suffered to proceed towards the fort. Captain Bishop of the 46th N. I., officiating as brigade major, was the only other victim in cantonments. Driving his wife and children to the fort, he had almost gained it when a trooper overtook him. Bishop, hoping to divert the ruffian's attention from his wife and children, and probably thinking he might also escape himself, sprang off the box and plunged into the ditch which surrounds the fort; the water, however, was too shallow to cover him, and he was soon wounded and cut down. So near to the fort wall was the spot where he was killed, that Captain Balmain, who with the Brigadier and others had already gained it, was on the rampart, and saw the attack on Capt. Bishop; seizing a musket, he fired two or three shots at the trooper, but the distance was too great, and the wretch was not to be intimidated; he did not leave his victim till life was extinct. Mrs Bishop saved herself by driving round to the fort gateway.

Without any defined plan for retreat having been arranged in the event of the sepoys rising, it was generally understood that the fort* would be the rallying-point, as furnishing the nearest asylum; and here the residents of the station had flocked, with the exception, as already noticed, of the officers of the 46th N. I.

* This old building belongs to the Rajah Tej Singh, the old Sikh general. It was perhaps most wise not to give out that this would be the rallying-point, for the only gate into it is *in one of the streets of the city itself*, and if it had been known that a general rush would have been made here, nothing would have been easier than for the troops to raise the city budmashes, and occupy the street leading to it. The absence of such a plan of retreat thus doubtless saved many lives.

From the civil lines also, which lay to the south-west of cantonments, a mile off, Mr Monckton and the Assistant-Commissioner, Lieutenant M'Mahon, with their wives, had hastened to the fort. The intimation they had received from Jhelum on the previous day made them augur the worst from the first sounds of unusual commotion in the station, and they started off at once under an escort of some new Punjab levies which were being raised in the district. With them the chaplain (the Rev. W. Boyle) also escaped. Having gone out the evening before to the civil lines, he acted on a hint given to him, and spent the night there, and thus reached the fort among the earliest.

Here was perpetrated a murder, which, for cold-blooded atrocity on inoffensive and helpless victims, was worthy of Delhi and Meerut butchers, and throws into the shade all the other sanguinary acts of that day. The Rev. J. Hunter, a Scotch Presbyterian missionary,* had a short time before moved out of the cantonments into the civil lines, for greater safety in the event of an outbreak in the station. The day had scarcely dawned, when tidings reached him that the sepoys had risen. Instantly placing his wife and child in a carriage, he started off for the fort. On his way, it was necessary to pass near the jail; either the troopers had been already here, or the civil sowars were in the plot; for, as he drove by, some of the *chupprasses* rushed out and

* There was another Presbyterian mission (American) close to the city; but these missionaries had left and gone to Lahore some weeks before.

attacked him ; he was first killed, and then his poor wife and babe.*

One most remarkable escape of that day, by which several lives were preserved, deserves to be especially noticed. Dr Butler and Lieutenant Saunders, of the 9th Cavalry, were living together in a large house in the centre of cantonments. This house was soon the object of attack ; and Dr Butler and Lieutenant Saunders, with their families, had only time to conceal themselves in a small outhouse, where they were preserved through the faithfulness of one of the servants, a chokedar (watchman). Many parties of sepoys and troopers came up to the very door of the outhouse, but their place of concealment was never discovered. For more than twelve weary anxious hours, on a July day, was this little party of twelve persons, eight of them young children, shut up in that miniature Black Hole. They could distinctly hear the parties of the mutineers entering the compound, rifling the house, and demolishing all they could not carry away. Later in the day the explosion of the regimental magazine added, if it were possible, to their alarm. However, as the day waned, the tumult began to cease; and when it was nearly dark, finding all around still and quiet, they came out of their hiding-place, and walked to the fort.†

* The resaldar (or native captain) of the civil sowars, and the subahdar of the police, were a few days after hanged for witnessing this atrocious murder without making an effort to save the innocent and unresisting victims, and for other negative proofs of disloyalty.

† One fine little boy of Dr Butler's never recovered the fright. After lingering for a short time in a distressing state of nervous excitement, he died at Lahore.

Here others also, who had been providentially preserved, were now coming in:—Colonel Farquharson and Captain Caulfield of the 46th N. I., with the sergeant-major and his wife, who had all been rescued by some of their own men and concealed in their lines; the inmates of the Roman Catholic seminary, who had been left unmolested through the daring devotion and tact of the priest; the patients of the Artillery Hospital, the sick soldiers, and those left on guard, who having with great promptness congregated in the dead-house, and fortified themselves there, giving ever and anon, as parties of the mutineers approached, proofs which they had no wish to challenge farther, that a warm reception awaited them. Among these was Mrs M'Ansh (the wife of Dr M'Ansh of the Artillery, who was absent with the column); at the commencement of the outbreak she had hastened with her children to the Artillery Hospital for protection, and thus escaped. All were now coming into the fort. Regarding the fate of the 46th officers great anxiety was entertained, as the night passed without their appearing. They, however, had effected their escape on the other side of the station, and after a ride of nearly forty miles under a scorching sun, had arrived safely at Goojranwalla.*

* They experienced the kindest treatment from the villagers along the road, who fed them, and even offered them money. One of them, Mrs Le Gallais, the wife of the adjutant of the 46th N. I., was in very delicate health, and by the time she had reached a small village called Budhpore, had become so faint and ill from the extreme heat and the shaking of the buggy, that she could bear the motion no longer. "The villagers," says one of the party, "rigged up an awning over a

After the bloodshed of the morning, the mutineers had spent the rest of the day in rifling the private bungalows and mess-houses, and carrying off all the property they could lay hands on. Very little that was of any value, and at all portable, escaped them; and wherever they bore any especial malice to the owner of a house, they committed the most wanton injury. The destruction of the kutcherry was complete—the liberated prisoners from the jail made this their special care. Tearing doors and windows off the hinges, and piling them, with all the tables and chairs, the books, papers, and everything combustible, in the centre room, they set fire to the whole; and as

> "The sheeted smoke, with flashes of light intermingled,"

rose up, there rose up, too, the yells and shouts of the infuriated convicts, revelling as they watched the destruction of this scene of their shame; and little remained but the bare charred walls to show where that handsome kutcherry had stood. Nor did the house of the Deputy-Commissioner fare much better: broken doors, windows, tables, chairs, &c. strewed that once beautiful and well-tended garden.

Happily, neither of the exquisite churches, for which Sealkote is so justly famed, was injured. The patrolling party from the fort, consisting of a few Sikh police and some of the new levies, were out early the next morning, and caught some wretches in the act

charpoy (native bed), and carried her across country to Goojranwalla."

of tearing up the benches in the larger church. They were seized, and quickly paid the penalty for their rashness, and the church was saved from further injury. The exquisite little chapel was not touched.

Having secured all the property they could carry away, not forgetting the old signal-gun—an act which reflects as much credit on their forethought as the use of it afterwards did on their artillery practice—the mutineers started, about four o'clock in the afternoon, towards Hosheyarpore, carrying with them crowds of camp-followers and servants,* expecting to be overtaken by a large body of their brethren from the 14th N. I., who, they were led to believe, had escaped, and were moving down in force to join them. They only marched ten miles that day, a delay which, as will be seen eventually, sealed their fate at the Ravee.

In the cantonment the demolition was chiefly the

* This was one of the peculiarities of the Sealkote outbreak. In almost all other stations domestic servants had been either faithful or at least neutral, but here they were clearly privy to the whole plot; and, with only a very few exceptions, every servant, whether Mussulman or Hindoo, proved false. In some cases, not even the claims of fifteen or twenty years' service with a family restrained them from now deserting their masters, or from being the first to help themselves in the general scramble. One instance (for the truth of which the writer has most unquestionable testimony) will suffice. In the service of Brigadier Brind was a bearer, an old and favourite servant. On the night of the 8th, Captain Chambers, who always slept at the Brigadier's, carefully examined all the pistols, &c., as was his nightly custom; for no one thought of being night or day without a loaded pistol or revolver at his side. The Brigadier's pistol was laid by his bed, loaded, capped, and ready for use. But in the morning, when the need of it came, the caps had disappeared—and no one had access to the Brigadier's sleeping-room but the old bearer. Indeed, the faithlessness of the servants was general. However, the majority of them paid dearly for it in the end.

work of Goojurs* of the neighbourhood, who flocked in like vultures to the prey.

When the mutineers left, they poured in, and pillaged till dark; and then all was quiet for the night—and that night, in all the wretchedness of that ruined dirty fort, many a one slept more soundly and fearlessly than they had slept for weeks before. *The mine had exploded, and they had escaped!* To the poor Brigadier it was a night of intense suffering, and before daylight he had breathed his last. He retained his faculties nearly to the end; indeed he had, with perfect self-possession, during the day, given his orders for securing the fort and making such arrangements as were possible. Throughout those six weeks of anxiety and danger, he had pursued, consistently and unswervingly, one line of conduct, which he believed to be alone possible to preserve quiet: he strove, by a seeming confidence in their loyalty, to win from the native troops a maintenance of order which he had no longer the means to enforce. He never lost his head, as so many did in less trying and perilous positions. He fell at his post; and in him his country lost a brave and fearless soldier,† to whose ability as an artillery

* The Goojurs of the Punjab are said, in the *Punjab Report of* 1849-50, to be more industrious and less predatory than their brethren of Hindostan. Those of the Sealkote district have now, at any rate, forfeited this distinction.

† Blame is sometimes imputed to Brigadier Brind for not at the first disarming, and thus disabling, the native troops. At Lahore and Peshawur the necessity had arisen—a deadly conspiracy had been detected; but not so at Sealkote—here they had shown no signs of disaffection. There had been no fires in the station; and excepting the one letter of a seditious character discovered in the musketry depot in

officer the campaigns of Gwalior, the Sutlej, and the Punjab, bore ample testimony.

It was eleven o'clock at night before the messenger from Sealkote reached Mr Montgomery at Lahore. At a single glance, he saw all the points at which danger threatened. Before midnight, one messenger was hastening to *Kangra* to warn Major Reynal Taylor, and to urge the disarming of the 4th N. I.; another for *Ferozepore,* to press on Brigadier Innes the necessity of taking away the horses of the 10th Cavalry, which up to this time they had retained; and a third (for the telegraphic wire made no sign) was journeying, post-haste by express mail-cart for *Umritsur,* to warn General Nicholson that he might throw his column on Goordaspore, disarm the 2d Irregulars there, and cut off the Sealkote mutineers at the Ravee.

Here was the possible contingency which had brought the Column up from Jullundhur.

To carry back our story a few hours. The Column had reached Umritsur on the 5th. On the morning of the 8th, the 59th N. I. had been paraded; and Nicholson, to remove the somewhat natural fear that they were to share the fate of the 33d and 35th N. I., had com-

February, not a symptom of a mutinous spirit had shown itself. Moreover, had they been disarmed when the European force was ordered to join the Moveable Column (after they left there were not the means of doing so), either the 52d Queen's must have been tied down to watch them, as the 81st were for so many months at Lahore, and thus have been lost to the Column, or else above one thousand native soldiers would have been left behind, degraded and exasperated; and what easier than for them to supply themselves with native weapons, and wreak their vengeance unchecked on the few remaining Europeans? *Then probably not one would have escaped.*

plimented them on their general good conduct, and assured them that he rejoiced in having no reason for disarming them. That day the telegraphic message came in from Mr Montgomery, reporting the imperfect success of the Jhelum affair. A necessity now arose, which had not existed a few hours before, although this upward march had been made in anticipation of its possibility; and the Column was now on the spot to meet it. On the following morning, the 9th of July, some wretched rebel was doomed to be executed. The general ordered down the 59th N. I., as well as the Column, to witness it. The spot always selected for this purpose was a large space of level ground between the city and Govindgurh fort, about a mile from the cantonments. The 59th marched down; the whole European Column, H. M. 52d Light Infantry, Dawes's troop, and Bourchier's battery, turned out and formed three sides of a square. The execution proceeded. When it was over, the 59th were suddenly ordered to "pile arms;" they were taken wholly by surprise; but with Europeans and guns in front and on either side, they obeyed without a moment's hesitation. They laid down 450 stand of arms, which were at once carried off to the fort; the Sikhs were ordered to fall out; and the regiment marched back to its lines.

It had been forgotten that only a part of the regiment were on parade, and that 450 only formed a small portion of their complement of arms. The corps proceeded to their lines crestfallen, but orderly; they went to the *kotes* (bells of arms), and brought out nearly

700 more muskets, which they gave up to their officers, and helped to pack away to be carried off to the fort! There could surely have been then but little treason in that corps, or, instead of thus voluntarily disarming themselves, they would have resented the disgrace to which they had been subjected, by shooting down their officers, who were wholly at their mercy.

This occurred on the morning of Thursday, the 9th of July. On that night, or rather early the next morning, the messenger arrived from Lahore reporting the Sealkote outbreak; and almost simultaneously another, direct from the scene of mutiny. A young band-boy named Macdougal, of the 46th N. I., had galloped off from the regimental parade-ground on a little tat, and by dint of borrowing and seizing fresh ones in the villages as he passed through, he finished his ride of some eighty miles into Umritsur, and hastened to the General's quarters just as the mail-cart brought in the Lahore messenger.

As soon as it was daylight, Major W. Baker, who commanded the left wing of the 9th Cavalry, received orders from General Nicholson to have a roll-call of his men in "Hindostanee dress" (without uniform or arms). Up moved a company of H. M. 52d Light Infantry, and drew up in front. Major Baker was requested to explain to his men what had taken place at Sealkote, in which their comrades of the other wing had taken a leading part, and to say that the General considered it necessary to demand their arms. A party from each troop was at once told off to bring away the arms, which the men had left piled by their tents; these were stowed away in carts ready at hand, and carried off to the fort of Govindgurh under a European escort. That afternoon orders were issued for a march; "the *horses* of the 9th Cavalry to accompany the Column;" the troopers were thus dismounted as well as disarmed, and were left behind under guard of a company of H. M. 52d and a couple of guns.

By nine o'clock that night the Column was in motion, consisting of Dawes's troop, Bourchier's battery, H. M. 52d L. I. under Colonel Campbell, and two companies of newly-raised Sikh infantry, with a few Punjab Mounted Police; and by daylight it reached Buttala, six-and-twenty miles on the road to Goordaspore.

"A halt was called for a couple of hours;* bread and rum, with an abundance of milk, were served out. All were aware what a terrific sunning we might expect; none knew it better than Nicholson, but he knew also the value of the stake.

"It was in a difficulty of this kind that his valuable qualities shone forth, in grasping the resources of the country. Two hundred pony carriages (ekhas), with all the ponies belonging to the grass-cutters of the 9th Cavalry, carried as many as possible of the 52d; while the cavalry horses were made over to the Sikhs.

"With these appliances even, many fell victims to the heat. When mounted, it was bad enough; but for an infantry soldier, with his musket and sixty rounds of ammunition in pouch, it was terrific.

* Colonel BOURCHIER'S *Eight Months' Campaign*, pp. 14, 15.

"Yet under these circumstances, trying as they were, the spirt of fun was not extinct; the artillery made *extempore* awnings of branches of trees over their gun-carriages and waggons, giving them the appearance of carts 'got up' for a day at Hampstead: officers crowned with wreaths of green leaves, were 'chaffed' by their comrades for adopting head-dresses *à la Norma.* Here might be seen a soldier on a rampant pony, desiring his companion on a similar beast 'to keep behind and be his "edge-de-camp;"' there a hero, mindful, perhaps, of Epping on Easter Monday, bellowing out his inquiries as to 'who had seen the fox?' Privates, never intended for the mounted branch, here and there came to grief, and lay sprawling on mother earth; whilst ever and anon some mighty Jehu in his ekha dashed to the front at a pace a Roman charioteer would have envied.

"All things must have an end. The artillery arrived at Goordaspore at 3 P.M. on the 11th, having been eighteen hours on the road; the infantry did not arrive until three hours later.

"Three artillery-horses were shot, and all were much knocked up; but the district was saved. The mutineers were only eight miles distant on the banks of the Ravee, never dreaming but that the Column was still at Umritsur." *

* Colonel Bourchier appears not to have known *how near* that discovery was being made. That evening Nicholson was walking down the lines of the 52d Light Infantry to speak to Colonel Campbell, when his keen eye detected, among the crowds of villagers who were pouring into camp with milk, eggs, vegetables, &c., for sale, two men whose

The Column, however, was not to enjoy, even here, much rest. By nine o'clock on the morning of the 12th, the tidings came in to Nicholson that the rebels were at the Trimmoo Ghat (or ferry), some ten miles off. Again the Column was on the move, though weary and foot-sore from the fatigues of the previous day; and by noon had come up within a mile of the river-bank. Here they could see the mutineers in the act of crossing, forming, and deploying as they landed —the 46th N. I. in the centre, with portions of the 9th Cavalry on either flank, and with videttes thrown out in advance.

With what feelings must the Column have thus confronted its old acquaintances of Sealkote! The Sealkote brigade, for such virtually it was, facing the Sealkote mutineers! The blood of the brave old Brigadier, of the kind-hearted *generalé doctor*, the respected Mr Hunter, and others, each and all of whom had friends in the Column, called aloud for vengeance. Thus they met—the murderers and the avengers of blood.

"The ground chosen by the enemy" (to quote again from Colonel Bourchier) "was most favourable for their operations; in their front was a deep narrow strip of

bearing attracted his notice. "Call the sergeant-major of the 52d," he said. "Sergeant-major, those two men are sepoys of the 46th—have them secured." The order was instantly obeyed; and the men confessed that they were, and were come to raise 2d Irregulars at Goordaspore. Had these men not been noticed, the tidings of the Column having arrived would have flown like lightning into the rebel camp; and they would probably have doubled back, and for a time have escaped.

water, over which was only one bridge, and their flanks were protected by villages. Scarcely had the artillery crossed the bridge, and were forming on the opposite side, screened by the Punjab levies, than down came the 9th Cavalry on their flanks (before the 52d could form to receive them), gnashing their teeth, and worked up to the utmost with intoxicating drugs; they cut right and left at the gunners and drivers. Away scampered the mounted levies back to Goordaspore; the enemy pushed out their skirmishers to within fifty yards of the guns, and a tremendous volley from the whole line, delivered as simultaneously as if on parade at Sealkote, made things at first look very ugly.

"In five minutes the scene was changed: not a trooper of the 9th Cavalry who charged the guns left the batteries alive. The infantry formed on our flanks, and a well-directed pounding of grape and shrapnell from nine guns, aided by the rifles of the infantry, soon told a tale. In about twenty minutes the fire of the enemy was subdued; in ten minutes more they were in full retreat towards the river, leaving between three or four hundred killed and wounded on the field.

"Had the General but possessed a squadron or two of cavalry, not a man would have escaped. The Sikhs, less done up by the sun than the Europeans, advanced, gallantly led by Lieutenant Boswell. The horses were nearly as much done up as the men, and could hardly get up a canter to the river-bank, where we took possession of all the baggage and stores crossed over by the enemy." *

* BOURCHIER'S *Eight Months' Campaign*, pp. 18, 19.

And thus closed the first scene of the Trimmoo-Ghat drama, with at least one important result gained, that the rebels, if not destroyed, had been driven back from the left bank of the Ravee.

Here, however, they found themselves in a dilemma they had little anticipated. The bank or strip of land by means of which they had crossed, and where they had again been driven back, divides the river into two channels—the southern one a deep and strong current, the other at times little more than a marsh, and almost always fordable ; but when the water rises (and it was now rising rapidly from the melted snow), this channel becomes flooded to such a depth as to be quite impassable. Thus it happened that the water which the rebels were able to wade through with some little difficulty on the 11th, was utterly unfordable two days after. The bank of land had now become an island. Here, with the dreaded Nicholson in front, the fear of a pursuing force from Jhelum in their rear, and the whole country around eager to catch and fleece them, they were in no enviable position. If, by chance, some clever student of one of the Government colleges, where mental culture is the *summum bonum*, and Christianity has no place, happened to be among them, he might have recalled to mind, and have translated into choice Oordoo, to his blood-stained companions, as aptly illustrating their own position, the reflection of that prince of traitors and murderers, Macbeth,—

> "There is nor flying hence, nor tarrying here."

Here they were to remain, but only till Nicholson could mature his plans for their annihilation. Lieutenant Boswell was left behind with his new Punjab Infantry to watch them, or, as a native would say, "to sit upon their heads," and also to guard the recovered property, while the Column returned for the night to Goordaspore.* The following afternoon they were out again, and moved down to the neighbourhood of the Ghat, and took up their ground, well out of reach of the old gun. The next day, the 15th, was spent in making preparations; boats were procured, and everything ready for an attack on the following morning. The mutineers, though thus hopelessly entrapped, were not idle; they ran up a breastwork close to the water's edge, behind which they placed the old gun; and, as if preparing for a desperate resistance, they tried to fortify the walls of a little village, *Meeadee*, on the northern point of the island. By daylight on the 16th, Nicholson brought down the guns to the river's bank, with orders to pour in shot and shell vigorously, so as to draw off attention, while he was moving down the infantry to a lower point from which he could cross them over unobserved to the southern end of the island. Nothing could be more successful; the rebels saw only the guns, and on them they sent charge after charge. The old gun had never done such a day's

* "It was long after dark before we arrived in camp, I can fairly say, dead beat. A sergeant died by my side of sheer exhaustion, and many of the 52d shared the same fate. None who have not experienced it know what those exposed on a battle-field suffer in India in the month of July. As we were returning to camp, my servant brought me a bottle of beer; I poured out a tumbler; a sergeant of the 52d passed me, and fairly turned round to stare at it: such a look of exhaustion I never before saw—he said not a word. I offered him the tumbler; his 'God bless you, sir!' was an ample reward."—BOURCHIER'S *Eight Months' Campaign.*

SKETCH

OF OPERATIONS AT

TRIMMOO GHAT

July 16th 1857.

W. & A. K. Johnston Edinburgh

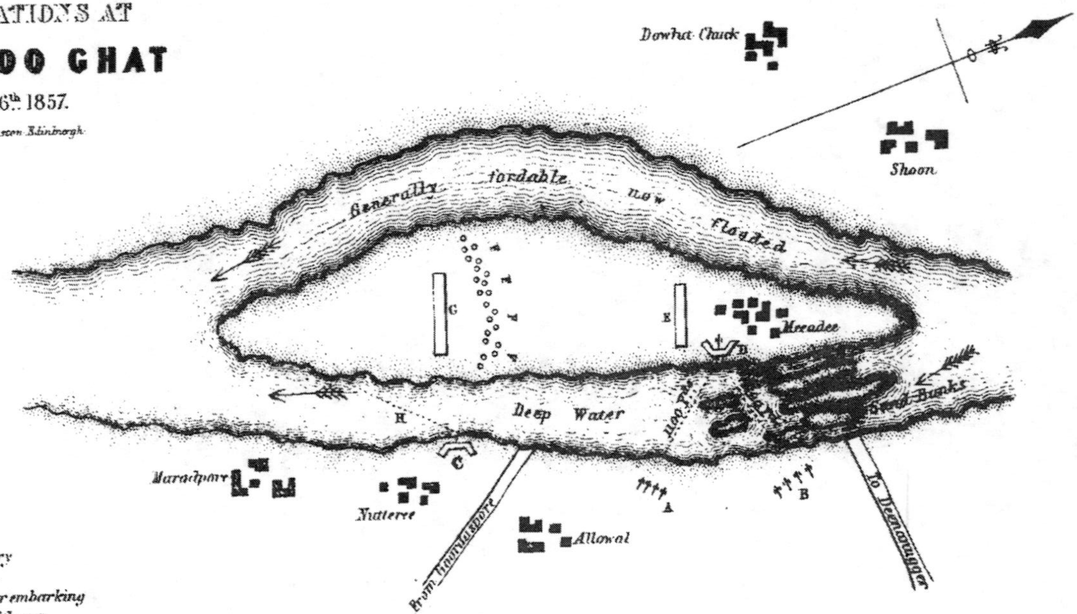

Reference

A Bourcheir's Battery

B Dawes's Troop H.A.

C Breastwork to cover embarking

D Enemy's Battery with gun

E Mutineers

F Skirmishers G Supports

H Passage of Force in Boats

work since it stood in a Sikh battery at Goojerat. But in the meanwhile H.M. 52d had moved down and crossed over, and were forming on the island, unnoticed by the mutineers. Nicholson, ever foremost, galloped ahead with a few sowars to reconnoitre the ground. It was thick brushwood, so he came almost on the picquets of the rebels. Out went the skirmishers of the 52d; back fell the picquets; the English words of command were heard at every point from the rebels; the gun was swung round, and brought to bear on the advancing column, but happily was elevated too high to do much harm. On pushed the 52d in admirable order, and when near enough went in at the double, seized the old gun, and bayoneted the few who stood at it. "It was now helter-skelter," says an eyewitness;* "they ran to the head of the island, were followed up by our fellows, and took to the water; many of them must have been drowned; numbers were like mud-larks on sandbanks and small islands; and how poor Pandy is to get out of it I do not know. There is deep water on the other side, and the villagers are up; there are only two or three places on this side where they can cross; these are all watched, and the zemindars are all alive." The few who did get over were soon seized, given up, and either hung or blown away from guns. Of those who escaped upwards in the direction of Jummoo, and attempted to skirt round the lower ranges of the hills, great numbers were caught by the villagers and police, or by the Maharajah's troops,† and

* Whose graphic letter was published in the *Lahore Chronicle*.

† Some, about 100, escaped, and were for some time protected in

were brought to Sealkote, where they were summarily dealt with as they deserved. The loss on our side was very slight: three officers were slightly wounded—Capt. C. M. Fitzgerald, Dep. Commissary-General, Lieut. Baillie of the 35th L. I., and Lieut. H. Harrington, of the Artillery;* the latter, though with a ball through his instep, would not leave his guns, and remained seated on a gun-carriage giving his orders to the last.

Thus ended a short week of inglorious mutiny.†

There was danger, too, at FEROZEPORE; the 10th L. Cav. still retained their arms and horses. This corps had certainly borne itself quietly in the outbreak; that was charitably taken for good service, and a complimentary order accordingly sent to them from head-quarters. On a subsequent occasion it had behaved really well; in the middle of June a faqeer had raised the standard of rebellion in the Nabba Rajah's territory, and a large gathering, said to amount to 4000 or 5000, threatened the peace of the district. Major Marsden took with him a wing of the 10th L. C. and two guns to attack the fanatics; the faqeer was caught and hung, several of his followers killed, and

Cashmere; but when the remonstrances of Sir John Lawrence to Maharajah Rumbeer Singh became unpleasantly strong, they were compelled to leave; and after wandering in the hills, first endeavouring to raise the Chinese on the border of Thibet, and baffled there, hoping to get into Oude, they were all caught at the head of the Kangra Valley in August 1858, by Lieut. Knox, Dep.-Commissioner of Kooloo.

* For a subsequent act of signal gallantry at Lucknow, Lieutenant Harrington received the Victoria Cross.

† For General Nicholson's Official Report, see Appendix L.

the rest dispersed; and the conduct of the 10th L. C. was declared to be "conspicuous and gallant." Still, after the outbreak at Sealkote, and the treacherous and bloodthirsty attack of the 9th Cavalry, it was considered unsafe to allow a single Poorbeah regiment to retain its arms, and the order came to dismount and disarm the 10th L. C.; which was carried out on the following morning, despite the indignant protests of the officers.*

One more change in this kaleidoscopic narrative: again the scene shifts, and the reader, if not already wearied out, must pass from the carnage and heat of the plains, the outbreak of Jhelum and Sealkote, and the retribution at Trimmoo Ghat, to the peaceful regions at KANGRA, where the mountain-breezes bear on their wings no echoes of the cannon's roar, and sweep over hills and valleys unstained by Christian blood.

The night on which the warning had been sent to Nicholson, had seen another messenger hastening off to warn Major Reynel Taylor to disarm the 4th N. I. at Kangra and Noorpoor. For nearly two months all had remained quiet here. The sepoys of the 4th had been perfectly orderly and respectful, and the district, after the first excitement had subsided, relapsed into its generally peaceful state.

On the 11th of July, Mr Montgomery's messenger reached Major Taylor. He also saw that the time was now clearly come to disarm the 4th N. I., for

* See page 104.

though not a shadow of suspicion rested on them, the fear was, that neither their loyalty, nor the fort, would be proof against a large body of rebels pouring down upon them; and it has been shown, on the safety of that fort depended the peace of the whole district. Major Taylor at once communicated his orders to Captain Younghusband, and by five o'clock that evening the wing of the 4th and the "Shere Dils" were turned out at short notice on the parade-ground of the former. Major Taylor addressed the sepoys, and said the order had come to take away their arms—not that there was a shadow of any imputation on their character, but a fear that they might not be able to escape the contagion of other mutinous corps supposed to be coming down on them. Their reply was, that "their arms were the property of Government, and they were quite ready to give them up at the request of their officers, and only regretted that any show of force had been made." * The bells of arms were then opened, the muskets and ammunition taken out, and carried into the citadel; and all was safe.

There still remained the right wing of the 4th N. I. at Noorpore, thirty-four miles off; where also was a fort, though much smaller and less important than that at Kangra. So having peaceably effected his purpose at

* The writer is indebted to the letter of an eyewitness for nearly all these details. "The men," says the same authority, "were very down-hearted; the officers used to visit them two or three times a-day in their lines, and laugh and joke with them, and set up some amusements to divert them, and thus the men soon recovered their cheerfulness."

Kangra, Major Taylor rode over that night to Noorpore, taking a hundred of the "Shere Dils," and sending on word to the commanding officer, Major Wilkie, of his intention of being there on the following morning, and the object he had in view. Here the news of the Jhelum and Sealkote outbreaks had already arrived, and the little station was actually in a state of siege.

All the ladies and families had collected in the fort; the guards had been strengthened, and extra ammunition served out; the Sikhs and Punjabees of the left wing* had gone out under Lieutenant Stothert to meet the Sealkote mutineers, and a steady resistance awaited them. So unwavering was the confidence of Major Wilkie in his men, that on receiving Major Taylor's intimation of his approach, and its object, he wrote back to beg that the "Shere Dils" might not be marched into the station, and at once went himself into the lines, and told the men of the 4th N. I. they were required to give up their arms. To their honour be it recorded, they obeyed at once; nay, more, they carried their arms to the bungalow of Major Wilkie, above a mile from the fort, having to pass through the city on their way! Their one feeling seemed to be that of pride at being so trusted, and a determination to requite that confidence as it deserved.*

* When the order had come, in the middle of June, for all Sikhs and Punjabees to be drafted out of the Poorbeah regiments, and sent off to Lahore, all those in the left wing at Kangra had been sent off to Noorpore, but halted there for further orders.

† It may be here also mentioned that when a report of the mutiny of the 2d Irregulars at Goordaspore reached Noorpore, Major Wilkie ordered out fifty men, twenty of them Punjabees, and thirty Poor-

Here was the last point touched by the ripple of the Jhelum disaster and the Sealkote outbreak. Not a Poorbeah regiment south of the Indus now retained its arms, and the Column was now free to push on for Delhi, 4000 strong, of whom 1200 were Europeans, with John Nicholson at their head.*

beahs, to oppose the advance of the cavalry. "This party having received the ammunition, marched to the Tehseel, where the muskets were kept, armed themselves, and after waiting some hours outside the town, the report proving false, went back to the Tehseel, lodged their muskets, and returned quietly and cheerily to the fort."

* The following stirring order was published by General Nicholson on the occasion:—

"CAMP, GOORDASPORE, *July* 17, 1857.

"The last remaining party of the Sealkote mutineers was yesterday morning destroyed, and its gun captured.

"The object of the forced march of the column from Umritsur to this place having been thus successfully accomplished, the Brigadier-General desires to return his sincere thanks to officers and men of all arms and grades, for the cordial and valuable assistance he has received from them throughout these operations.

"The Brigadier-General considers that the column has reason to feel proud of the service it has rendered the State within the last few days.

"By a forced march of unusual length, performed at a very trying season of the year, it has been able to preserve many stations and districts from pillage and plunder, to save more than one regiment from the danger of too close a contact with the mutineers; and the mutineer force itself, 1100 strong, notwithstanding the very desperate character of the resistance offered by it, has been utterly destroyed or dispersed.

"It will be the pleasing duty of the Brigadier-General to bring prominently to the notice of Government, in detail, the services rendered by officers and men on this occasion, and he entertains no doubt but that those services will be appreciated and acknowledged as they deserve."

CHAPTER XIII.

[JULY 1857.—PART III.]

MOOLTAN—PESHAWUR—THE FRONTIER—FORT MACKESON—NORINGEE.

WHILE the central districts of the Punjab were being thus cleared out, the mutinous regiments that remained either quietly disarmed or annihilated,.the frontier was not without its anxieties.

Mooltan *seemed safe;* like the Punjab, it was for the present quiet. By the disarming of the sepoy corps on the 10th of June the snake had been scotched —though not killed. Reinforcements, too, were almost daily coming in; though so pressing were the demands of the Punjab that there was no alternative but to push them on; however, their very presence as they passed through was not without its effect. On the 14th of June three companies of the 2d Punjab Infantry (Green's Rifles), from Dehra Ghazee Khan, had come in; this had enabled Captain Hughes with his 1st Punjab Cavalry to push on for Ferozepore and Delhi. A week after, a wing of the 1st Bombay Fusiliers had arrived from Scinde, but were at once passed on to Lahore.*

* The heat was so intense that, on the first march out of Mooltan, eight men died from sunstroke.

Thus Mooltan was gaining little in actual strength; nor, indeed, from the middle of May to the 10th of June, was its position more critical, or treason more rife, than at this period. Secret meetings were being constantly held in the Shewallah, but the designs of the traitors were so craftily covered that it seemed impossible to lay hands on the ringleaders. So cunning were they, especially those of the 69th N. I., that whenever they found a man unwilling to join in their treason or likely to betray them, he was at once reported to the commanding officer as a "dangerous character;" and so implicit still remained the faith of the commandants in the stanchness of their men, that a native officer had only to bring such an imputation against an obnoxious man to obtain his instant discharge. Thus, while the plot was thickening, the chief obstacles to its success were being one by one got rid of.*

However, by the end of July Mooltan had become much strengthened by reinforcements. The 1st Belooch battalion had arrived from Scinde under Colonel Far-

* One of the men who had been in this way reported and discharged as a "dangerous character," bolder than the rest, openly declared that he was only "put out of the way." To Major Crawford Chamberlain, who heard them, these words furnished a clue which he never lost sight of. Several of the sowars of the 1st Irregular Cavalry, disguised as faqeers, would straggle into the lines of the 69th N. I., and wheedle secrets out of the men; and information has thus, day by day, been accumulating, which enabled the authorities at last to take decisive measures. Many arrests were made; the subahdar-major, whose arrest has been already mentioned, and several others, were brought to a court-martial, convicted, and blown away from guns. This duty was performed by native gunners, who showed no delay or hesitation. It is true, there were half-a-dozen European artillerymen, fusee in hand, close to each gun.

quhar, and the remaining wing of the 1st Bombay Fusiliers under Major Hogge. Nor must we forget to mention the services of Golam Mustapha Khan Kugwarree, a very influential Pathan chief of the district, who, at a hint from the Punjab Government, had raised and organised a *resalla* (troop) of cavalry, an example which proved invaluable in its influence over the other Pathan chiefs.

Now the worst was over; Mooltan had safely tided over the danger, could hold her own, and without risk push on further succours into the Punjab. The 2d Punjab Inf. had moved on for Ferozepore as soon as the Belooches began to arrive, and Golam Mustapha Khan's resalla, soon fit for service, joined General Van Cortlandt's force at Sirsa. The attitude assumed by the neighbouring chiefs, some openly doing good service, and none apparently holding back, kept the district in a state of quiet. Not that the predatory tribes had lost their inherent love of plunder, for which they, no doubt, were as ready as ever at a moment's notice; but feeling sure they would have no encouragement from their chiefs, who were committed to Government, and, moreover, having no sympathy with the mutinous sepoys, they remained quiet.

Only one event occurred to break this quiet; and it was promptly suppressed. About seventy miles from Mooltan, and twice as far from Lahore, is the town of Gogaira, where there is a small civil station, with its usual adjunct of a gaol, always well filled with convicted cattle-lifters and other marauders of the district.

In May the Gogaira force had consisted of one company of the 49th N. I. from Lahore, under a native officer, with about eighty of the *Kutar Mookhee* police battalion, and a part of a resalla of mounted police. Lieutenant Elphinstone, the Deputy-Commissioner of the district, directly he heard what had been done at Lahore, with great promptness and tact disarmed the company of the 49th N. I. by the aid of these trusty police. This precautionary step enabled him early in June to detach a large portion of the Kutar Mookhees and the whole of his mounted police, in order to reinforce General Van Cortlandt, who was moving down from Ferozepore on Sirsar and Hissar; and he had subsequently raised in the district a resalla of cavalry, and pushed them on in the same direction. Thus by the end of July his available force, as the guard upon the gaol, had been reduced to *sixteen* Kutar Mookhees, when, on the night of the 26th, a desperate attempt was made by the prisoners in the gaol to effect their escape, and to raise the neighbouring district. However, Lieutenant Elphinstone, aided by Mr Berkeley, with this handful of stanch Kutar Mookhees, was too much for the prisoners, though above 200 in number. His vigour and energy kept the mastery, and the convicts paid dearly for their rashness: some fifty were shot down in their attempt to get over the wall, and only eighteen contrived to effect their escape. There can be little doubt that a couple of hundred of these desperate fellows, had they once got out among their lawless brethren of the district, would in a few hours have thrown the whole country into commotion, ripe, as it was afterwards proved to be, for rebellion; nor could either Lahore or Mooltan at that time have spared any troops, even to settle a riotous rabble; they were too busy watching their own disarmed Poorbeahs. Before daylight, however, all was quiet; the few who had escaped, skulked away into the jungle; some of them were captured and brought back, and the rest could offer little temptation for a general rising, when they could but confess that two Englishmen and sixteen police had been more than a match for two hundred rioters.* The attempt was a signal failure, and for a while longer the district remained quiet.

Along the Dherajat frontier matters looked hopeful. For the regiments which had been withdrawn, new levies speedily sprung up to take their places. Under the magical influence of the reports which now came up regularly from Delhi of a golden reign of plunder, enlistment seemed as free and hearty here as it had been in Peshawur; and that long line of frontier, intrusted to its own mountaineer recruits, remained perhaps more peaceful than when it was lined by the Punjab Irregular Force, who had been originally placed there to overawe their marauding tendencies.

At Peshawur itself little change had taken place. Enlistment still continued the rage; the mountain tribes were still crowding in for service.

In the beginning of July, however, other reports

* The Hindoo portion of the prisoners appear not to have taken an active part in the *emeute*.

came up—of deaths before Delhi, in "the Guides," Cokes's Rifles, and other corps, and a reaction was dreaded. But Colonel Edwardes was prepared ; from an exchequer, wholly inadequate to meet even its own pressing demands, *pensions* were at once given out liberally to widows, children, brothers, parents, of any who had fallen, and the first risings of a discontent among families that suffered were at once suppressed, an additional claim established on their fidelity, and enlistment went on more briskly than ever.

About this time an event occurred which strikingly illustrated the true position of that frontier. To the south-west of Peshawur, about seventeen miles off, and within three of the Kohat Pass, stands Fort Mackeson, so called in honour of one whose name is so gloriously connected with the first years of our rule at Peshawur, and who fell at his post by the hand of the assassin.* In this fort was a detachment of the 24th N. I. disarmed. It became known to Colonel Edwardes that these traitors were carrying on a correspondence with the Bussee Kheyl Affreedees in the hills close by, pledging themselves to give up Fort Mackeson to them in return for a safe passage through the hills. Edwardes at once made the Affreedees his friends, urged them to persuade the traitors of the 24th to give them a written promise that they would give up the fort. The Affreedees fell into Edwardes' views, obtained the promise, and placed it in his hands. That night Captain Brougham, with two of his mountain-

* Colonel Mackeson was murdered in Kutcheree, in September 1853.

train guns, 150 Mooltanee Horse, and a similar force of new foot-levies, moved out of Peshawur; one-half of this force pushed on in advance, and made a circuit, so as to come round on the rear of the fort, while Edwardes brought up the rest by the direct road. The day had not yet broken when both parties almost simultaneously reached the fort walls on opposite sides. Edwardes' precautions had been perfect, the keep had been already secured.* A young officer of Brougham's battery was ordered to ride into the fort. He shall tell his own tale:—"I rode into the fort, and told the commandant to have a parade, sharp, to hear an order read. The men came and fell in. I then told him to march them on to the parade outside the fort; the men hesitated a good deal, and I thought our revolvers would come into play; however, at last out they came. It was still very dark, so that they did not twig anything until they got about seventy yards from the gate, when we heard the word of command—'Punjab Rifles,

* "Edwardes deserves great credit," says a correspondent whose letter was published in the *Times* newspaper, "for this peaceful termination of his expedition; for, knowing the fort, he had taken the precaution of seizing the keep, the fort itself having no gates. Had the mutineers been able to get into the keep when the Colonel summoned them to lay down their arms, they certainly would have fought; but the day before, he sent off a Pathan havildar and eight sepoys, with two mules and a couple of empty panniers. All that he told the havildar was to take the panniers into the keep, and make them over to the officer who resided there, and who commanded the garrison. The Pathan was further instructed to be very particular to close the gates at night, and not to open them again on any account till the sun next morning was pretty high. He obeyed his 'instructions to the letter,' and the appearance of the force before the fort next morning showed him the reason why he had been told to keep the gates shut."

double march'—and a guard of about twenty-five men rushed at the gate, boned the guard there, and shut the doors. At that moment the garrison men heard on their left flank a neighing of horses, answered soon by neighing in their front; then a sort of jingling of chains was heard on the right flank, which seemed to surprise the gentlemen paraded. The dawning of the day soon showed that it was caused by the mountain-train, escorted by 100 Rifles. The game was now up. There was the fort in the rear, the cavalry in front and on the right flank, and the guns on the left." A roll-call was now held; only one man was missing, but he was the arch-traitor of the party, and was at that very time away in the hills. He was at once given up by the hill chief, and two days after suffered the penalty of his treason. The whole affair was a complete success. Not only was the fort safe—and that without the withdrawal of a single European soldier from Peshawur, for Edwardes had accomplished it with only frontier levies—but, what was of infinitely more importance, at a time when it appeared that the hill-tribes were open to negotiation with the disarmed Poorbeahs, and every hill-chief might not have proved as faithful to us as this one did; it established a spirit of mutual mistrust and suspicion between the two races, and struck a blow at all future similar intrigue.

There was another point on the Peshawur frontier, from which danger threatened during the latter part of this month. Across our border line, on the edge of the Euzofzaie country, is a village called Noringee.

Here a moulvie, a well-known turbulent character, had unfurled the green flag of the Prophet, and was preaching a crusade against the "Nazarenes."* On the morning of the 21st of July, the occupants of this little hamlet were just entering on their daily peaceful occupations, the cattle going out to graze, the labourers to their khets (fields), when they suddenly found themselves confronted by a force which had come out from Nowshera and Hotee Murdan.

This moulvie had come *too near*, and the population were too inflammable for safety; so a small force, three of Brougham's mountain-train guns, and a detachment of 2d Punjab Cavalry, and the 4th and 5th Punjab Infantry, the whole under Major Vaughan, had gone out and presented themselves, as described, at the entrance of the valley. It does not take a borderer long to draw in defence of his hearth and home; a few minutes sufficed to convert each peaceful labourer into an armed soldier, and every hut into a little fortress; out rushed several Ghazees (Mohammedan martyrs), but they were quickly cut down by the 2d Cavalry; and the lower part of the village was soon mastered and set on fire: but the remainder still held out desperately. The heat of the sun and flames was become

* "The Ghazees came with the moulvie at their head, and planted their standard (embroidered with butchery from the Koran) on the heights of Norinjee. This mountain village was so strongly situated that the police scarcely dared to go near it, and it became a refuge for every evil-doer. Its inhabitauts, about 400 in number, welcomed the moulvie with delight. The holy war seemed auspiciously opened with every requisite—a priest, a banner, a fastness, a howling crowd of bigots, and several days' provisions."—Col. Edwardes' "Report."

irresistible, and the force fell back on Sewa, purposing to renew the attack the next morning. That night an express came summoning the 4th Punjabees (Wilde's) off to Delhi. Thus weakened, the force, anticipating a severe struggle, had to wait for reinforcements from Peshawur; these, consisting of two 24-pound howitzers, 150 Europeans, 50 from each of three corps, with Enfield rifles, under command of Captain Barnes of H. M. 27th, 150 of Cave's Sikhs, with a troop of Mooltan Horse under Sultan Jan, joined them on the 2d of August. On the morning of the 3d, the force thus strengthened again made its appearance at the mouth of the valley. This time the villagers were ready for them, and had planted themselves in force at the entrance of the village, expecting as before to be attacked in front. But while the main body were advancing by the direct route, Lieutenant Hoste,* of the 55th N. I., had been detached, with a small party of 87th Fusiliers and 5th Punjab Infantry, with orders to mount the hill by a side-path, which would bring him round to the top of the village. "It was a pretty sight," said one who witnessed it, "to see the hill-side forced. Hoste pushed on rapidly; his reaching the head of the village was the signal for the main body to move on into the lower part of it, while from the opposite hill appeared a party of the 5th Punjab Infantry, sent round with a view to cut off retreat." The enemy at once saw that the force was too strong, and, making

* Who but a few months before had returned to India, rich in experience gained in the Crimea.

little show of resistance, were soon in retreat. The moulvie, of course, was clear away; he and the leading fanatics had gone off the night before; the cattle also, and all valuables, had been removed in anticipation of such a result. The village, however, was utterly destroyed; the loss on our side only seven, that on the side of the rebels about eighty. But still more important was the lesson which it taught them, that Peshawur was strong enough to master above 3000 disarmed traitors, to overawe the city, to hold all the forts, and yet detach a Moveable Column, strong even in Europeans, for border warfare! *

Thus had passed ten weeks since that fatal May morning which told of Meerut and Delhi; and the Punjab, despite pressure from without, treachery from within, delay before Delhi, and impatience everywhere, was still ours.

* So well did they learn this lesson, that all *this portion* of the frontier remained quiet until the end of October.

CHAPTER XIV.

[AUGUST 1857.—PART I.]

THE CRITICAL POSITION OF THE PUNJAB STATIONS—THE OUTBREAK OF THE 26TH N. I. AT MEAN-MEER, AND THEIR ANNIHILATION AT UJNALA—THE EMEUTES OF THE 10TH L. CAVALRY AT FEROZEPORE; AND THE FATE OF THE 51ST N. I. AT PESHAWUR.

IF the quiet which rested on the Punjab in the month of July was deceptive, still more so that which brooded over it in the month of August. There was a lull; but it was the lull that foreboded a coming storm. The clouds were gathering around, the thunder muttered deep and low. Now again was seen the flash: but providentially it spent its force on some isolated point; the flame was extinguished before it could spread beyond. First Lahore,* then Ferozepore, and lastly Peshawur,

* There was a danger, too, though not generally known at the time, which emanated from Subathoo. Under a noble *toon* tree on the parade-ground of that station stands a small temple of considerable note, where there had resided for many years an old *byrajee* (priest) named Ram Persaud, of some repute for sanctity, and still more for wealth. He was looked on as a harmless old man, who was known to combine with his priestly functions the cares of a money-lender, but even in those days of general mistrust was never regarded by the authorities with suspicion. One day, however, towards the end of July, a letter was intercepted at the Umballa post-office from this worthy to the chief *pundit* of the Maharajah of Puttiala, calling upon him, as a most holy Brahmin, to use all his influence to alienate his chief from the "unclean cow-slaying English;" that now was the time to strike the blow; every hill rajah and rana were ready to rise, and

felt the shock, and for the moment trembled; but it passed off, and all again relapsed into that portentous lull. Not that the public generally were conscious of the danger; they could see only the flash and its effect; but they who in silent stern resolve swayed the Punjab knew too well that the whole political horizon was surcharged with the electric fluid, which might at any moment set the whole country in a blaze, and add to the horrors of a Poorbeah mutiny the crowning desolation of a Punjab rebellion.

First for Lahore. All the Hindostanee regiments there, as has been already described, had at the first outbreak been disarmed by that master-stroke of the (*still unrewarded*) Brigadier Stuart Corbett. The Sikhs had been soon after detached, and formed into a body, and had received back their arms; the *Bhojporees** also, who were believed to be free from the seditious taint, were drafted out of these corps; and thus the Poorbeahs alone remained degraded and watched. This

looked only to their liege lord for the signal; that the hill stations were utterly denuded of English; that there remained only "*wounded men, widows and children;*" that the Goorkhas of the Nusseree battalion at Seharunpore were prepared to join; and the English could be annihilated without difficulty. This valuable missive was soon in the hands of Mr Barnes the Commissioner, its contents communicated to the Maharajah (who indignantly repudiated the imputation), and the *Byrajee*, as he sat in fancied security under the shadow of his own tree, was seized, brought down to Umballa, tried, convicted, and hanged. His fate was not without its warning for good. If there was truth (as perhaps there was) in the statement that the hill chiefs were ready to rise, its failure gave them little encouragement; still less so did the noble unswerving loyalty of the Maharajah offer any countenance to such treachery. Thus, with the old priest the intrigue began and ended.

* Men of Bhojpore, a district of Behar, which was still quiet.

state of surveillance was little suited to the taste of "Jack Sepoy," who had been hitherto so petted and pampered. He writhed under the sense of detected treachery, and was for ever plotting for revenge or escape. Hitherto no opportunity had offered ; for two months and a half they had remained in sullen passiveness, nursing up their discontent, their imagined wrongs, and their spirit of rebellion.

Rumours had, indeed, been from time to time floating about that a rise was meditated ; but the cry of "wolf" so often heard, came to be little heeded. Nor even when, during the latter days of July, the rumour began to assume more shape—when even the very manner and time of the outbreak were mysteriously hinted at—was any notice taken of it, or any more than ordinary precaution adopted. However, as the mid-day gun fired on the 30th July, there came up ominous sounds of shouting and yelling from the lines of the 26th N. I. ; Major Spencer, who commanded, at once hastened down to see the cause, and found the whole regiment in mutiny. Unarmed as he was, he went forward and endeavoured to reason with them : but in vain. The tide had set in too strong to be now stemmed. A sepoy, stealing up behind, felled him with a blow from a hatchet (for though deprived of their arms, they had no difficulty in subsequently supplying themselves with native weapons), others rushed on him, and he who had grown up among them from boyhood—who had lived among them, and, it might be said, *for them*—and there were few who would have been said to be more beloved by their men—*he was hacked to pieces by his own* BABAS.* The sergeant-major also, who attempted to rescue him, was knocked down and killed. The men then broke off into parties, and made for their officers' bungalows, bent on killing every one they found. Providentially the officers were at the mess-house, and so escaped. A large body of the sepoys then rushed to the house of the chaplain, the Rev. F. Farrer (who lived in the same lines), threatening to murder him; but he became aware of the danger in time to escape. Springing into his buggy, he drove out of one gate of his compound (estate) as the fiends were pouring in at the other. Baffled everywhere, they returned to their parade-ground, and then beat a retreat. The artillery were above a mile off. It took time to give orders, and to bring the guns up in pursuit; and when they reached the lines, they found them empty, and the rebels clear away. A dust-storm, too, came on; so furious was the wind, and so dense the darkness, that pursuit was impossible. It was not even known what route they had taken. It was thought that Hurreekee Ghat, on the Sutlej, with the chance of pushing down to that focus of rebellion, Delhi, was the most probable point that they would make for; and Captain T. Blagrave started off with a small body of his new Sikh levies in that direction, while Lieut. Boswell was ordered up to the same point

* Literally *children*, a term of endearment which was commonly used by officers of sepoy regiments when speaking of or to their men. It is sad to reflect how such misplaced confidence, ay, and *affection*, have been requited.

from Umritsur, with a few of his Punjabees and some Towana Horse, to be ready for them should they effect a crossing. However, with a view doubtless to hand on the torch of mutiny to the other disarmed Hindostanee regiments scattered over the *Manjha* country, they took the very opposite direction; bearing due north, they worked up the left bank of the Ravee. They had not gone above five-and-twenty miles, when, in their attempt to cross a ghat, they were confronted by a sturdy Punjabee Tehsildar with a handful of police, and were for a time kept at bay. News of their position soon came into Umritsur; Mr F. Cooper, the Deputy Commissioner, flew off with a small body of mounted police, and by a forced march came upon them on the afternoon of the 31st. He found them in a sorry plight; famished and footsore, on an island, with no means of defence or escape. It was a second Trimmoo Ghat, only without the old Sikh gun or the Enfields, for the best weapons they could muster were hatchets and knives. By an ingenious arrangement,* Mr Cooper succeeded in getting them all off the island, and landing them on the shore, in such small detachments that they were outnumbered, and bound with ropes, and thus secured were marched off, 500 rebel sepoys, under guard of scarcely a quarter that number of police, to Ujnala, the nearest police-station. Here, on the following morning, a general execution took place; and within forty-eight hours of the outbreak at

* This is described at some length in the *Crisis in the Punjab*, p. 94-99.

Mean-Meer, the 26th N. I. had ceased to be ; and the peace of the Punjab was still secured.*

From Lahore and Ujnala we pass to Ferozepore. The month was scarcely half over when the *emeute* of

* The circumstances of this execution have been most unsparingly, and perhaps not altogether unnaturally, censured in various quarters, either for party purposes, or in ignorance of the real state of the country, or both. Not only has Mr Cooper been condemned, but even Sir John Lawrence and Mr Montgomery have been included in the censure, for daring to approve of the tremendous retribution inflicted on the 26th N. I. Let the reader think only of the really critical position of the Punjab at that time, and he will at once see that that stern policy was the only safe one ; and that the fate of the 26th mutineers, murderers and deserters as they were, was both *just* and *necessary ;* nor would it have called forth a single word of condemnation, but for the glowing terms of exultation in which Mr Cooper so unfortunately described their annihilation. On this whole question, who so capable of judging as Mr Montgomery himself ? and his statement must silence all further cavil.

" Under the facts above stated," says Mr Montgomery in his official review of the whole case, " there arise three questions :—

" *First.*—Were the men legally and morally liable to the punishment of death ?

" *Second.*—Was this punishment, under the circumstances, necessary as well as just ?

" *Third.*—Was it possible, under the said circumstances, to select men for various degrees of punishment, or to wait for a formal trial ?

" On each of these questions a few words may be said.

" *First,* then, Were they legally and morally liable to the punishment of death ? Now it will have been seen that they were murderers, mutineers, and rebels, in the broadest sense. As such they were taken *in flagrante delicto.* And for such an offence the punishment of death is adjudged both in law and morals. The whole body were directly or indirectly participating in the murders, the mutinous rising, the escape, the resistance. If this be so, then the whole body were justly executed. Where many blows were struck, it was impossible to say which hand was most guilty. Subsequent inquiries seemed to point to a particular man as having dealt a fatal blow to Major Spencer ; but at the time the whole regiment were banded in one accord, and none would inculpate the other. They stood, acted, and fell together.

" *Secondly,* Was the punishment necessary as well as just ? Now at that moment the Lahore Government was literally in extremity. Its last available European troops had been despatched to Delhi. There was but one weak European regiment to guard the whole Lahore the 10th Cavalry there threatened, if not to convulse the Punjab, at least to throw a fresh force of mounted traitors into the rebel army at Delhi, at a time when

division, containing the two capitals of Lahore and Umritsur. Within this circle there were three disarmed regiments at Lahore (besides the 26th), and two at Umritsur. At Goordaspore, some forty miles distant from Umritsur, there was an armed regiment of Irregular Cavalry, which, though still obedient, might easily be tempted by the spectacle of successful mutiny. There were disarmed troops at the neighbouring stations of Noorpoor and Hosheyarpore. The Punjab population, both Sikh and Mohammedan, was known to be in a feverish state. The country was drifting or tending towards rebellion, as was afterwards evident from two partial insurrections which actually did take place. British power at Lahore was in the air, with no support either above, or below, or on any side. When, therefore, any rising took place, it was absolutely necessary to strike any blow that could be struck. The crisis did not admit of any leniency being shown to mutineers. Things were at such a stage that either the mutineers must be executed, or else the lives and honour of the English must be sacrificed. When the 26th N. I. broke out, the English believed themselves to be in imminent danger; none knew to what extent the disaster might spread; all apprehended a general rising of the disarmed troops, which could hardly be put down, and which, if not put down, must lead to a general insurrection, and the ultimate destruction of British power in the Lahore division. When, therefore, the English heard of the destruction of the 26th N. I., they felt joy and gratitude for the deliverance which Providence had vouchsafed. The circumstances were perfectly known to all at the time, and none doubted the necessity and justice of the retribution which had befallen the mutineers.

"*Thirdly*, Was it possible for Mr Cooper at the moment to select men for various degrees of punishment, or to wait for a formal trial? Now, it is to be remembered that the place of capture was thirty miles distant from the nearest station, Umritsur. How was he to guard and transport thither the mutineers, when he had scarcely sufficient men to seize and execute them summarily? Of the force he had with him some were untrustworthy, and had to be sent back to Umritsur. The few raw Sikh levies that remained were hardly numerous enough for the short and sad duty that had to be done. If Mr Cooper had tried to transport the prisoners to Umritsur, they might very probably have overpowered their guard on the march, and then all the evils mentioned in the preceding paragraph would have been precipitated. If he had chanced to succeed in transporting them to Umritsur, then there was no jail large enough to hold them; there was a large body of Hindostanee comrades ready to fraternise; there was no available our holding on there, already opposed by such overwhelming numbers, was a matter of grave anxiety.

The previous conduct of the 10th Cavalry, their

European force; and the risk of an outbreak at the most critical point—namely, the religious capital of the Sikhs—would have been extreme. Therefore the immediate execution of the men was almost unavoidable. In fact, had Mr Cooper, through dread of responsibility or any other reason, *attempted any other course than that he actually pursued*, the attempt would probably have failed, and failure might have brought on the most disastrous consequences. That some of the prisoners died in confinement during the brief interval which preceded the execution, was an unhappy and unforeseen accident. Had the crisis been less perilous, had there been European troops at hand to uphold the law, then of course they would have been tried, and selections would have been made for various degrees of punishment. But this was, in the case under discussion, simply impossible. In all times and in all countries, the complexion of guilt and the severity of punishment are affected by the circumstances of the moment. And at that time, death was, in justice and necessity, awarded to all mutineers. Those of the 26th who were captured separately, and tried by court-martial, were sentenced to the same punishment as that inflicted by Mr Cooper on their comrades.

"From this explanation the true character of the affair will be understood. The necessity of inflicting such stern justice on so large a body of criminals is to be lamented. But it was justice nevertheless. Though Mr Cooper's acts may be well vindicated, yet the style of his narrative is much to be regretted. His conduct could only be justified by necessity. Supposing (of course erroneously) that the circumstances would be understood everywhere, he omitted to explain fully in his narrative the necessity which really existed, and to express adequately the sense which he doubtless felt of the sad and painful nature of the task which had fallen to his lot. His error lay, not in the act itself, but in the way of describing it.* And it is hoped that his countrymen will, after learning all the facts, show a just consideration towards a British officer who evinced great energy and moral resolution under circumstances of extraordinary trial and difficulty.

"R. MONTGOMERY,
Lieutenant-Governor, and formerly
Judicial Commissioner of the Punjab.

"LAHORE, *April* 1859."

---

* Lord Canning, in his minute on the services of the civil officers, says of Mr Cooper: "I hope (he) will be judged by his acts, done under stern necessity, rather than by the narrative of them."

behaviour in cantonments on the 13th May, the ready service of the detachment in the Fyzulke district, where they seized and gave up emissaries from Delhi caught in their camp, their unflinching attack on the village of Jeytoo under Major Marsden—indeed, their general orderly behaviour, whether in camp or in quarters, during those months of excitement—require that their outbreak at the last should be dwelt on at greater length than the event itself perhaps demands.

The circumstances were these :—

The Jhelum disaster and Sealkote outbreak in July had shown that at such a time not a Hindostanee regiment was to be trusted. Instantly on the receipt of the tidings from Sealkote, Mr Montgomery had (as the reader will remember) sounded forth the note of warning to every point of danger, and among the others to Ferozepore. Brigadier Innes saw the risk from the 10th Cavalry still retaining their horses and arms ; his resolve was at once made to disarm and dismount, but at the same time to show every consideration compatible with the public safety to men who had hitherto borne themselves well, and even now had not come under any direct suspicion. The intimation from Lahore reached him on the 9th July, and the following morning the whole regiment * was assembled in front of the barracks of the 61st Queen's. A dismounted

* From the first, Brigadier Innes had taken the precaution of separating the two wings ; the one was moved into tents between the European infantry barracks and the intrenchment, while the other remained in their own lines, the two wings changing places every week.

parade was held; the men were told what had occurred at Sealkote, and were ordered to file past and lay down their sabres; the pistols were in the meanwhile being quietly taken out of the holsters, where the horses were picqueted close by. There was no demonstration of force, though the means of coercion were at hand if needed: behind the barracks the 61st were drawn up under arms, the guns on that face of the intrenchment all shotted, and Woodcock's battery ready alongside. But there was no necessity to use force: the men obeyed without hesitation. Their lines were also searched, and all private arms taken away; and thus the disarming was complete, without any sign of resistance. And then, to show as much confidence as possible in the men, their horses were all left picqueted close by the tents, near the European lines.*

But Delhi still held out; the artillery were losing horses, and there were no Government studs left to supply remounts; so, early in August, there came an order from Lahore, that one hundred of the horses of the 10th Cavalry should be sent to fill up the gaps caused in the artillery. Then a few days later, fifty more were called for, for the use of the Cashmere contingent, which was marching down to Delhi. Both batches were withdrawn without a word or sign of remonstrance from the men. But a further trial was

* It so happened that one squadron was absent under Captain Dumbleton, having gone on escort duty to Umballa. On their return to Loodiana they heard what had taken place at Ferozepore, and were also ordered to give up their arms and horses, which they did without any hesitation.

awaiting them, and secret influences were at work to make them less willing to bear it. New levies of Irregular Cavalry were springing up in every quarter; the Peshawur frontier, the Salt range, the Manjha country, all were sending in claimants for service; and to mount them a further call was necessary on the horses of the dismouted corps, which were now standing idle; and among other regiments, the 10th Cavalry were required to give up what still remained, with the veterinary surgeon, the European non-commissioned officers, and syces. In the meanwhile, emissaries from Delhi had been among them; in spite of the strictest *espionage,* letters breathing sedition would find their way into the lines; then two of the Irregular Cavalry corps, sent back from Delhi under a cloud, passed through; a wing of the 17th Irregular Cavalry, bound for Leia, under Captain P. R. Hockin, who had dropped seventeen suspicious characters *en passant,* to be taken care of in the Ferozepore jail; and the 9th Irregular Cavalry, under Captain Campbell, *en route* to Bunnoo—a corps which contained, as after-events showed, some desperate traitors, and spread sedition wherever it passed.*

This order was issued from Lahore on the 12th of August, to the effect that all the horses, &c., of the

* The author would on no account be understood as reflecting on the character of the *whole* regiment. It contained, no doubt, many good men and true; but past events before Delhi proved, and after-events still more, that it had in its ranks some desperate traitors. They alarmed the men of the 10th with hints that Government was preparing to send them down the Sutlej in boats, and to sink them in the stream!

10th Light Cavalry were to be sent to the "remount depot" which was being formed there under Captain Snow of the 9th Cavalry. It reached Ferozepore on the 14th; but so anxious was Brigadier Innes to spare the 10th Cavalry this further trial if possible, especially as the order for their being disarmed and dismouted in July had been accompanied by the assurance that, in acknowledgment of their good conduct, they should be the first regiment to receive back their horses and arms when the time might arrive for such a step, that he pleaded that an exception might be made in their favour. On the 18th the answer came that the demand of the public service did not admit of such an exception. That night the order became known; and the following day came the struggle.

There had been little to portend such a desperate *emeute.* It was known, indeed, that a spirit of discontent was beginning to work among the men: they would complain that the thanks of the Government and of the Commander-in-Chief proved but empty praise; for that now, without a single act of disobedience on their part, their arms, horses, and non-commissioned officers, all that constituted them a regiment, were to be taken from them, and all feeling of self-respect was gone.

About one o'clock, the most unguarded hour of the day—the men at their dinner, the officers enjoying their *siesta*—a rush was made on the guns of Woodcock's battery from the tents, where the men of the other wing had been noticed thronging in; out came clubs, sticks, stones, that had been concealed under their white sheets; the sentry was knocked down; the guard turned out, but were overpowered by numbers; the guns were seized and turned on the barracks; the heel-ropes of the horses cut; and the mutineers seemed for the moment to have all their own way—when out poured the artillery in force from the nearest barrack, and from the next the depot of the 61st;* the mutineers were quickly driven from the guns, and a few minutes more would have seen all of them either cut down or captured, and quiet restored, when suddenly a gun from the nearest bastion of the intrenchment opened fire—a most unhappy, insane step—it covered the horses; the grape swept through them, and over they rolled, killed and wounded, while some in their fright broke loose and tore away to their old stables. So utter was the confusion caused by the fire from this gun, that the mutineers were able to move off with but trifling loss,† and made away leisurely, taking with them every horse they could lay hands on—such of their own loose troopers as they could catch, any chargers found in their officers' stables, grass-cutters' ponies, *bazaar tats*, all were seized; and thus, with the exception of about one hundred who remained quiet, the whole regiment made good their retreat. Captain

* The regiment had gone to Delhi when relieved by a wing of the Bombay Fusiliers, leaving only the depot of women and children and sick under a small guard.

† Seventeen of them only were killed, whereas above twice that number of horses were either killed, or so severely wounded that it was necessary to shoot them on the spot.

Salmon's young Sikh recruits were quickly out to clear the cantonments; a small force, consisting of such of the Bombay Fusiliers as could be spared, and a couple of the guns from Woodcock's battery, went in pursuit, joined by Major Marsden, with a few mounted police and Puttiala Horse; but the mutineers had too good a start; moreover, they had judiciously chosen their line of road—nullahs, ravines, and jungles defied pursuit—and they got clear away. The day, too, was closing in; and with a station, and above all such a magazine to care for, the Brigadier, finding the pursuit hopeless, hastened back to cantonments, where he was soon joined by Major Marsden, who, even with his mounted force, could make but little way after the rebels, and had drawn off his men.*

Thus the storm burst and passed on.† The mutineers bore away in a south-westerly direction towards Hansi,‡ and the Punjab was free of them.§

* The more wisely that some of the men with him were not over-stanch or over-brave.

† There were two casualties among the Europeans: the sentry who was knocked down died of his wounds a few days after, and Veterinary-Surgeon Nelson was cut down by some troopers as he attempted to escape to the Fort.

‡ Some ten or twelve of the fugitive mutineers were caught in the Loodiana district, and hung, after trial, by Mr G. Ricketts, C.S. The body of them made their way through Hansi to Delhi; but there (as report says), instead of a hearty welcome awaiting them, all their shortcomings in treachery were remembered against them, and they were refused admission into the city.

§ The author cannot leave this part of the subject—Ferozepore and its Brigadier—without noticing briefly a most painful incident connected with it,—the temporary removal of Brigadier Innes from the brigade-staff of the army.

At the outset Brigadier Innes was thanked officially and privately.

But the month was not to close without another—and, though the last, the most dangerous—outbreak. Peshawur had been for weeks in a state of siege.* All the disarmed Hindostanee regiments had indeed been

Mr Montgomery, the Judicial Commissioner, on hearing of the Ferozepore doings, called them a "success," and wrote, "I congratulate you most sincerely." The Commander-in-Chief, General Anson, expressed his "perfect approbation of the judgment, vigour, and decision with which the Brigadier had acted." General Gowan, at Lahore, offered officially his "thanks and acknowledgments for the promptitude and energy" shown by him; and privately wrote, "I myself have full confidence in you," &c. Yet a few weeks after, apparently from some private source, reports reached Sir John Lawrence of a want of energy and zeal at Ferozepore; and the Chief Commissioner wrote to Government, begging that Brigadier Innes might be removed—a request which was at once complied with, without any opportunity being offered of explanation or defence.

It is possible to understand how an impatience of anything which fell short of that high pressure of energy under which he himself lived and worked, and a consequent readiness to believe any reports of shortcomings or delay at any point, might prompt the Chief Commissioner, in those days when our tenure of the Punjab—our very existence—trembled in the scale, to pass a hasty censure; but how a condemnation so severe—not to say wholly undeserved—should have been dealt out against a well-proved officer, is a subject of as much surprise as regret.

Men living all those troublous weeks at Ferozepore, daily *feeling* the effects of the Brigadier's conduct, may be accepted as no incompetent judges. All classes—officers in civil employ, commanding officers, and private soldiers—all openly affirmed their opinions. They who would have been the loudest to cry out about his mismanagement were the loudest in his defence. The soldiers' wives in the barracks declared they "owed their lives to him." The native tradesmen of the bazaar wrote in their farewell address, "To you we owe all, our lives and our property." Old friends who knew his past career wrote, "There must be some great mistake here." Mistake indeed there was—hasty *misrepresentations,* and perhaps thoughtless ones; but they involved a wrong that was little contemplated or intended, and which time did not admit of then refuting.

However, a more calm investigation of the case by Lord Clyde, in the days of returning peace, has in some measure retrieved the wrong—the charge is refuted, the stigma on a brave officer removed.

* The real state of Peshawur cannot be better depicted than in the "Memorandum," issued early in August. See Appendix M.

allowed to remain in their own lines, but under close surveillance, for it was known that they were deep in intrigue in every quarter; and now and again some would-be ringleader of mutiny was detected, convicted, and summarily made an example of. Nothing but the unwearied vigilance of Colonel Edwardes and the prompt energy of General Sidney Cotton had kept them down so long. They had been living on the whole time in passive rebellion, only waiting an opportunity to break out; and the opportunity came, but not exactly with the result they had wished.

In the end of August the authorities received sure information that arms were being purchased in great numbers, and were most probably being secreted in the native lines; and it was resolved to institute such a search as should defy all evasion, and set at rest all such attempts for the future, and at the same time to throw the suspected regiments out into camp in "the open," where every movement could be still more closely watched. The 27th N. I. and 51st N. I. were the two corps most suspected; and on the 28th of August they were ordered to move out into tents on the plain beyond their respective parade-grounds; every precaution being taken to meet the possibility of the order being resisted, and becoming the signal for an outbreak. Captain Cave brought down his Sikhs to the lines of the 27th N. I., to superintend their move, and to take possession of their huts when vacated; while H. M. 87th R. I. Fusiliers, under Colonel Murray, with a squadron of the Peshawur Light Horse and a couple of guns, lay in their own barrack-square alongside, in readiness to overawe the sepoys, should they attempt any resistance. The 51st N. I. fell to Captain Bartlett and his young Afghan levies; and in the adjacent barrack-square were H. M. 27th and 70th regiments, with another squadron of the Peshawur Light-Horse, and two more guns, the whole under command of Colonel Kyle. Such were the arrangements. The process of vacating the lines began early in the day, and had gone on quietly for some hours; each regiment moving out *en masse* to its camping-ground, leaving behind only the regimental guards, while fatigue-parties kept moving to and fro, carrying out the property. When all had been removed, the work of search began. In the lines of the 27th N. I. all was quiet; the men obeyed in sullen passiveness. But not so the 51st N. I. About mid-day, as Captain Bartlett was sitting on the edge of a tank in the centre of their lines, looking on at his Afghans in their work of search, the sepoys at the quarter-guard made a sudden rush at him, and simultaneously (as no doubt by concert) the whole regiment rose, to use Captain Bartlett's own expression, "with a whirr like a covey of partridges," broke, and made a dash, some for their lines, and others for a field close by. Captain Bartlett sprang into the tank, and kept off the villains by pointing his revolver at them, until some of his own men ran to his rescue. The alarm was sounded: out ran the Afghans from the huts, and threw themselves on the advancing sepoys. In a few moments more the

Inniskillings, the Light-Horse, and guns, were pouring out of the barrack-square, and the struggle began. The guns opened fire; the Inniskillings were thrown out in detachments on either flank to prevent their spreading; the Afghans pressing them in front. The sepoys fought well, but were soon mastered, and then infantry, cavalry, and guns—European, Sikh, Afghan, and Mooltanee—all joined in pursuit. "Then began that memorable fusillade, which commenced on the parade-ground at Peshawur and ended at Jumrood."* The rout was complete. The sepoys were cut down or captured by dozens; some few succeeded in skulking away, and hiding in the *khets*, nullahs, and ravines, but were soon caught and brought in by the district police; and of the 870 men who, on the morning of the 28th, composed the 51st N. I., within eight-and-forty hours not the odd 70 survived; and a few days after, it was reported on credible authority that only 19 famished fugitives lingered on in the neighbouring hills.

It has been noticed, that in all probability the rise was thoroughly premeditated; champions for the "poor sepoy" there were, and perhaps ever will be, ready to assert that, they were the victims of persecution, that they were all either frightened or driven into mutiny; the whole transaction being nothing more than the result of a sudden fear, followed by flight, which in the excitement of the times was summarily punished as

* Colonel Edwardes's official account, published in the *Punjab Mutiny Report*.

mutiny. Let such weigh well the following facts: When the search was resumed, arms were found everywhere; under floors, in walls, in roofs of huts, wherever a weapon could be concealed, *tulwars* (native swords), spears, knives, hatchets, matchlocks, cartridges, powder, were brought to light. Nor only in the lines of the 51st N. I.: in those of the 64th, which had been vacated long before by the withdrawal of that regiment to the forts, was a tank, in which, all round the sides just below water-mark, were found a row of *tulwars*, buried up to the hilt, so as to be completely out of sight, yet within easy reach when required. In the huts several *ghurrahs* (native water-pitchers) were, on examination, discovered to be full of powder! Again, in the 24th N. I. lines, in the house of a native officer, bundles of balled cartridges and boxes of caps were discovered—wrapped up, too, in a copy of Sir Henry Lawrence's proclamation to the sepoys in Oude!* The field, too, adjoining the parade of the 51st was full of concealed arms; to this, as noticed, a portion of the regiment made a rush, and from it many shots were fired, and several muskets were afterwards dug up there. Yet with all these discoveries the Peshawur authorities openly confessed that "not a quarter of the arms that *they knew* to have been lately purchased had yet been discovered!"

Besides these proofs of premeditation, other circum-

* A copy of this proclamation had been sent by Sir John Lawrence, early in June, to every native officer in the Hindostanee regiments in the Punjab.

stances tend to show that even the *time* was all arranged—at least, that as the intention to move out the corps was somehow known or suspended the day before, they had laid their plans accordingly;* and that the 51st N. I. were to take the lead in the *emeute* (being acknowledged to be the best of the disarmed corps), while the 24th and 27th were pledged to follow, in the hope that not only the two Irregular Cavalry regiments, which were still armed, but, perhaps, even the 21st N. I., might join; the outbreak was then to become general, and an appalling massacre to close our reign at Peshawur. But the dispersion of the different regiments, their unexpected withdrawal from their *depots* of concealed arms, and inability to communicate with each other, placed them in a hopeless dilemma; simultaneous action was impossible, and anything short of that would be madness. Thus, when the 51st gave the sign, the other regiments, too far off to see or even hear what was going on,† remained

* One officer, that very morning, on his way to the parade, was asked by one of his native officers if he would drink some *sherbet*—in itself apparently a mere act of courtesy; but the expression is a well-known *double entendre: sherbet* is supposed to be the beverage of the gods, and the speech probably implied in that case, that the officer would be out of this world before long. The same morning another native officer was heard to say it was the last parade they should attend there. Some persons were tempted to think that it was Captain Bartlett's presence that actually caused the outbreak at that moment. Now there can be no doubt that he was the object of intense personal hatred to the Poorbeahs, from his unenviable position as postmaster and cantonment magistrate: in the one capacity intercepting all their correspondence, and in the other having to superintend all executions. But it needed not such spark to fire a mine so long laid.

† "In the lines of the 27th N. I.," says Captain Cave, in a note to the author, "*we did not hear a shot fired.*"

quiet till it was too late to act. The fate, however, of their comrades, so sudden and condign, struck such terror into their minds, that from that day their whole bearing underwent a change. They were thenceforth kept out in tents doubly guarded and watched, without the possibility of again procuring arms, or of escaping; and they knew full well that a single hand lifted up, or a single voice raised in mutiny, would irrevocably seal their fate.

This was the last danger from that source.

With these failures fell for ever the Poorbeah's hope of mastery, or of escape.

CHAPTER XV.

[Aug. 1857.—Part II.]

THE GENERAL STATE OF THE PUNJAB POPULATION—THE CHANGE FROM FRIENDS TO FOES AND FOES TO FRIENDS IN EVERY PART—PESHAWUR, SEALKOTE, JULLUNDHUR, AND THE CIS-SUTLEJ STATES—REINFORCEMENTS—SIEGE-TRAIN—ENLISTMENT—POPULATION BECOMING DISTURBED—THE POSITION OF THE CHIEF COMMISSIONER.

In the absence of more stirring events, it may not be mistimed to take a cursory review of the actual condition of the various classes composing the population of the Punjab.

To begin with the Peshawur valley. It had been one main principle of the Punjab administration that Peshawur should always be held by European and Hindostanee troops;* in Huzara and the Dherajat were Sikh and Punjabee corps, with their occasional sprinkling of mountaineers from the frontier; but Peshawur itself was a position of too great importance to be garrisoned, in however slight a degree, by men from the neighbouring frontier tribes. Here the native force was purely Hindostanee. The ordinary strength of Peshawur was rather above 10,000 men;

* *First Punjab Report*, para. 56.

of these about one quarter were Europeans, consisting of two European infantry regiments, and a force of artillery, some 500 strong, with four or five regular native infantry regiments, one of regular, and two of irregular, cavalry. At the end of the year 1856, a third European regiment had been brought across the Indus and located in the valley at Nowshera. Thus, as has been already described, there were, in May 1857, about 2450 Europeans, including the artillery, and 6500 Poorbeahs, in Peshawur itself; at Nowshera, 900 Europeans and 1500 natives; at Hotee Murdan and the forts, 2500 more—altogether, about 3350 Europeans, and 10,500 natives (almost entirely Poorbeahs). In August there remained the three European regiments, greatly weakened by sickness, as also by the volunteering into the Peshawur dragoons and the artillery. Of the artillery, one troop, one battery, and a reserve company had been pushed down, leaving behind one troop, one battery, and two reserve companies. Of the Hindostanee infantry regiments, two, the 55th at Hotee Murdan, and the 51st at Peshawur, had been annihilated, four remained disarmed. the regular cavalry corps was disarmed, one irregular corps disbanded, and the other two, though retaining their arms, so much suspected and watched as to be worse than useless. In the place of these had sprung up one regiment of Sikhs and Punjabees, and three of frontier Pathans. So the European force was reduced to 2400; but 2500 irregulars appeared on the stage, and of the 10,500 Poorbeahs there remained only 6500, of whom more than half were without arms. The station into which hitherto an Afghan or an Affreedee might not have entered armed, was now patrolled, garrisoned, virtually held by them. The Poorbeah, so long regarded as our only strength, now proved our weakness. The Pathan of the frontier, who had hitherto been our fear, had now become our safeguard and hope!

It was the same in Huzara; Rothney's Sikhs had pushed down to Delhi, their places taken by Pathans; and so in the Dherajat, Wilde's Sikhs, Green's Rifles, Vaughan's Punjabees had left the frontier to be held by the mountain levies.

In the Punjab Proper and the Cis-Sutlej States the change was no less remarkable. Four months before, there had been between the Indus and Umballa eight regiments of European infantry and one of cavalry, mustering some 8000 men.* Of European artillery there were six troops, four companies with light field-batteries, and five reserve companies, mustering in all rather more than 1000 men—the whole European force on this side the Indus being about 9000 strong. Against these were to be set a native force of above 20,000 men of all arms,† comprising three troops of horse, five companies of foot-artillery, twenty regi-

* H. M. 24th at Rawul Pindee, 52d L. I. at Sealkote, 81st at Lahore, 61st at Ferozepore, 8th at Jullundhur, 75th at Kussowlee, and the 1st and 2d Bengal Fusiliers at Dugshai and Subathoo, and the 9th Lancers at Umballa.

† Of native infantry, the 3d, 4th, 5th, 14th, 16th, 26th, 33d, 35th, 36th, 39th, 45th, 46th, 49th, 57th, 58th, 59th, 60th, 61st, 62d, and 69th regiments. Of regular cavalry, the 4th, 6th, 8th, 9th, and 10th; and of irregular cavalry, the 1st, 2d, 9th, 16th, and 17th.

ments of native infantry, five of regular, and five of irregular cavalry.

By the beginning of August three regiments of native infantry had been destroyed in the act of mutiny,* three disbanded,† four had mutinied and escaped,‡ one, the 39th N. I., had been removed to Dehra Ismael Khan; and there remained nine disarmed and watched.§ Of the native regular cavalry corps, one (the 6th) had mutinied and escaped, and four had been deprived of their arms and horses.‖ On the other hand, of the eight European regiments *only two* remained—the 81st at Lahore, tied down watching the disarmed Poorbeahs, and the 24th, distributed between Rawul Pindee and Umritsur, with a detachment of 100 of the 8th at Jullundhur, and a similar body at Philour, some 200 more at Umballa, besides about 100 sickly and wounded in the hill-stations; so that, in round numbers, there were in the Punjab scarcely 2000 Europeans against nearly 10,000 disarmed Poorbeahs.

Now let us take each station separately. In Rawul Pindee the change was perhaps least perceptible; a portion of the 24th remained, and the 58th were disarmed.

* The 14th N. I. at Jhelum, the 26th N. I. at Ujnalla, and the 46th N. I. at Trimmoo Ghat.

† The 45th and 57th at Ferozepore, and the 5th at Umballa.

‡ The 60th at Rohtuck, the 36th and 61st from Jullundhur, and the 3d from Philour.

§ The 58th at Rawul Pindee, the 33d, 35th, and 59th at Jullundhur and Umritsur, the 4th at Noorpore and Kangra, the 16th and 49th at Lahore, the 62d and 69th at Mooltan.

‖ The 4th Cavalry at Umballa, the 8th at Lahore, the 10th at Ferozepore, and a wing of the 9th at Umritsur, the other wing having mutinied at Sealkote.

At Lahore there remained the European corps, H. M. 81st, and three out of the four disarmed native regiments.

Sealkote, in succession to the earlier station of Wuzeerabad, had been originally designed by Sir Charles Napier for a force of some 10,000 men. Sir Charles's motives for the selection of this station he has placed on record. Regarding all Indian princes as at best faithless allies and reluctant subjects, he especially mistrusted Gholab Singh, whom he calls "a modern Tiberius of cruelty and villany;" he remembered his trimming policy both in the Sutlej and Punjab campaigns, and he believed that any serious difficulty in the newly-annexed territory of the Punjab might be a signal for him to break faith and rush down upon us. Sealkote, then, presented an important point of observation, being within sight of Jummoo; and the strong force permanently located there would present a formidable barrier to his advance on the most direct route by which he could enter the Punjab. Again, the district of Sealkote contained a turbulent population, from which a large portion of Runjeet Singh's army, especially his artillery, had been raised. It was but a short distance from the Manjha country, the most dangerous portion of our new territory, as having been the home, and now being the refuge, of the greater portion of the Khalsa army. Thus Sealkote stood out, a defiance to the Jummoo Rajah* on the

* Gholab Singh is here regarded as the "Jummoo Rajah," not as the Maharajah of Cashmere (Jummoo was his hereditary territory,

one side, and the Manjha Sikhs on the other. It had subsequently been reduced from a strength of 10,000 men to a single European infantry corps, one troop and one battery of artillery, one regiment of native regular cavalry, and two of native infantry. At the outbreak, the whole of the European force, with one regiment of native infantry and one wing of cavalry, had been withdrawn, and the remaining regiment and wing had, in the month of July, perpetrated a bloodthirsty mutiny. Thus that station, which had been originally designed to keep in order a turbulent district, to overawe the Manjha Sikhs, to look defiance at Jummoo, was in August 1857 held by a few levies raised in the district itself, while the Jummoo Rajah was pouring down through it a contingent of 2200 men to strengthen our army before Delhi!

Then, again, in the Jullundhur Doab was perceptible as remarkable a change as at Peshawur and Sealkote. This district had been annexed after the battle of Sobraon in 1846. In its two chief stations of Jullundhur and Hosheyarpore was then placed a force of 12,000 men of all arms. On the annexation of the Punjab, the latter station had been nearly abandoned, and the force in the district reduced to about 8000. In May 1857 it numbered scarcely 7000, consisting of a troop of European and one of native horse-artillery; one European regiment, H. M. 8th; two regiments of native cavalry, and five of native infantry; being in all

Cashmere transferred by the English after the Sutlej campaign). It was from Jummoo that the advance would be made.

scarcely 1000 Europeans to 6000 natives. In August 1857, of this large force there remained about 100 Europeans at Jullundhur, as many more at Philour, two guns at Kangra, the 33d N. I., disarmed, at Jullundhur, while two Punjab infantry corps* were being raised in the district. Punjabee and Sikh were pressing in for enlistment; but besides — perhaps more than all this—as a means of keeping the district and the city in order, the Kuppoorthulla Rajah, Rundheer Singh,† the grandson of him who had been the *turban brother* of Runjeet Singh, the son of the man who had been degraded by us a few years before, placed his troops and his money at our service, raised new levies at his own expense, kept down the city, guarded the civil lines and cantonments, protected the trunk-road from the Sutlej to the Beas, and virtually held the Bist.‡

The Cis-Sutlej States presented a still more remarkable appearance. Umballa and the hill stations were almost denuded of Europeans, the Hindostanee regiments dispersed or disbanded, the whole available force being pushed on to Delhi; while the native cities, towns, and the whole district, were kept in order, and the Umballa cantonment and grand trunk-road guarded, by the very native chiefs to overawe whom the forces had been originally cantoned there.

* The 1st at Jullundhur, under Captain Tulloh, and the 2d at Loodiana, under Captain Nicolls.

† See Appendix N.

‡ The Jullundhur Doab is so called, as lying between the rivers Beas and Sutlej.

At Ferozepore, on the mutiny and subsequent disbandment of the 45th and 57th, a wing of the 61st had been withdrawn, and the peace and security of the city maintained by the Rajah of Fureedkote. At Loodiana and that district was the brave young Rajah of Nabba; at Kurnaul, the Nawab; at Paneeput, Lursowlie, Rae, and Alipore, the Jheend Rajah's troops, the Rajah himself in the camp doing noble service during the whole siege. And though last, chiefest of all, at Umballa itself, and throughout the centre of the division, even to Hansi and Hissar, was the Puttiala Rajah. In short, with men, money, example, influence, he was everywhere, supporting the Government when it seemed at its greatest need, strengthening it in its hour of weakness, and holding all till we should be able to re-occupy. Thus was the country in the hands of our trusty allies.*

The crisis was at hand: the final struggle, which was to recover Delhi, or lose all!

Every day saw succours passing on for the siege. The Trimmoo Ghat, as has been mentioned, had set free the Moveable Column. Nicholson, perhaps more impatient than even those under him, to be at Delhi, lost no time, when once the permission to move down

* The following statement of forces supplied by these rajahs shows the amount of aid they so nobly gave:—

	Guns.	Horse.	Foot.
Puttiala, . .	8	2156	2846
Nabba, . . .	2	600	600

Of the Jheend Rajah's forces the author has been unable to get accurate returns.

reached him. The whole Column was quickly on its way, gathering strength as it came.

Then the arsenals of the Punjab were putting forth all their strength. The siege-train, which had been originally despatched from Philour, while it had been sufficient for the mere defensive operations maintained along the ridge, had been at once pronounced by Lieutenant Alexander Taylor of the Engineers, when he took charge on the withdrawal of Major Laughton, to be utterly inadequate to the purpose of a regular assault, especially against an enemy in possession of the whole of our vast Delhi arsenal. A first-class siege-train of the heaviest metal was consequently called for, and the magazines at Ferozepore and Philour* were put into request to prepare one that would effectually breach the walls of the rebel city. Towards the end of August, the whole was ready. Six 24-pounders, eight 18-pounders, four 8-inch howitzers, with 1000 rounds of ammunition per piece, besides a similar quantity for all the howitzers and mortars already at Delhi, moved out from Ferozepore, and, as it passed through Loodiana, received an augmentation from Philour of four 10-inch mortars, with 1000 rounds for each; and the

* The amount of metal and ammunition supplied by the Philour magazine from first to last may be thus summed up: 50 pieces of ordnance of various sizes, with 80,000 rounds of shot and shell, and nearly 500,000 pounds of powder; besides these, 5000 muskets, and nearly 3,000,000 rounds of balled cartridges, with a similar number of percussion caps. From Ferozepore, the entire supply passed down to the camp exceeded 2000 cartloads. For these valuable particulars, the author is indebted to his kind friends Captain Lewis, Commissary of Ordnance at Ferozepore, and Lieutenant Griffith of Philour.

whole rolled on its ponderous length of gun-carriages, tumbrils, ammunition-carts, extending over *thirteen miles of road.* The leading cart had reached the new camping-ground before the last of that long line had started on its march.

Enlistment was everywhere the order of the day.

Some idea of the energy and activity called forth to supply the place of the traitor Poorbeahs by trusty Punjabees may be gathered from the following statement:—

There were originally 6 Punjab infantry regiments. There were now being raised, 3 at Peshawur, by Captains Cave and Bartlett, of the 21st N. I., and Major Shakespear, 24th N. I.; 1 at Nowshera, by Lieutenant Brownlow, 1st N. I.; 2 along the frontier; 1 at Bumoo, by Captain Gardner, 29th N. I.; and 1 at Khohat, by Captain Thelwall, H. M. 24th Regiment; 1 at Rawul Pindee, by Captain Doran, 24th N. I.; 3 at Lahore, by Captains Blagrave, 26th L. I., and Larkins, 49th N. I., and Lieutenant Shebbeare, 60th N. I.; 1 at Jullundhur, by Captain Tulloh, 33d N. I.; 1 at Loodiana, by Captain Nicolls, the Assistant Commissioner,* and subsequently by Captain Macpherson, H. M. 24th Regiment; 1 at Philour, by Lieutenant Stafford, 4th N. I.; 1 at Umballa, by Captain Garstin, 5th N. I.; 1 at Ferozepore, by Captain Salmon, 57th N. I.; and 1 at Mooltan, by Captain Dennis, 62d N. I.†

* Captain Nicolls was not allowed to retain command, because he could not be spared from civil employ.

† These 16 corps were afterwards enrolled in the Punjab Irregular Force, from the 7th to the 22d regiment inclusive. At a later period, 3 more were added; the 23d, composed of a part of Van Courtlandt's

There was now a lull; but, as has been already said, it was an ominous one—it foreboded a coming storm; the whole political atmosphere was charged with electricity—the "subtle fluid" might burst forth at any point; it might throw the whole country into a blaze, and all might still be lost. Delhi must be the lightning-conductor, and that speedily. There was less hope than ever of any succour from below; *from England no hope at all.* The mail of the beginning of July had arrived, but it brought the cheerless intimation that while England was appalled with tidings of the Meerut and Delhi massacres, Lord Ellenborough had launched the thunders of his eloquence on the head of Lord Canning for subscribing to a missionary society, and Lord Clarendon had promised that reinforcements should be sent *as soon as possible round the Cape!*

Moreover, a fresh danger threatened, and that at our own doors. The Sikhs had hitherto remained quiet, tolerably contented in the peaceful times which, under us, had followed their reign of anarchy and terror. Lacking sympathy with the Poorbeah, their hands full with an abundant harvest, for two months and a half they had looked on with hope for a speedy return of order; and had but sparingly, at the first, enlisted into our ranks, though those already in our service had fought faithfully and bravely for us. But Sir John

force; the 24th, formed of the brave little Muzbee Sikhs, before Delhi; and the 25th, a Hazara Goorkha regiment.

Besides these, some more cavalry regiments had also sprung into existence, Lind's and Cureton's Mooltanees; and, later still, several Sikh cavalry.

Lawrence had not failed to detect a change which was gradually, yet perceptibly, coming over them. It shall be described in his own powerful words:—"As months wore on, they saw that our power in the Punjab was being wasted away, as troops were despatched for Hindostan, without any reinforcements arriving from Europe. They discovered, too, that it was going hard with us elsewhere in India. Incendiary letters came day after day, describing, in highly figurative phrase, the utter isolation of our position. These things sank deep into their minds; they began to think (what they could hardly have believed at first) that the end of British rule was really approaching. Then latent embers of disaffection began to glow; people commenced, as it were, to make up their political book against the coming revolution; individuals thought of securing their own future position and influence, of conciliating those who would become formidable when the hand that ruled all alike should be removed; even our real well-wishers, our loyal agents, would take precautions for the safety of themselves and families in the troubles which they feared were inevitable; dreams floated about, not, perhaps, of nationality, or of a restored Sikh commonwealth, but of the possible revival of separate parties like the original Sikh *Misls;* the idle and the vicious everywhere hoped for congenial excitement; chiefs living idly in their country-seats thought once more of mixing in strife; in the southern waste tracts men looked forward to resuming predatory habits; in the northern hills they sighed for independence." "They would stand by us, and risk their lives for us, while we could hold our own; when we could not do that, they would be forced to turn against us.*

Nor were the Mohammedans on the frontier uninfluenced by the same causes. Once more the cloud was gathering over Peshawur. The fort of Michnee was attacked by a band of Mohmunds, led on by a fanatic moulvie: the plea was that they had been dispossessed of some lands, and now, in the day of its weakness, they thought to extort restoration from Government, or take possession for themselves. A force could ill be spared from Peshawur to punish them, for disease was beginning to thin the European ranks; so Edwardes tried negotiation. He sent out to remonstrate; if they had any grievance, that was not the way to obtain redress, much less to gain favour; let them withdraw in peace, dismiss the fanatics, and make a respectful representation of their case, and it should be calmly reconsidered. This dignified attitude, this assumed confidence, which looked so like a consciousness of strength, awed the Mohmunds; they retired, and the danger—never perhaps greater during the whole period—was averted. Yet it showed too plainly that the frontier was again becoming dangerously excited; it was clear that, after all, the Mohammedan fanatic thought "the good time coming" when a blow might be struck for the supremacy of his race and religion, and for the extirpation of the infidel.

If, a month before, Sir John had felt the need, it

* *Fourth Punjab Report*, para. 150.

now, alas! was more imminent than ever, that Delhi *must fall, and that by Punjab troops.* What he had done to effect this has been already mentioned—more he could not do; the last man that could be spared had been pushed on to Delhi, and the issue was with Heaven.

"History dwells with admiration on the calmness of the Roman Senate, who, at a crisis unexampled in the varying fortunes of Rome, thanked one consul for not having despaired of the safety of the state, and with an enemy flushed with victory advancing on one road, despatched by another a reinforcement to strengthen an over-matched general, in a distant province. With similar admiration, we think, will history point to Sir John Lawrence as a man who, with a failing treasury, an excitable population, and a newly-raised force, despatched his last trustworthy body to the gates of Delhi, and then sat himself down calmly to await the result." *

* *Frazer's Magazine* for June 1858, p. 688.

CHAPTER XVI.

[AUG. 1857.—PART III.]

IMPROVEMENT IN CAMP—CONFUSION INCREASING IN THE CITY—THE BUKRA EED A FAILURE—THE BATTERY AT LUDLOW CASTLE CARRIED BY SHOWERS—THE ARRIVAL OF THE MOVEABLE COLUMN—GREATER DEPRESSION IN THE CITY, BOTH AMONG THE SEPOYS AND THE SHAHZADAS—TIDINGS OF THE DEATH OF SIR HENRY LAWRENCE—HODSON'S AFFAIR AT RHOTUK—NICHOLSON'S VICTORY AT NUJUFFGHUR.

AT Delhi the tide had turned: the new *regime* was restoring health and hope. Order was beginning to return. Although the assaults of the rebels were at times very desperate, they were less frequent, and the men, recruited by the new system of reliefs, were far better able to meet them. Then the severity of the the rains, after the first few days, somewhat relaxed. Cholera, which had been raging during the preceding month, appeared to be passing away. The sanitary measures for draining and cleansing the camp had succeeded in mitigating the discomfort as well as disease to which the troops had been hitherto subject. The sick-list, indeed, was still very heavy—a fifth of the whole force! Still the admissions into hospital were daily becoming less numerous, the attacks milder, and less frequently fatal; and with improving health came a very perceptible improvement in the effectiveness of the force. On the whole, the prospect was brighter, or, as perhaps should be more correctly said, less dark and hopeless than it had been a month before.

The actual force in camp at this time may be set down, in round numbers, at 5600 of all arms; of these some 3500 were Europeans, and about 2100 natives; but then of the former more than 800, and of the latter about 300, were in hospital, so that there remained fit for duty not more than 2700 Europeans and 1800 natives. But a few days would see them strengthened by the Moveable Column, which, having done its work in the Punjab, was hastening down to take its share in the crowning assault.

In the city, on the other hand, confusion was becoming worse confounded. In the end of July arrived the Neemuch Brigade, with the Kotah Contingent, and some of the Gwalior Artillery. In one sense, the arrival of this force was inopportune to the rebels themselves. Nothing could have promised better than the arrangement effected by that mistress of intrigue, the *Begum Zeenat Mahal*, which was to secure the succession of her son Mirza Jumma Bukht to the empire, with the promise of the appointment of "Commander-in-Chief" and "Governor-General of India" to General Mohamed Bukht Khan, if only he would take the British batteries. But with the Neemuch Brigade there appeared on the stage a new candidate for favour and power. General Ghaus Khan had his "following" and his rival claims. The 31st of July was to have seen an overpowering attack of the combined brigades, but between the feud of the rival generals and a heavy downfall of rain the assault was abandoned. But the 1st of August was the *Bukra Eed*, and they were resolved to signalise this high Mohammedan festival with the utter extermination of "the unbelievers." Their fanaticism was at its height. The Jumma Musjid resounded with prayers louder and wilder than ever ; the Koran witnessed oaths sterner and more bloody ; the battle-cry which had led on the Moslem bands in desolating fury over the fields of Spain in the thirteenth century,

> "Glory for all, but heaven for those who bleed,"

could scarcely have called forth a fiercer spirit than that which seemed to inflame the minds of the fanatics of Delhi, in anticipation of that great day's achievement. All the rivalry between the different brigades, all jealousy of Generals Ghaus Khan, the Neemuch champion, and Bukhtawur Khan of Rohilcund, which had paralysed all efforts during the preceding month, seemed to be for the time suspended. A royal salute announced the day, and put the camp on the alert. But it was not till about sunset that the advance was made. The plan of attack was indeed most formidable ; each brigade in its turn was to hurl itself on our batteries, and to be relieved every four hours. The day was far advanced when out the rebels turned in full force, and the city gates were closed behind them. They commenced by an attack on Metcalfe's House, on our extreme left, and soon spread along our whole front. It was a desperate struggle; through the whole night they kept pouring up fresh bodies as one after another they were repulsed from our batteries. Not a man of ours advanced from under cover; from behind the breastworks our picquets and supports plied them incessantly with musketry, while our field-pieces played grape and round-shot through their ranks. The day dawned, and the fight still went on; and it was past noon, when, finding how little they had gained, their zeal began to flag; down poured the rain, and still more damped their ardour; the coveted martyrdom was too wholesale to please them; and in spite of prayers and oaths, they gave up the attack and returned to the city!

Never, perhaps, was seen such a Bukra Eed in the city of the Great Mogul. Not a cow was killed within the walls; even Mohammedan faith was compelled to yield this point to Hindoo veneration. The King himself did not take his wonted place at the head of the gorgeous procession, which, in Moslem fanaticism, was accustomed year by year to thread the streets of the city on its way to the Jumma Musjid. His presence might have been offensive to his Hindoo soldiery; so he remained shut up within the walls of his own palace, and performed his devotions in private, sacrificing, so report has it,* with his own hands, a camel instead of a cow!

* ROTTON'S *Siege*, p. 176.

This day, too, the intelligence from below was far from cheering to the rebel cause. A large body of fugitive sepoys from Cawnpore arrived in the city, and brought authentic intelligence of Neil's retribution there, and glowing exaggerations of the force Havelock commanded, consisting of "demons" in petticoats (Highlanders), and broad-shouldered "fiends," who could carry the heaviest cannon on their backs (the Naval Brigade).

Reports, too, came of the advance on Lucknow, and the heart of the Poorbeah turned towards his own *bustee* (village), and applications for leave to visit their own homes poured in fast to the palace. The sepoys were put off with excuses and promises: if they would only wait and carry the English batteries, they should then have all arrears of pay, and go off to the rescue of their *bhaibunds*.

On the 2d of August, a large body, some 10,000 in number, had gone out with the view to repair the bridges on the canal which we had destroyed in our rear, especially that at Bussaye ; this they rebuilt, but two days after the water rose and washed it all away. On the 3d another advance was made on Aleepore, but the rain fell so heavily that they abandoned it, and on their return made an attack on our batteries, where they were repulsed with very heavy loss. Our men were kept well in hand and suffered little (about twenty would cover our loss) ; but among them a brave and excellent officer (one of the old officers of the Punjab Irregular Force), who had distinguished himself in many a border fight—Capt. Eaton Travers, of Coke's Rifles.

On the 6th, a joint attack of the Neemuch and Nusserabad brigades, under *Generals* Sirdhara Singh and Buldee Singh, was made on our right batteries with like success, the loss on our side being very slight: the force on that day, however, had to lament the loss of Lieutenant J. H. Browne (33d N. I.), attached to the Kumaon battalion of Goorkhas, who was killed; and Captain Kennion (Artillery), Lieutenant Somerville and Lieutenant Temple, wounded.

The 7th was memorable for the explosion of a powder-magazine in the city. The old magazine—the scene of Willoughby's heroism on the 11th of May—was considered to be dangerously near our batteries, for shell would occasionally find their way into it; so the rebels had established a working magazine on the other side of the city, far beyond our range: it was this which, with fifty maunds of gunpowder, blew up and destroyed five hundred workmen. It was at once considered the act of an incendiary, and, by a device of Hodson's* suspicion rested on Ahsan-Oollah, one of the King's most trusted advisers. An instant rush was made upon his house, which was quickly plundered and gutted. Two days after, suspicion pointed more correctly, and our friendly moulvie, Rujjub-Ali, had a price set upon his head, and was obliged to escape for his life, after having been for three months the invaluable medium of all city news in the

* HODSON'S *Twelve Years, &c.*, p. 261.

intelligence department so admirably conducted by Hodson.

On the 8th of the month a second attempt had been made to establish a battery at Ludlow Castle. For two or three days they caused considerable annoyance in the Metcalfe outposts, and it was resolved to seize them. General Nicholson had ridden into camp a few days in advance of his Column, and had been promised this little exploit as practice for his Column directly it should arrive. However, the fire was too galling, and the rebels, left in undisturbed possession, had become too confident: so General Wilson resolved to have them taken at once without waiting for the Column. On the night of the 11th all was settled. A small column, made up from H. M. 75th, 1st and 2d Fusiliers, Coke's Rifles, and the Kumaon Battalion under Brigadier G. Showers, who, having recovered from his wound of the 23d of July, was again in his saddle. By four o'clock in the morning, the Brigadier had his whole force ready for the advance. They managed, in the stillness of the morning, to move down unobserved within convenient distance of the battery, and so completely took the rebels by surprise that they were scarcely able to fire a single round from their guns before they were overpowered. Four guns were captured and brought into camp in triumph; Lieut. Owen of the 1st Fusiliers, who was severely wounded, and several of the men, came in riding on the guns. However, complete as was the success, it was not achieved without considerable loss; our list of killed and wounded being about one hundred; among them Lieut. Sherrif, 2d Fusiliers, killed; Brigadier Showers again wounded; also Major Coke (of Coke's Rifles), Lieutenant Lindsay (Horse-Artillery), Lieutenant Maunsell (Engineers), Captain Greville and Lieutenant Owen (1st Fusiliers), and Lieutenant Innes (70th N. I.), orderly officer to the Brigadier.

The following morning saw the Punjab Moveable Column march into camp with General John Nicholson (who had ridden out to join them), at their head, the band of H. M. 8th playing them in. Its strength now was— Bourchier's battery * of 9-pounders, H. M. 52d Light Infantry under Colonel Campbell, mustering 600 strong, 200 Mooltanee Horse under Lieutenant Lind, and 400 newly-raised Military Police. On the way it had picked up the left wing of H. M. 61st, nearly 400 bayonets, relieved from Ferozepore by a wing of the 1st Bombay Fusiliers, and by about an equal strength of the Belooch Battalion, pushed on from Mooltan; and at Lursowlee they were further strengthened by Green's Rifles (2d Punjab Infantry), some 700 strong. While hastening on behind came Wilde's Punjabees (4th Punjab Infantry), summoned down from Norinjee, bringing with them 100 recruits for Rothney's Sikhs; and, lastly, three more companies, nearly 250 strong, of H. M. 8th (who were holding Jullundhur and Philour),

* Dawes's troop, to the general sorrow of the Column, had been halted at Umballa, and was subsequently sent down to Meerut to be ready for service in any flying brigade that might be formed there. It was considered that his light field-pieces (6-pounders) would be comparatively useless before Delhi.

on being relieved by a detachment of H. M. 24th, ordered down from Rawul Pindee. The whole force amounted to about 4200 men, of whom nearly 1300 were Europeans.

In the city, in the meanwhile, difficulties were daily increasing: the men were becoming more and more dispirited, and, tired of waiting for the promised leave, were deserting in large numbers for their own homes; those who remained becoming more clamorous for pay. The King was each day growing more disheartened, and threatened to abdicate; at one time he demanded a right to resign in favour of one of the Shahzadas, and to retire to the Kutab in peace; at another, he would walk out and give himself up to the English!

Every day found the sepoys more disorganised and more reluctant to face our batteries. The knowledge that such strong reinforcements were pouring into camp, and, moreover, that a heavy siege-train was on its way down, did not tend to raise their spirits. If anything was to be done, it must be done at once. So on the 15th a council of war was held; all the native officers of the rebel force attended. Each one threw a pinch of salt into a *lotah* of water, thereby pledging themselves that, as the salt dissolved in the water, so might each one perish who proved faithless or a coward; to do or die was their vow. However, as the issue proved, they had not the heart for either; the salt melted away, and so did their courage.

The real condition of hopeless despair which pervaded the whole city may be admirably illustrated by the following incident :—Behind the little army which was frowning defiance upon them beyond the ridge, they felt that there was a ruling power which they dreaded almost more than our bayonets, and that was Sir John Lawrence. It was not many years since he himself had been a magistrate in that city ; his name was still well remembered ; the indomitable will, which now held the Punjab, had made itself felt in the bazaars of Delhi and the surrounding district ; and the very name made them quail. It has been well said that it was worth a brigade. Many, it is believed, were the plots vainly concocted in Delhi for his assassination : but he still lived. So they resorted to the following device :—Some luckless Cashmeree, with almost European fairness, was caught in the city, dressed up in English clothes, handcuffed and shackled, and paraded through the streets as the veritable Sir John Lawrence, a prisoner, to give confidence to the rebels !

Nor was this hopelessness confined to the sepoys or the populace ; even the *Shahzadas* began to feel their condition very perilous, and tried to open negotiations with the authorities. "I am beginning to get letters from the princes," writes Mr Greathed, on the 19th of August ; "they declare they have been all along fondly attached to us, and that they only want to know what they can do for us. They must find out for themselves, for I shall not answer and tell them." *

About this time came tidings which spread a deep gloom over all—the corroboration of the report which

* GREATHED'S *Letters*, p. 205.

had previously reached camp, but which men shrunk from believing, that Sir Henry Lawrence was really dead. How many of that band had known him in bygone days, as resident at Lahore under the Regency, or as Chief Commissioner of the Punjab on its annexation! Who had known him, and not loved him? Of that heart, gentle as a child's, with all its fire—that manner so courteous, so winning of confidence—that form, manly though spare—all the traces of character which endeared him to all who worked with him and under him, and which ennobled him in the memory of that country which he served, and for which he died—of all this will the far abler pen of one who knew him well and mourned him deeply tell with characteristic vigour and genial admiration. Suffice it to say, in camp the general feeling was, and it often found vent in words, that India was only half saved if Henry Lawrence was gone.

From this passing allusion to Sir Henry Lawrence, the narrative of events carries us to the only two incidents which varied the monotony of camp-life during the latter part of this month, and which reflected honour on two men whose value the discrimination of Sir Henry Lawrence had first detected, and on whom, in their different degrees, he had first conferred posts of honour—John Nicholson, and Hodson of the Guides.

Allusion has been frequently made to the dangers that threatened our camp from the rear. Twice, towards the latter part of August, was that danger most imminent; and in the absence of more stirring events in the camp itself, a full account of the dashing gallantry by which the danger was both times averted will be read with interest.

The districts of Paneeput and Rohtuk had been always regarded with suspicion; lying in the direct road between Delhi and Kurnal, they were a constant source of anxiety lest they should "rise," and the communication be closed. In the midst of a generally peaceful Jât population are small communities of *Ranghurs*, a turbulent and predatory class of Mohammedans, of Rajpoot origin—from among whom our irregular cavalry regiments are to a considerable extent recruited. The natural lawlessness of these tribes was now, of course, greatly aggravated by the presence of bodies of their brethren, either "on leave" from their corps, or belonging to regiments that had mutinied. The whole country round was accordingly affected, and the revenues were resolutely withheld by some of the villages. In the month of July it was found necessary to make a demonstration. A small force was sent from Kurnal to bring them to order, under Captain Hughes of the 1st Punjab Cavalry. Taking 250 of his troopers, he made for a place called *Bulleh*, lying some twenty-five miles from Kurnal, the head Jât village of that district, which had refused its revenue. Here he found the people assembled in force, at least 900 matchlockmen and a few mounted sowars; the gates of the town were barricaded with heavy timbers, and everything ready for a determined resistance. Captain Hughes's demands for the arrears of revenue were met by a savage yell and a volley, which brought down one of his men and two or three horses. He saw that to carry the principal gate required a larger force than he could command, with guns and infantry; however, observing on the left another which appeared less strongly defended, he made a desperate dash at it and carried it, the sowars dismounting and tearing down the barricades to effect an entrance; but an inner barricade defied them, and he was compelled to withdraw his men, leaving two or three of them dead, but having killed some twenty of the enemy, and wounded as many more.

He at once despatched a messenger to Kurnal for reinforcements; and encamped for the night a short distance in front of the town. During the night the Ranghurs flocked in from the neighbouring villages to the number of some 3000, and in the morning turned out in full force; and, under shelter of a small jungle and the banks of a canal, kept up a harassing fire. In vain had Captain Hughes been trying to lure them away from their cover, when two guns of the Nawab of Kurnal * and 50 Sikhs (Puttiala men), with 20 of the Nawab's troopers, arrived, and coming up

* The praiseworthy conduct of Ahmud Alli Khan, Nawab of Kurnal, has been already alluded to. He from the first appreciated the emergency of the crisis, and on *the 14th of May* predicted to Captain Martineau the defection of the whole native army. He admitted that his position might be a critical one—only seventy miles from Delhi, with the villages around filled with turbulent Ranghurs, and the whole of the districts to the eastward in arms; but he said, "Confide in me, and I will do my best to keep the peace of the Kurnal Pergunnah, and all my resources shall be at your disposal." Nobly he kept his word.

unnoticed by the enemy as Captain Hughes was withdrawing his cavalry, they suddenly appeared in front, and a few rounds of grape quickly cleared the jungle and the canal banks. Then the cavalry, by a flank manœuvre, got between the rebels and the town, drove them into the open, and cut up about 100 of them. The guns were now brought to bear on the gateway, and the place quickly surrendered; the revenue was paid up, and a fine of 1000 rupees was inflicted, which was given to the troopers of the 1st Cavalry to replace the horses they had lost.*

A month passed away, and these Ranghurs began to forget the punishment they had received on the 14th July. In the beginning of August, reports came into camp that they were collecting again in great force, headed by one Baber Khan, and it was known that a considerable body of rebels had gone out in that direction from the city: so it was feared that they might greatly impede the advance of the siege-train, now on its way to Delhi.

Hodson started off on the 16th of August, taking with him 233 of his own troopers and 103 of the mounted Guides (in all 336 sabres), and 25 riflemen of the Jheend Rajah's men. On arriving at a small village called Kurkowdah, about twenty miles from Rohtuk, he came upon a party of "leave men" belong-

* The cavalry lost in all two native officers, and three troopers killed and fifteen wounded, besides several horses killed and wounded. Captain Hughes's own horse was wounded in three places. This corps, it will be remembered, had been sent out of Delhi with the 9th and 17th.

ing to irregular cavalry corps, and other corps, under no less a man than one Bisharut Ali, a ressaldar of the 1st Irregulars, a man lately decorated with the Order of Merit, who ought to have been otherwise engaged. This village was surrounded: the little party of mutineers was soon mastered, and the ressaldar shot down by Hodson himself, five other "leave men" and some twenty rebels killed. Intelligence having now reached Hodson that Rohtuk was the rallying-point of the rebels, and that they were determined to oppose his advance, on the following afternoon he started his small force, and reached Bohur; then, after a short halt, pushed on for the old civil station of Rohtuk, which he reached about four o'clock the next afternoon; here he formed his men out of sight of the town, and rode forward with two officers and a few sowars to reconnoitre. The enemy were lining the walls in considerable numbers, and opened fire on him directly he advanced. He then brought up his men, and detaching two troops to the right, and the same number to the left, with orders to take up positions so as to prevent any one escaping, with the remainder made a dash at the main gate: but it was instantly closed; a few only of the rebels straggling outside were cut down. A circuit of the city soon showed it would defy all attempts by cavalry alone; so Hodson withdrew his men to the old Kutcherry compound, and there bivouacked for the night; having established picquets and patrols commanding the three roads to Delhi, Bohur, and the town of Rohtuk, which converge at this point. About seven o'clock in the evening, some of the head men of the city came in, "having grass in their mouths," in token of abject submission, and declared it was only a few *budmashes* who had offered resistance, but the city was ours. However, Hodson received them very coldly, and told them that if the gates were not thrown open in the morning, and the place surrendered, no mercy would be shown, and the town should be burned to the ground. They promised everything; but about seven in the morning, Hodson, who had gone out a short distance in advance of the camp to reconnoitre,* suddenly galloped back, and shouted out to "mount and turn out sharp," and with about twenty troopers he galloped to the front and formed up. There were the enemy, about 300 cavalry and a cloud of matchlockmen, from 600 to 700, dashing down the road at the camp. But when they saw the bold front of Hodson and his twenty sowars, they halted, wavered, and as the other troopers, now saddled and ready, galloped up and fell in, they darted off right and left, and were soon lost among the trees and gardens that surrounded the city; here, under shelter, they incessantly poured in a galling fire, which could only be feebly replied to by the handful of the Jheend Rajah's men.† So long as the rebels were under cover the cavalry could not act, and were

* "Hodson rode on in front to reconnoitre, and there," says an eyewitness, "not 400 yards from the matchlockmen, with bullets whistling by him from every point, he made his observations as coolly as if on parade."

† "Gough," says the same eyewitness, "coolly dismounted, and, making a rest of his saddle, with his Enfield rifle dislodged a party of the enemy who were creeping up to a favourable position near our centre."

being picked off fast: the only hope lay in drawing them out: to effect this, Hodson sent out one troop to the right under Lieut. Wise (of the 4th Cavalry), and a second to the left under Lieut. Macdowell (2d Fusiliers), his adjutant, and placed the rest under Captain Ward in the centre; pushing the Guides to the front under Lieut. Hugh Gough. Thus disposed, they defied the efforts of the rebels to outflank them, presenting a front wherever they appeared. Hodson then ordered them to retire slowly by alternate troops. The manœuvre succeeded admirably; on seeing the cavalry retiring, out the rebels came, yelling and shouting, and followed up Hodson's party. When he had drawn them about three quarters of a mile out in the open—"*Three's about, charge!*" was the word, and quick as thought round went the gallant fellows, and bore down on the astonished and discomfited enemy in every direction. The Guides, being in the rear as they retired, were now foremost in the charge, and right well did they maintain their high name. The Ranghur cavalry rode for their lives, and many rode in vain; the matchlockmen threw away their matchlocks, and made for shelter as they best could. Hodson's Horse, young in fame, emulated the well-proved gallantry of the Guides, and the rout was complete. They followed the rebels up to the very walls of the town, marking their way with dead; some eighty were left on the field, and the rebels admitted that they had also 150 wounded. That night saw their force still more diminished; the rebels slunk away under cover of the dark, and Hodson, who had bivouacked outside, was left undisputed master of the field and of the town. His loss was trifling—one sowar killed, Lieut. H. Gough and seven sowars wounded.

Thus concluded Hodson's memorable "Rohtuk affair," and the gallant band returned to camp to receive their meed of praise: but just too late to take part in another excursion, for a share in which the heart of the indefatigable, insatiable Hodson was bent, and which may be regarded as *the* most dashing and brilliant success of the campaign.

The heavy siege-train, which was to bring low the ramparts of the beleaguered city of the Mogul, was now dragging its portentous length along, and its near approach had been duly notified. Expectation was at its height; in anticipation of its arrival, men were planting the several batteries in imagination, and picturing to themselves the broad breach already crumbled under its heavy fire, by which Delhi should at length be in our hands. Nor were the rebels in the city in ignorance of its approach, or unconscious of the danger it portended to them. To intercept it was clearly most important, and Mohammed Bukt Khan, still smarting under the taunt of having lost a battery at "Ludlow Castle" on the 12th, offered to take out the newly-arrived Neemuch and Rohilcund brigades and cut off the train, and bring it into Delhi, or die in the attempt.

How the braggart fulfilled his promise we will now proceed to tell.

In the course of the 24th our spies brought intelligence that this large force, numbering at least 6000 of all arms, with sixteen guns, had left the city that morning. A picked brigade, under General Nicholson, was at once ordered out in pursuit, consisting of Tombs's, Remington's, and Blunt's troops of Horse-artillery, 100 of the 9th Lancers under Lieutenant Sarel,* 250 of H. M. 61st Regiment under Colonel Rainey, 200 of the 1st Bengal Fusiliers under Major Jacob, 400 of the 1st Punjab Infantry (Coke's Rifles) under Lieutenant Lumsden, 400 of the 2d Punjab Infantry (Green's Rifles), 100 2d Punjab Cavalry under Lieutenant C. Nicholson, 200 Guide Cavalry under Captain Sandford, 300 Mooltanee Horse under Lieutenant Lind, and a detail of sappers and miners under Lieutenant Geneste, of the Engineers. The plan of the rebels was suspected to be to make for Kurkowdah, cross over the canal at Burrah Thana, and come down on the siege-train at Rae. Nicholson's object, on the other hand, was to thwart these kind intentions by overtaking them, and so utterly crippling them as to leave the road open and safe for the train.

By 4 A.M. on the following morning (August 25th) the column was on the move. But what with having to drag the guns over a cross-road and ploughed fields, at some parts up to the axletrees in water, and the rain pouring down in torrents all the morning, it was 11 o'clock in the day before even the advance had accomplished ten miles. Here a halt was sounded, to allow

* These numbers differ from those published in the official report; but the author has every reason to believe the numbers given here are correct, the state of the regiments not admitting of their making up the complements as originally intended and ordered.

the entire column to close up. Sir Thomas Metcalfe, who had volunteered to accompany the column, and whose knowledge of the whole country around rendered his presence of the greatest value, now pushed on ahead with a couple of officers to reconnoitre the road. He knew that some five miles further on they would come upon a *nullah* running across the road, and the fear was that this might be now so flooded as to be impassable for guns. Just before reaching this nullah the ground rises. Metcalfe and his companions, as they mounted this high ground, came suddenly in view of the rebel camp. Under a garden-wall, on the other side the nullah, they saw an elephant and two sowars asleep, and detected the tops of the tents rising up among the trees about half a mile beyond. A cavalry vidette on this side the nullah observed them, and made a desperate dash to cut off their retreat; but they were well mounted, and a hard ride brought them back safe to the column, with tidings of the rebels' whereabouts. The force having in the meanwhile enjoyed an hour's halt, were again in motion, and in a couple of hours more had arrived at the ridge above the nullah, within sight of the enemy.

The position of the rebels may be thus described: near the village of Nujuffghur, the road by which the rebels had come crosses the Nujuffghur Jheel Canal by a bridge, over which they had passed, and were encamped on the other side. They had taken up their advanced position at a serai, which they held in force with four guns; they also held two villages, one on

SKETCH
ILLUSTRATIVE OF THE
ACTION OF
NUJJUFGHUR.
from memory by
Lt. M. G. GENESTE.
Bl. Engineers.
W. & A. K. Johnston, Edinburgh.

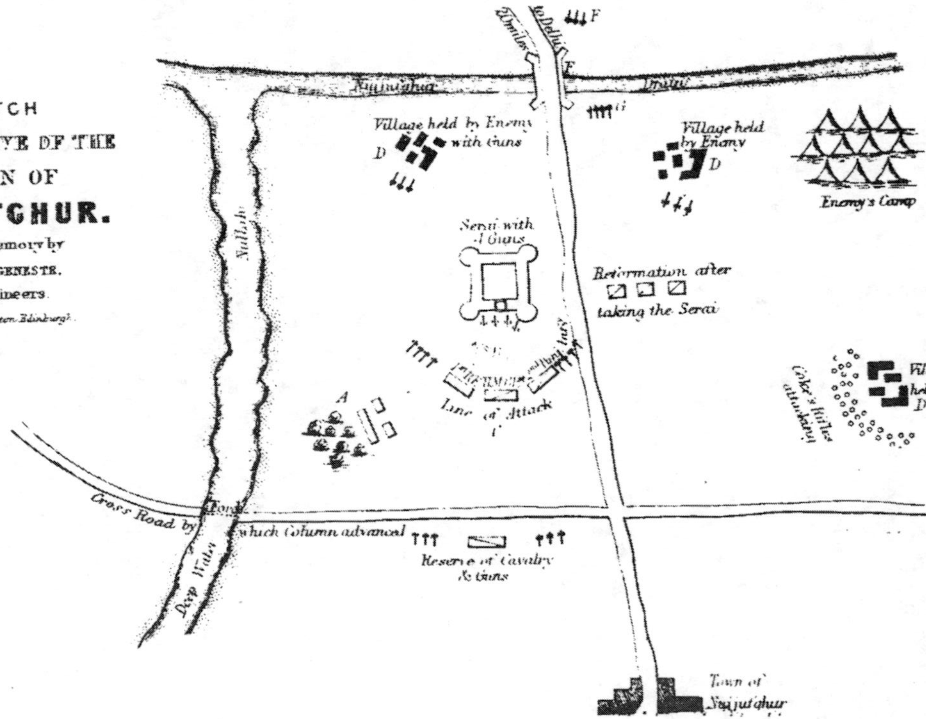

REFERENCE

A. Garden where the Enemy were first seen.
B. Rising ground in front of our advance.
C. Line of Attack on Serai consisting of H.M. 61st Regt. 1st Bengal Fusrs. on right 2nd Punjab Inf. (Green's) on left.
D.D.D. 3 Villages held by Enemy.
E. Bridge 84 feet long, 27 broad, blown up to prevent Enemy threatening our rear.
F. Guns brought by Enemy to play on Bridge when held by us.

either side in rear of the serai. Nicholson's advance had been by a cross-road, so that he came down on their right flank, with the nullah flowing between them.

His plan of attack was instantly formed. The commissariat stores and baggage were left behind at the village of Baproolee, about a mile from the nullah, under a strong guard of the 2d Punjab Cavalry under Lieutenant C. Nicholson, 100 Mooltanee Horse under Lieutenant Caulfield, some detachments of the infantry corps, and a couple of guns under Lieut. Lindsay. A small force was pushed on with guns to cross the ford, and to cover the advance of the main body. As soon as the whole had crossed, which they effected under heavy fire of shot and shell from the serai, and musketry from the nearest village, and through water which, even at the ford, was breast high, Nicholson disposed his attack in the following order:—The serai being the first and chief point to be gained, in front of it were drawn up the European portion of the force, the 1st Bengal Fusiliers in the centre, H. M. 61st on the right, with Green's Rifles on the left, some 800 men in all; Tombs's and Remington's guns were on a slight ridge in advance, with the Guides out in skirmishing order to keep down the enemy's fire. The village of Nujuffghur, beyond the serai, on our right, was consigned to Lumsden with his Rifles (Coke's); that on the left, which seemed more strongly occupied, was made over to Captain Blunt, with four guns and a small detachment of cavalry, to watch till the infantry should be available for an attack. The reserve was composed of Blunt's two remaining guns and the rest of the Mooltanees under Lieut. Lind. Such was the disposition of the force. Nicholson advanced to the front of the line, whom he had ordered to lie down, and thus addressed them: "Men of the 61st, remember what Sir Colin Campbell said at Chillianwallah, and you have heard that he said the same to his gallant Highland Brigade at the Alma; I have the same request to make to you, and to the men of the 1st Fusiliers. Hold your fire till within twenty or thirty yards; then fire, and charge, and the serai is yours."

After some beautiful practice from Tombs's and Remington's guns, the General gave the word for the main line to rise and advance;—up they sprang over the hillock and across the marshy ground; pushed on at the double, steady as on parade—though sometimes ankle-deep in water—on they went; grape and musketry were pouring in amongst them as they advanced, but not a shot did they return, till, within twenty yards, the order was given to "charge," and then, with a volley and a cheer, they carried the guns.

The rebels offered a desperate resistance, and a bloody hand-to-hand encounter ensued, in which the towering form and death-dealing arm of Nicholson were conspicuous. Poor Gabbett of the 61st, a fine, brave soldier, twenty yards in advance of his men, made a rush on one of the guns; his foot slipped, and he was bayoneted by a gigantic Pandy;* but Captain

* General Nicholson declared that, had he lived, he would have recommended Gabbett for the Victoria Cross, so gallant was his conduct.

Trench, of the 35th N. I., who was A.D.C. to General Nicholson (that moment rising from the ground, his horse having been shot under him), quickly avenged his death by bringing down the rebel with his revolver. The guns were soon mastered, the drivers and gunners cut down, and the serai carried at the point of the bayonet.

In the meanwhile Lumsden had been carrying out his part of the programme on the village to the right, with his Rifles; at a given signal they rushed forward "with a frontier howl," and cleared it in gallant style. Having done this, he crossed over along the rear of the line, to strengthen the attack on the other village to the left, on which the guns had been playing all the time. Here the enemy had a stronger position, surrounded too by high grass and corn-fields; Coke's Rifles, flushed with their success in the other village, rushed on with a cheer; but they soon had to deplore the loss of their gallant young leader, who was shot down at their head. As soon as the serai was cleared, a small guard was left to hold it, and a part of the 61st sent off to support the attack on the second village, while the rest re-formed to attack the enemy's camp and the bridge in their rear. The rebels at once suspected this latter object; and as in that bridge lay their only chance of retreat, they did not wait for the advance of the Europeans, but *bolted* from all sides, and succeeded in dragging two of their guns over the bridge. But all their camp-baggage, stores, camels, horses, and an *English buggy*, fell into our hands; large quantities of ammunition, seventeen tumbrils full, were abandoned. The powder was blown up, and all the baggage, tents, &c., burnt, there being no carriage available to bear off the goodly spoil. Thirteen guns were captured; and to crown all, the bridge was blown up, thus effectually closing that road for the future. The rebels confess to a loss of above 800 men, while ours was only sixty killed and wounded; but, alas! among the former the gallant young Lumsden, who proved himself worthy of the name he bore; Gabbett of the 61st, whose bravery has been mentioned, and also Lieutenant Elkington of the same corps, who lingered for some days, but at length died of his wounds. Dr Ireland was dangerously wounded, but recovered.

It was subsequently discovered that only the Neemuch Brigade were engaged, the Rohilcund force being a few miles in the rear, and either unable or unwilling to come to the succour. The heaviest loss of the rebels was in their artillery, and several of the *7th Scindiah's Contingent** were among the killed. The action had commenced about half-past five in the afternoon, and by the time all was over the evening had closed in. The troops received orders to bivouack on the bank of the river, and there these gallant fellows passed the night, weary and worn, without covering, and, what was perhaps worse, without food and grog, for they had not broken their fast since four o'clock in the morning, and all the commissariat supplies had

* The presence of these seems unaccountable; however, the fact is indisputable, as the *regimental buttons* showed.

been left at the village under the rear-guard. The next morning the General gave them the choice of halting for the day, or marching back at once; they chose the latter, and reached camp about seven o'clock in the evening, having marched above thirty-five miles and beaten a force strongly posted, three times their own number, in less than *forty hours!* A fitting reception awaited them in camp; the regimental bands turned out to play them in; hundreds crowded round to greet them, and to offer their ungrudging welcome and congratulations on so triumphant an exploit.*

"For the glorious result of these operations," in the General Order which they elicited, General Wilson declared himself "indebted to the judgment and energy displayed by Brigadier-General Nicholson, the steadiness and gallantry of the troops in action, and the cheerfulness with which they bore the fatigue and hardships they were called on to undergo."

Thus ended the month of August, and with it rose the fame of the young General.

* For General Nicholson's Despatch, see Appendix N.

CHAPTER XVII.

THE ASSAULT OF DELHI—THE SIEGE-TRAIN ARRIVED—THE BREACHING BATTERIES—THE ASSAULT—NICHOLSON WOUNDED—FAILURE AT KISSENGUNGE—CRITICAL POSITION OF THE ARMY—THE SURRENDER OF THE KING—THE DEATH OF THE SHAHZADAS—DEATH OF NICHOLSON—DELHI OCCUPIED.

"Woe to the bloody city! it is all full of lies and robbery. . . . . Behold, I am against thee, saith the Lord of hosts." *

IN the dead of night—before the day had yet dawned—on Thursday the 14th of September 1857, these words, uttered 2570 years before against Nineveh, were read in more than one tent on the Delhi camping-ground; they came as a cheering omen of success to men awaiting the order to fall in for the "assault." A few hours later they were read in many a family circle, and in at least one church,† in the daily morning-service; and to many an anxious heart that knew the momentous crisis to be at hand, in which husband, or son, or brother, or friend might stand unscathed in the breach—or perhaps be left a lifeless corpse—did they sound forth their note

* Nahum, iii. 1. The first lesson for September 14th. The whole chapter is awfully descriptive of the horrors of an assault.

† Simla, where daily morning prayer was always said; and during this momentous week, evening prayer also, by the Rev. F. O. Mayne, chaplain.

of solace, and soothe the intensity of personal anxiety with the mingled assurance of national success.

A few hours more, and the telegraph flashed up from the very walls of the bloody city, "Delhi has been assaulted." Who shall attempt to describe the feeling of exultant gratitude which filled the heart of every Englishman in the Punjab? The die was cast, *Delhi taken, and the Punjab safe.*

To make the doings of that day intelligible, the reader must be carried back to the point at which our history of the siege left him, and trace in their order the steps by which the breach was carried.

The siege-train had arrived. Over miles of flooded road, through a country teeming with a disaffected population, and exposed at almost any point to an attack from the rebels, with no escort but Farquhar's Beloochees and a detachment of H. M. 8th Regiment, did it drag its ponderous length along. As it drew nearer, and the risk of attack increased, a body of infantry and cavalry were sent out for its protection, and, thus escorted, it rolled into camp on the 3d of September. While it was yet on its way, the note of preparation for its arrival was heard on every side, so that once safely landed on the ridge, little would remain to be done to bring it into full play. Gabions, fascines, sand-bags, were ready in thousands, and a few hours would suffice to run out advance-batteries, and mount some of the heaviest guns within more effectual working-distance of the walls. All the reinforcements, too had now arrived. The Moveable Column in full force; the remaining wing of the 61st from Ferozepore (with whom Nicholson had already proved his generalship at Nujuffghur); Meerut had spared a few more Carabineers and artillery;* Wilde's Rifles, let loose from the far Peshawur country, had come in; the Jheend Rajah had strengthened his gallant little band with a few more hundred picked men; and, last of all, the Cashmere Contingent marched in.

Now the siege may be said to have begun in earnest. Hitherto we had done little more than defiantly hold our own—nominally besiegers, really *besieged.*

The north face of the city, which comprised the whole length of wall between the Lahore Gate and the river, and contained the Moree, Cashmere, and Water bastions, and the intervening curtains, was resolved on as the side for the assault. Our own position along the ridge already commanded it; the intervening ground, although (as has been already said) broken up with ruined houses and gardens, and towards the right intersected by large ravines and stone quarries, still presented the only space by which an advance could be made; while at every other point along the land-face, the suburbs of the city, covered with the crumbling palaces and mosques and houses extending for miles to the south, in a wilderness of ruins,—telling their tale of a succession of former cities, the growth and decay of nearly a thousand years, from the Indraprestha of the Tuar dynasty to the now "Old Delhi" of Feroze-

* For General N. Penny had thrown new life into that station.

shah,—defied all advance. Then again, inside the walls, this part of the city, having been chiefly occupied by European residents, presented in its open space greater facilities for the assaulting columns, when they had once cleared the breaches, to re-form and advance, and more effectually fight their way, than in the narrow lanes and alleys with which the rest of the city was intersected. Towards this face, then, it was resolved to push forward the batteries.*

General Wilson † then addressed his men to brace

* The nature of the line of defence is thus described in the official report of Colonel Baird Smith, which the author has extracted from the *Siege of Delhi*, by the Rev. J. E. W. ROTTON, p. 267.

"These (defences) consist of a succession of bastion fronts, the connecting curtain being very long, and the outworks limited to one crownwork at the Ajmeer Gate, and Martello Towers mounting a single gun at such points as require some additional flanking-fire to that given by the bastions themselves. The bastions are small, mounting generally three guns in each face, two in each flank, and one in embrasure at the salient. They are provided with masonry parapets about twelve feet in thickness, and a relief of about sixteen feet above the plane of site. The curtain consists of a simple masonry wall or rampart sixteen feet in height, eleven feet thick at the top, and fourteen or fifteen feet at bottom. This main wall carries a parapet loophole for musketry, eight feet in height and three feet in thickness. The whole of the land-front is covered by a berm of a variable width, ranging from sixteen to thirty feet, and having a scarp-wall eight feet high; exterior to this is a dry ditch of about twenty-five feet in height, and from sixteen to twenty feet in depth. The counterscarp is simply an earthen slope, easy to descend. The glacis is a very short one, extending only fifty or sixty yards from the counterscarp; using general terms, it covers from the besiegers' view from one-half to one-third of the height of the walls of the place."

† On the 7th of September, General Wilson's address to the troops at Delhi on the expected assault ran as follows:—

"The force assembled before Delhi has had much hardship and fatigue to undergo since its arrival in this camp, all of which has been most cheerfully borne by officers and men. The time is now drawing near when the Major-General commanding the force trusts that their labours will be over, and they will be rewarded by the capture of the them up for the coming struggle. Volunteers were called for from the cavalry corps (for in the assault there would be little work for them), to relieve the artillery, who were already well-nigh sinking under

city for all their past exertions, and for a cheerful endurance of still greater fatigue and exposure. The troops will be required to aid and assist the engineers in the erection of the batteries and trenches, and in daily exposure to the sun as covering-parties.

"The artillery will have even harder work than they yet have had, and which they have so well and cheerfully performed hitherto: this, however, will be for a short period only; and when ordered to the assault, the Major-General feels assured British pluck and determination will carry everything before them, and that the bloodthirsty and murderous mutineers, against whom they are fighting, will be driven headlong out of their stronghold, or be exterminated; but to enable them to do this, he warns the troops of the absolute necessity of their keeping together, and not straggling from their columns. By this can success only be secured.

"Major-General Wilson need hardly remind the troops of the cruel murders committed on their officers and comrades, as well as their wives and children, to move them in the deadly struggle. No quarter should be given to the mutineers; at the same time, for the sake of humanity and the honour of the country they belong to, he calls upon them to spare all women and children that may come in their way.

"It is so imperative, not only for their safety, but for the success of their assault, that men should not straggle from their columns, that the Major-General feels it his duty to direct all commanding officers to impress this strictly upon their men; and he is confident that, after this warning, the men's 'good sense and discipline' will induce them to obey their officers, and keep steady to their duty. It is to be explained to every regiment that indiscriminate plunder will not be allowed; that prize-agents have been appointed, by whom all captured property will be collected and sold, to be divided, according to the rules and regulations on this head, fairly among all men engaged; and that any man found guilty of having concealed captured property will be made to restore it, and will forfeit all claims to the general prize; he will also be likely to be made over to the provost-marshal, to be summarily dealt with. The Major-General calls upon the officers of the force to lend their zealous and efficient co-operation in the erection of the works of the siege now about to be commenced; he looks especially to the regimental officers of all grades to impress upon their men, that to work in the trenches during a siege is as necessary and honourable as to fight in the ranks during a battle.

the unceasing labour.* Trenches were dug on the artillery park, and every evening detachments of infantry might be seen at escalade practice, that they might be the more ready to mount the breach when the time for the assault came. To relieve the overcrowded hospitals, a general hospital-delivery took place;† as many sick as could be moved were sent out of camp to Umballa and the hills. And with the bright jewels and untold wealth of the reputed richest city in India,—the whole to be given up to the army,‡ —prize agents were appointed: Captain Fagan of the Artillery, to represent the Staff; Captain Sir E. Campbell, Bart., of H.M.'s 60th Rifles, for the Queen's troops; and Captain Wriford, of the 1st Bengal Fusiliers, for the troops of the Company. Such were the preliminaries.

Some distance in advance of Hindoo Rao's house,

"He will hold all officers responsible for their utmost being done to carry out the directions of the engineers, and he confidently trusts that all will exhibit a healthy and hearty spirit of emulation and zeal, from which he has no doubt that the happiest results will follow, in the brilliant termination of all their labours."

* One battery was entirely worked by volunteers from the 9th Lancers.

† ROTTON'S *Siege of Delhi.*

‡ When Delhi had been taken, and communication was once more open with Calcutta, the army found that this pledge, given by General Wilson, that all the property of the rebel city should be regarded as "prize," was ignored by the Supreme Government. This unfortunate order gave rise to the indignant waggery—which aroused so tremendously the wrath of Government—of some soldier (name unknown), who gave vent to his feelings by writing on the barrack wall, "Delhi taken for thirty-six rupees ten annas," which sum exactly represented his six months' batta. However, on reference to England, the word of the General given to the gallant English soldier was allowed to be as binding as that given to the blood-stained King of Delhi.

the last spur of the ridge towards the Moree Bastion spreads out into a plateau; on this tempting position a battery of six 9-pounders and two 24-pounders had been planted under command of Captain Remington, as an initiatory step, to play upon the Moree Bastion; and the first real advance was made from this point. A dry nullah runs down from the ridge—this served for a parallel; and a battery (No. 1) was run up on the night of the 7th, within 700 yards of the walls, consisting of two parts, that on the right mounting six guns, "to smash the Moree;"* that on the left with four guns, to keep down the fire of the Cashmere Bastion; the whole under Major J. Brind.

This step, following up the planting the light battery on the plateau, evidently misled the rebels; nearly all the hard fighting had hitherto been in this quarter, and the advance of these two batteries confirmed them in the idea that the assault, whenever it was made, would be made in this direction; so they were wholly unprepared for the next advance, which was on Ludlow Castle. This important position had always formed an advance picquet of the enemy, even after they had lost their guns there on the 12th of August; but, apparently not contemplating the possibility of advance here, they were taken so utterly unawares that they offered scarcely any resistance, and Ludlow Castle fell into our hands almost without a struggle.

* *A Year's Campaigning in India*, by CAPTAIN MEDLEY, p. 74.

Here a battery (No. 2), a little in front, also consisting of two parts, was soon planted under Majors Kaye and Campbell.* In the right division were seven 8-inch howitzers and two 18-pounders; in the left, nine 24-pounders—the one to play on the Cashmere Bastion, the other on the curtain beyond, where the main breach was to be made. To the left of this, still in advance, stood the Koodsia Bagh; and here, under shelter of the ruined gateways, a mortar battery of ten pieces to clear the Cashmere Curtain was established under the gallant Major Tombs; but it was kept masked till all the left batteries were ready, that they might open fire simultaneously. On again, nearer still, without parallel or covered-way, was now made an advance without precedent in the world's history of siege operations. A little in front of the Koodsia Bagh stood what once had been the "Customhouse," of late years used as a private residence, now a pounded, riddled, charred ruin, and attached to it a small ruined outhouse. Perhaps its proximity to the city wall —for it was within 160 yards of the Water Bastion—made the rebels look upon the occupation of it by themselves as useless, and by us as impossible. From whatever cause, it was left unoccupied, and our engineering party quietly walked in and took possession. However, the enemy soon found out their mistake; the noise of the working parties, though carefully suppressed, could not fail to reach the sentries on the wall, and shot and

* Major Campbell was wounded on the evening of the 11th, when the command devolved on Captain Johnson.

shell were soon pouring in, and in spite of the cover of the walls the men fell fast. However, the work went on in the face of the enemy's fire, and a battery (No. 4) under Major Scott was established. This completed the line of breaching batteries; the whole formed between the 7th and the 13th — a goodly week's work!

Brind's battery to the right had been at work ever since the morning of the 8th, pounding away on the Moree Bastion, and dropping long shots into the Cashmere Gateway; two days after, the Ludlow Castle batteries opened; the next morning the Koodsia Bagh battery was unmasked, and, with that of the Custom-house, took up the game. And now some fifty pieces of heavy artillery were in full play on the doomed city. Day and night the pounding went on; the Moree Bastion was soon silenced, and the line of parapet which sheltered the sharpshooters between it and the Cashmere Bastion was fast disappearing. The Cashmere Bastion itself was "silenced in ten minutes after the Ludlow batteries had opened on it;" * and the massive stone-work, only a few months before restored and strengthened by the English Government for the protection or beautification of the city of the Mogul, soon began to crumble away under the play of English 24-pounders. Now a round-shot dislodged a block of masonry, and rattled it down into the ditch; now a ponderous shell, judiciously pitched, lodged on the crumbling wall, and, as it exploded, tore down yards of battlement. The

* MEDLEY, p. 87.

Water Bastion fared almost worse; the fire from the heavy guns at the Customhouse at 160 yards' range played with fearful effect; the guns were dismounted and smashed, and the breach opened; while under the play of Tombs's mortars the curtain between was literally stripped.

Yet dearly was all the success bought; every hour told its tale of death or wounds. Foremost, and most lamented, perhaps, of all who had yet fallen, Fagan of the Artillery, than whom the whole army had not a kinder-hearted or a braver man, fell a victim to his gallantry; Hilldebrand, too, of the Artillery followed, and many others; and among the working parties the losses were very heavy. For not only did the enemy pour in a deadly fire of grape and round-shot from the walls, and musketry from the jungle and trenches in front, but they had contrived to plant an enfilading battery on the right in Kissengunge, out of sight of the guns on the ridge, so that not one of the batteries there could play upon it, and within grape range from the city walls, so that it could not be carried without heavy loss—a loss that could not then be borne.* A round-shot from this would now and again plough through, not only Brind's battery on the right, but those at Ludlow Castle too; while the Customhouse and Koodsia Bagh batteries were similarly enfiladed by a rebel battery established across the river. Add to this the intense heat, the almost unceasing fatigue, the anxious sleep-

* MEDLEY, p. 91.

less days and nights,* wearing out body and mind alike, cholera, too, raging among them—and who will wonder at so heavy a list of casualties even before the grand struggle had come? Yet in spite of all this danger and difficulty, men's hands were ever ready and hearts light, and they laboured on with an energy and strength borrowed from the hope that a day or two more and all would be over.

By mid-day on the 13th it was clear that the crowning assault was only a question of hours.

The day before, a council of war had sat, and everything was arranged for the assault, the time only remaining a secret. On the afternoon of the 13th the breaches at the Cashmere and Water Bastions looked so inviting that an examination was resolved, and four young Engineer officers, Lieutenants Greathed, Home, Medley, and Lang, were ordered out on this perilous expedition. Let one of the exploring party describe the adventure in his own words:—

"It was a bright starlight night, with no moon, and the roar of the batteries, and clear, abrupt reports of the shells from the mortars, alone broke the stillness of the scene, while the flashes of the rockets, carcasses, and fireballs lighting up the air ever and anon, made a really beautiful spectacle. The *ghurees* struck ten, and, as preconcerted, the fire of the batteries suddenly ceased. Our party was in readiness; we drew swords, felt that our revolvers were ready to hand, and leaving the shel-

* Colonel Brind, for instance, never took off his clothes or left his guns from the hour they opened on the 8th till the 14th!

ter of the picquet, such as it was, advanced stealthily into the enemy's country.

"Creeping quietly through the garden, we quickly found ourselves under a large tree on the edge of the cover; and here we halted for a moment, conversing only in whispers. The enemy's skirmishers were firing away on our right, some thirty yards from us, and the flashes of their muskets lit up the air as if they had been fireflies. The shells and rockets of the enemy at one moment illumined the space around, as they sailed over our heads, and then left us in total darkness. We now left the Rifle officer, Lieutenant H——, and his twenty men in support, and with the six men who were to accompany us Lang and I emerged into the open, and pushed straight for the breach. In five minutes we found ourselves on the edge of the ditch, the dark mass of the Cashmere Bastion immediately on the other side, and the breach distinctly discernible. Not a soul was in sight. The counterscarp was sixteen feet deep, and steep; Lang slid down first, I passed down the ladder, and, taking two men out of the six, descended after him, leaving the other four on the cope to cover our retreat. Two minutes more, and we should have been at the top of the breach; but quiet as we had been, the enemy was on the watch, and we heard several men running from the left towards the breach. We therefore re-ascended, though with some difficulty, and, throwing ourselves down on the grass, waited in silence for what was to happen. A number of figures immediately appeared on the top of the breach, their forms clearly discernible against the bright sky, and not twenty yards distant. We, however, were in the deep shade, and they could not apparently see us. They conversed in a low tone, and presently we heard the ring of their steel ramrods as they loaded. We waited quietly, hoping they would go away, when another attempt might be made. Meanwhile we could see that the breach was a good one, the slope easy of ascent, and that there were no guns in the flank. We knew by experience, too, that the ditch was easy of descent. It was, however, desirable, if possible, to get to the top; but the sentries would not move. At one time the thought occurred to me of attempting the ascent by force. We might have shot two or three of them from where we lay, and in the surprise the rest might have run, and we could have been to the top and back before they had seen how small our party was; but the extreme hazard of the attempt, and the utter impossibility of rescuing any one that might be wounded in the ditch, made me abandon the idea, when I further reflected that we had, in reality, gained all the needful information. After waiting, therefore, some minutes longer, I gave a signal; the whole of us jumped up at once, and ran back towards our own ground. Directly we were discovered, a volley was sent after us; the balls came whizzing about our ears, but no one was touched. We reached our support in safety, and all quietly retreated to the Koodsia Bagh by the same road we had come. Lang went off to the batteries to tell them they might open fire again, and I got on to my horse and galloped back to camp as hard as I could, to make my report to the chief engineer; the roar of the batteries as I rode off showing that they had once more opened fire on the breach."*

Greathed and Home also returned untouched, and reported the breach at the Water Bastion practicable, though it would have been all the better for a few hours more pounding, had the time admitted of it.

About midnight the order flew through the camp, "The assault at three o'clock in the morning." The plan had been already determined on, and it only remained to carry it out. The whole force was to be divided into "four assaulting columns and a reserve;" the first to storm the breach at the Cashmere Bastion, the second that in the Water Bastion, the third to blow open the Cashmere Gate, and the fourth, on the extreme right, to clear Kissengunge and enter by the Lahore Gate; while the "reserve" was to follow up in the wake of the first three columns, and throw in supports wherever necessary.

The post of honour and of danger was claimed by General Nicholson. He had been sent down by the Chief Commissioner "to take Delhi." It was no disparagement to those to whom rank gave a priority in that army to say that all eyes were turned to him. His arrival in camp gave a new vigour to the troops, a new hope to the Punjab: even jealousy, where it existed among those whom he superseded, rose into emulation in the hearts of the nobler ones; among others, if such

* MEDLEY'S *Year's Campaigning*, p. 97-100.

there were, it learned to be silent. Then Taylor of the Engineers, though only a young subaltern, was regarded by all, and felt by all, to be the life, the moving spring, of the engineering department. During the interval between Major Laughton's withdrawal and Colonel Baird Smith's arrival, the sole charge lay with him; and even afterwards, when a subordinate, it was acknowledged by all that his was virtually the directing hand.* Early in the breaching operations, Colonel Baird Smith was wounded by a splinter from a shell, and consequently the duty of directing the assault necessarily devolved on Lieutenant Taylor, and he accompanied Nicholson at the head of the first column.

Ludlow Castle was the rendezvous for the three columns on the left and the reserve. By three o'clock A.M. they had all fallen in, of the following strength:—

---

* It is scarcely necessary to support the above statement, for it is borne out by the concurrent testimony of all who were before Delhi.

General Wilson, in his despatch of the 22d of September, speaking of him, calls him "gallant and eminently talented," and thanks him and the whole of the officers and men "for having planned and successfully carried out, in the face of extreme and unusual difficulties, an attack almost without parallel in the annals of siege operations."

A brother Engineer writes thus of him:—

"He virtually directed the whole siege operations in the field, from the commencement to their triumphant conclusion. No one but his own brother officers knew the great responsibility that devolved upon him, and the amount of anxiety, labour, and exposure that he underwent in consequence." It was sometimes thought Lieutenant Taylor's services were not duly recognised. Gazette after Gazette brought its list of honours without his name being included; but no sooner did he emerge from the chrysalis of the subaltern, and appear in the full glory of a captain, than the well-won honours which the rules of the service had hitherto forbidden now clustered round him, and he was made a Lieutenant-Colonel and C.B.

The 1st Column, under General Nicholson, consisted of—

300 men of H.M. 75th Regt., under Lieut.-Col. Herbert;
250 „ 1st E. B. Fusiliers, under Major Jacob;
450 „ 2d Punjab Infantry, under Captain Green;

with Lieutenants Medley, Lang, and Bingham, of the Engineers, attached.

The 2d Column, under Col. W. Jones, of H. M. 61st, of—

250 men of H. M. 8th Regt., under Lieut.-Col. Greathed;
250 „ 2d E. B. Fusiliers, under Captain Boyd;
350 „ 4th Sikh Infantry, under Captain Rothney;

accompanied by Lieutenants Greathed, Hovenden, and Pemberton, Engineers.

The 3d Column, under command of Colonel G. Campbell, of H. M. 52d L. I., consisted of—

* 250 men of H. M. 52d Regiment, under Major Vigors;
500 „ 1st Punjab Infantry, under Lieut. Nicholson;
250 „ Kumaon Battalion, under Captain Ramsay;

also the soldier-hearted civilian, Sir T. Metcalfe, who knew the streets of Delhi as no one else there did, with Lieutenants Home, Salkeld, and Tandy, of the Engineers, attached; and

The Reserve Column, under command of Brigadier J. Longfield, consisted of—

250 men of H. M. 61st Regt., under Lt.-Col. C. Deacon;
200 „ Bellooch Batt., under Lieut.-Col. Farquhar;
550 „ 4th Punjab Infantry, under Captain Wild;
200 „ Jheend Force, under Colonel Durnsford;

with Lieutenants Ward and Thackery, of the Engineers, attached;

while in advance of all, under cover of the trees that lined the road, and concealed in the brushwood

* This is given on regimental authority. General Wilson's report states it to have been only 200.

which stretched up within musket-shot of the walls, the gallant 60th Rifles, under Colonel J. Jones, spread themselves along, ready to sweep the parapets, keep down the fire of the rebels, and cover the advance of the columns.

All had collected at Ludlow Castle before daylight.

The 1st column turned off to the left into the Koodsia Bagh, ready to rush out on the main breach; the 2d column passed on beyond to the "Customhouse garden," their duty being to mount the breach at the Water Bastion; while the 3d column moved out along the high-road, prepared to march on the Cashmere Gate when blown in. The explosion to be effected here at daybreak was to be the signal for a simultaneous advance of the three columns.

But as the day began to dawn it was observed that Pandy had been busy at work during the short respite from our guns, and the breaches had been filled up with sandbags and a *chevaux-de-frise* improvised. The order flew along through the batteries to open fire again, and knock down this new obstacle; and the columns were ordered to lie under shelter until the breach should be cleared; and then the advance of the Rifles to the front with a cheer was to be the signal for the batteries to cease fire, and the columns to rush out to the assault.

At the head of the 3d column stood the gallant "exploding party," consisting of Lieutenants Salkeld and Home, of the Engineers; Sergeants Carmichael, Burgess, and Smith, of the Bengal Sappers; Bugler

Hawthorne, of the 52d L. I. (who accompanied the party to sound the advance when the gate was blown in); and eight native sappers, under Havildar Madhoo, to carry the bags of powder. At the edge of the cover the powder-bags had been transferred to the European soldiers.* Here stood this heroic little band, forming a forlorn hope, feeling themselves doomed to almost certain death, waiting in almost agonising suspense for the appointed signal. It came: the firing suddenly ceased, the cheer of the Rifles rang through the air: out moved Home with four soldiers, each carrying a bag of powder on his head; close behind him came Salkeld, port-fire in hand, with four more soldiers similarly laden; while, a short distance behind, the storming party, 150 strong,† under Captain Bayley of H. M. 52d, followed up by the main body of the column in rear. The gateway, as in all native cities, was on the side of the bastion, and had an outer gateway in advance of the ditch. Home and his party were at this outer gate almost before their approach was known. It was open; but the drawbridge so shattered that it was very difficult to cross; however, they got over, reached the main gate, and laid their bags unharmed.

"So utterly paralysed," says Lieutenant Medley,‡ "were the enemy at the audacity of the proceeding, that

* The sergeants and the havildar accompanied Home, carrying the first four bags.—ROTTON'S *Siege of Delhi*, p. 272.

† Fifty men of H. M. 52d L. I., fifty of Kumaon Battalion, and fifty of 1st Punjab Infantry (better known as Coke's Rifles).

‡ MEDLEY'S *Year's Campaign*, p. 109.

they only fired a few straggling shots, and made haste to close the wicket with every appearance of alarm, so that Lieutenant Home, after laying his bags, jumped into the ditch unhurt. It was now Salkeld's turn. He also advanced with four other bags of powder, and a lighted port-fire. But the enemy had now recovered from their consternation, and had seen the smallness of the party, and the object of their approach. A deadly fire was poured upon the little band from the top of the gateway from both flanks, and from the open wicket, not ten feet distant. Salkeld laid his bags, but was shot through the arm and leg, and fell back on the bridge, handing the port-fire to Sergeant Burgess, bidding him light the fusee. Burgess was instantly shot dead in the attempt. Sergeant Carmichael then advanced, took up the port-fire, and succeeded in the attempt, but immediately fell, mortally wounded. Sergeant Smith, seeing him fall, advanced at a run, but, finding that the fuse was already burning, threw himself down into the ditch, where the bugler had already conveyed poor Salkeld. In another moment a terrific explosion shattered the massive gate. The bugle sounded the advance, and then with a loud cheer the storming party was in the gateway, and in a few minutes more the entire column; and the Cashmere Gate and Main Guard were once more in our hands." *

* Thus was accomplished one of the most daring acts probably on record. Salkeld, Home, Sergeant Smith, and Bugler Hawthorne, received the Victoria Cross. But poor Salkeld, after lingering several days, died of his wounds; and the gallant Home, after his hair-

And where were the other columns? Each had carried its breach.

The darkness to which they had trusted for a surprise had passed away, and the day had broken when they moved out, each from its cover, in solid advance to the assault. A shower of grape from the flanking guns of both bastions, and a perfect sleet of musketry, greeted them, and many a gallant fellow fell before the glacis was reached. At the edge of the ditch there was a check; the fire was so terrific that man after man was knocked over before the ladders could be got down into the ditch, which were to help them up the opposite side. The ladders once down, the men sprang in, mounted the scarp, scrambled up over the debris of the crumbled wall, and were on the breach. Ever foremost in daring, Nicholson, in advance of his men, was the first on the wall, at the head of his part of the column; Major Jacob, Captain Greville, and other officers of the Fusiliers, were the next moment by his side; the other portion, with the 75th in advance, diverged a little to the right to escalade the adjoining bastion; here a brave young officer of the corps, Lieutenant Fitzgerald, was the first to mount, and fell mortally wounded. A lodgment was now effected, and in spite of a fire from the church, the Kutcheree, the Government College, and even the Selim Gurh in the distance, which raked the top of the wall, they stood firm: resistance was in vain; the rebels were hurled

breadth escape, met death accidentally soon afterwards, while blowing up the fort of Malagurh.

back, or fled on every side; and, running down the ramp, the whole column were under shelter of the Main Guard, where they re-formed.

The 2d column to the left had also carried the breach at the Water Bastion, though not without heavy loss. At the given signal it emerged from the cover of the Customhouse, gallantly led by Colonel W. Jones, of the 61st Queen's. A deadly fire greeted it as it approached the ditch, and among the first to fall, severely wounded, were the two Engineer officers, Greathed and Ovenden, who bravely headed the advance-party with the scaling-ladders; and of the thirty-nine ladder-men twenty-nine were rendered *hors de combat* within a few minutes.* However, "English pluck" triumphed; on the column pushed; the ditch was crossed, the scarp mounted, and the breach carried in gallant style.†

The three assaulting columns had now fairly effected a lodgment within the walls; and a call was made on Brigadier Longfield to bring up his reserve, in order to

* MEDLEY, p. 108.

† "And here a little incident deserves notice; and the more so, as it affects the reputation of a very young and inexperienced, but, notwithstanding, very valuable officer, since dead, Ensign Everard Aloysans Lisle Phillips, formerly of the 11th Regiment of Native Infantry. In co-operation with some Rifles placed under his command, he most gallantly carried the Water Bastion, and turned the guns which he found therein, with all possible speed and dexterity, against the retreating rebels."—ROTTON'S *Siege*, p. 271.

This young officer's gallantry was acknowledged by the Horse Guards giving him a commission in the 60th Rifles; but he was not destined to enjoy the honour, or even to know that it had been conferred upon him. Two days after he was killed in the Delhi Bank House.—*Ibid.*, p. 308.

occupy the positions as they were taken, thus leaving the columns free to push on.

Colonel Campbell first moved his column out of the Main Guard, and diverged to the left to clear the Kutcheree and church, while General Nicholson, having re-formed, filed past his rear to the right, and entered the narrow lane called the Rampart Road, which runs the whole circuit of the city within the wall. Such a line of advance was evidently never anticipated by the rebels; for, with the exception of the riflemen on the ramparts, scarcely a man was here to dispute their progress. They soon cleared the ramparts, and, with very slight loss, carried the Moree Bastion, and also the Cabul Gate, and were pressing on towards the Lahore Gate, their *point d'appui*, which they were to open from inside for the 4th column, under Major Reid.* They had gone on some distance, H. M. 75th in front, when, at a curve in the road, a gun on the Burun Bastion opened fire upon them; in the lane, too, was a slight breastwork with a brass gun to dispute the road; but this was soon withdrawn before the brisk fire of the 75th. Unhappily, no rush was made to capture it: the men in advance hesitated, and fell back to the Cabul Gate, with three officers—Captain Freer (of the 27th), Wadeson, and Darrell—wounded. Here Nicholson, who had mounted the Moree Bastion

* Major Reid, in a letter to Mr Rotton, published in the Appendix to his *Siege of Delhi*, p. 356, says he was to have entered the city at the *Cabul Gate*, but General Wilson's despatch, and Medley, p. 103, in the programme of the operations, expressly mentions the *Lahore Gate.*

to reconnoitre the movements of the enemy outside, joined them, and found the aspect of affairs suddenly changed. In the lane, which had before been comparatively clear, one of the guns (originally placed at the Lahore Gate to sweep the Chandnee Chouk) had now been run some distance down the lane, and another placed at the entrance to support it; the windows and roofs of the low houses on the left were also now swarming with riflemen, and, where a short time before a vigorous rush might have cleared the almost empty lane, and taken the gun, and carried the Lahore Gate in flank, with probably but little loss, now every inch of ground had to be fought, and the advance made in the face of deadly fire from the field-piece, through the lane alive with a concealed foe. Nicholson saw the emergency, and resolved on recovering, if possible, the lost ground. He pushed on the 1st Fusiliers, who answered to his call right gallantly. One gun was taken and spiked; twice they rushed at the second; the grape ploughed through the lane; bullets poured down like hail from the walls and houses; Major Jacob fell mortally wounded at the head of his men; Captain Speke, Captain Greville, were disabled; the men were falling fast; there was hesitation; Nicholson sprang forward, and while in the act of waving his sword to urge the men on once more—alas for the column, alas *for the army*, for INDIA!—he fell back mortally wounded, shot through the chest by a rebel from a house window close by, and was carried off by two of the 1st Fusiliers. The command of the column devolved on

Major Brookes, of the 75th Regiment, who, on Colonel Herbert's retiring wounded at the glacis, had taken command of that regiment They now fell back on the Cabul Gate—which was for some days to be our advanced position.

The delay had lost us the Lahore Gate — *and Nicholson.*

To return to the 3d column. On moving out at the Main Guard, Colonel Campbell turned to the left, cleared the Kutcheree and church, the Delhi Press, and Skinner's House, where some rebels still held on ; and leaving these positions in the hands of Wilde's Punjabees, who came up from the reserve, he then pushed on through the "Begum-ke-Bagh" into the lower end of the Chandnee Chouk, then across this, the main thoroughfare of the city, into a narrow street or lane which leads up to the Jumma Musjid. The column had fought its way gallantly for some distance, when, at a turn in the lane, where, a hundred yards ahead, that majestic pile, the pride of the Mohammedan of Hindostan, towered into view, they found themselves confronted by a massive gateway, with the side arches bricked up and the heavy gate closed. Without an engineer—for they had all fallen, two killed and the third wounded at the Cashmere Gate; without artillery —for the drawbridge was so broken and the gate so blocked up with the ruin caused by the explosion, that not a gun had yet been able to enter the city ;* with-

* Bourchier's battery was lying outside ready, and as soon as the bridge and gateway admitted of it, in it came, and did noble service.

out a powder-bag—they were utterly at fault. In spite of a heavy musketry-fire playing on them from adjoining houses, they yet held on, hoping succours might come up: at length, when Colonel Campbell learnt that Nicholson had not gained the Lahore Gate, and that the rebels were mustering strong in the Chandnee Chouk, finding his men falling fast, and himself slightly wounded, seeing no hope of support, he resolved to fall back, and drew off his men to the church. In the meanwhile a noble struggle had been going on in the Chandnee Chouk. Major Ramsay, with his Goorkhas (Kumaon Battalion) and about 100 of the 52d L. I., had been detached by Colonel Campbell to push up the street and seize the Kotwallee. They carried their point in gallant style, and, fearing to be cut off, fell back to the main column, leaving a few men to hold the building. Three times did they clear the road and the adjoining houses; and for some five hours the Kotwallee was in their hands; but Major Ramsay, also finding himself without support, and afraid to risk the danger of so isolated a position, was compelled to abandon it and join Colonel Campbell at the church.

The reserve column under Brigadier Longfield had from the first been broken up to meet the demands of the assaulting columns; the whole of the 60th Rifles, under Colonel Jones, had distributed themselves along the line of advance to cover the attacking columns; while the Belooch Battalion was first thrown into the advanced batteries, and subsequently sent to the support of Reid's column to the right. On the assaulting columns advancing, H. M. 61st Regiment, under Colonel Deacon, had pressed on in support; while the 4th (Wilde's) Punjabees and the Jheend Force occupied the points as they were taken by Campbell's column, and then, under Major Wilde, made a gallant rush on the Government College, still held by the rebels, which they carried with trifling loss.

Such was that day's work within the city, thus summed up in the official telegraphic message at half-past two o'clock, "*We hold the line of the city from the Cabul Gate to the College Gardens.*"

It only remains to describe the progress of the 4th column, whose work lay on the extreme right. The policy of an attack upon this point at all has been sometimes questioned, as embracing too large a range of assault. It has been urged that the troops concentrated here, if distributed over the other columns, would by the increase of numbers have made the advance at the other points more vigorous, and the success more certain and complete. In this there may be some truth; but, on the other hand, it is only just to consider that the advance of numerically* the largest column on this quarter was not without its object: it served as a *feint*, confirming the rebels in their expectation that the main attack would be here, and thus drawing off their attention from the other points of assault. It has been sometimes hinted, too, that the General was greatly deceived as to the strength of the enemy in the Kissengunge, that he had been led to be-

* Though a very large proportion were the Cashmere Contingent.

lieve them to be in no great force there, and that they could be easily mastered; to which it may be replied, that though possibly the exact strength of the enemy in this strong position was not actually known, still so much was known, that they were a formidable body, and that their location here was not without its object, that object being to turn the flank, attack the rear, master the camp, and murder all the sick and wounded while the army were engrossed in the assault! So that the advance of this column on the Kissengunge, though unsuccessful, did effect its twofold object—it acted as a *feint*, and it saved our rear and camp.

At the appointed hour all the troops told off to compose this column, 50 men of the 60th Rifles, 160 of the 1st Fusiliers, with 200 of the Sirmooree Goorkhas, and 200 Guides, and the Crows' Nest picquet drawn in, 80 of H. M. 61st Regiment, 65 Kumaon Battalion, and 25 Coke's Rifles, with the Cashmere Contingent, formed up behind the Goorkha stronghold, Hindoo Rao's house, and then moved down the hill to the main road, close to the advanced picquet in the Subzee Mundee, where they were disposed by Major Reid for the attack; three guns were also attached to this column, but there was considerable delay in their arrival, and when they did arrive, they were so deplorably under-manned as to be of little use.* Two Engineer officers, Lieutenants Maunsell and Tennant, accompanied this column.

The enemy had occupied the Kissengunge Serai in great force, planting two strong batteries in front, and

* ROTTON, p. 281.

running out two breastworks with light field-pieces across the road leading up to it, one a short distance from the wall, the other far in advance, close to the canal bridge. Major Reid's plan was, after carrying the first breastwork, to divide his column into two parts, and, branching off with one half on each side, to push on in parallel lines to the flanks of the batteries and the serai, making at the same time a feint on their front; and then, having carried the guns and cleared the building, to make for the Lahore Gate.

From the unfortunate delay in the arrival of the guns, it was now broad daylight: not only was surprise no longer possible, but their intention was known, and reinforcements were seen pouring in to the rebel position from the Lahore Gate. While all was being prepared for the advance, firing was suddenly heard on the right. It was the Cashmere Contingent, who for some cause were prematurely engaging the enemy. The advance now sounded; a handful of Rifles and the Sirmoorees rushed at the first breastwork, and carried it at once, though with the loss of two gallant officers, Captain M'Barnett, 55th N. I., and Lieutenant Murray, 42d N. I., who were attached, the former to the 1st Fusiliers, and the latter to the Guides. Major Reid was now arranging for the substantial attack on the serai, when (in his twenty-sixth engagement*) he was severely wounded in the head, and compelled to resign his command. The whole plan of attack was now disconcerted—the heavy guns from the rebel batteries swept the road

* See Appendix O.

with grape; the Cashmere Contingent on the right, finding the enemy far more numerous than they expected, gave way, and could not again be brought up;* any further attempt was hopeless, and it only remained to draw off the rest of the column with as little loss as might be, which was effected by Captain Muter of the 60th Rifles, who succeeded to the command on Major Reid being wounded.

There remains one portion of that gallant little army to be accounted for, which could not take their place in any of these columns—the cavalry, comprising the 9th Lancers, the 6th Carabineers, Guide cavalry, and Hodson's Horse, and portions of the 1st, 2d, and 5th Punjab Cavalry,—in all, what with losses in action, and from disease, and volunteers to the artillery, only mustering about 600 sabres. These were concentrated by the side of Brind's battery on the right, so as to prevent any flank movement on the assaulting columns. They gradually moved down towards the city walls, and came close under the Moree Bastion, and were for some time most critically placed, suffering heavy loss from the grape and musketry of the rebels. Their post was perhaps the most trying of the whole force on that day: without any of the thrilling excitement of the assault, they were compelled to hold their ground for some three hours, a stationary target for the enemy, losing men every instant, yet unable to avenge the deaths of their fallen comrades; until at length, the

* The native commandant, Joalla Sahai, resorted to the very common native mode of avoiding the disgrace of defeat by poisoning himself.

lodgment fairly effected in the city by the other columns, they were enabled to retire from their exposed position, bearing with them, alas! a heavy though honourable roll of wounds.

Thus ended September 14th. With daybreak, it might be said, the carnage had begun. On the edge of the glacis—even before it was reached—many a brave fellow had fallen: the ditch, the breach, the Rampart Road, the Chandnee Chouk, the smaller streets, all had their victims. The troops had scarcely crowned the breach before the doolies (native litters) were bearing off their loads of wounded to the field-hospital tent, which had been pitched just beyond Metcalfe House. Soon it became a line, then a perfect stream; and so it flowed on for hours, load after load: some poor fellow with shattered limbs, groaning with every movement of the doolie, others lying senseless and motionless, exhausted from loss of blood; others again in the agonies of death-thirst, craving for water, and breathing their last in delirious moans, while others were past suffering or want. On they swept along the cantonment road; and as each load was deposited at the hospital tent, back hurried the bearers with the empty doolie for another, and another. There seemed no end:—for some six hours the struggle lasted, and the melancholy stream of doolies flowed along. What a roll of killed and wounded! 66 officers and 1104 men had fallen since morning! *

* Something like one-third of the whole number engaged.—MEDLEY, p. 114.

Then pass into the tent. What pen can describe, in all their sickening reality, the horrors of a field-hospital on such a day! There lie England's sons, as brave in suffering as in action. The cheery greeting of some slightly wounded—the scarce-suppressed moan of agony forcing itself from the lips of some old soldier, of many a fight and many a wound—the shriek of suffering from the frail youth, the soldier of yesterday—the reckless curse—the muttered prayer of faith—are some of the Babel sounds that meet the ear; while in the midst of all, calm, self-possessed, not daring even to give utterance to the sympathy with which, despite familiarity with suffering, their hearts are overflowing, the surgeons move noiselessly about from patient to patient; and the chaplains,* too, are there, sick at heart in such a scene of woe, and only sustained by the sense of their high office, striving to minister so far as may be to the needs of each. On such a scene the sun set on that day of blood.

The next day no further advance was attempted: indeed, the position of the force was too precarious. For while it is only due to the brave army to record the manner in which the order of General Wilson was obeyed, and they only warred with *men*, sparing women and children, and even old men, with such noble forbearance as to give in this particular an honourable pre-eminence among assaults to that of Delhi; still, it must be confessed, the besetting vice, the bane of the English soldier, proved wellnigh fatal. His love of

* The Revs. F. Ellis and J. E. W. Rotton.

drink was too well known by the natives not to be taken advantage of; bottles of beer, wine, and brandy were literally piled in the deserted shops and along the pavement. The soldiers, parched with thirst after hours of fighting under a broiling sun, caught at the bait; and that night and the next morning so utter was the disorganisation in the whole force, that any attempt at an advance would have been certain failure and defeat. Never, perhaps, did victorious general find his victory so fraught with danger: the advance even of the assaulting columns only partially successful; not one-sixth of the city occupied; the Lahore Gate on the one side, the Magazine on the other, and the Palace and Selim Gurh beyond, still defiantly keeping up a steady fire of shot and shell; the mass of the troops literally *hors de service* from intoxication—separated, moreover, from the camp by a distance of nearly three miles, over an utterly unprotected line of road; the camp itself very insecure, exposed on the rear, and, now that the attack on the Kissengunge had failed, on the right flank also, without any force available for its defence; for every man that could be spared had been thrown into the assault. In such a position, it perhaps was scarcely to be wondered at that thoughts of vacating the city, and falling back on the camp to wait for reinforcements, should have entered the mind of General Wilson. Providentially, it became known that such a step was being thought of; indignant remonstrances, in no whispered or measured tones, resounded through camp, as men looked around and saw in the thinned ranks the cost at which the city had been taken. Loudest and deepest came the remonstrance from the dying bed of Nicholson; and, happily, the matter never assumed the form of an official reference to Sir J. Lawrence, whose reply, had it ever been submitted to him, may be readily imagined. So the 15th was devoted to making defensive arrangements; the points already held were in some sort fortified; sandbags were piled on the flat roofs of Skinner's House, the Press House, the College, and other houses, to form breastworks; riflemen distributed over them to keep down the enemy's fire; and by this means the whole position was strengthened: and as the day advanced order was being restored, and the causes for the panic of the morning passing away.* The only onward step taken this day was to plant a battery on the left of the College to breach the magazine, which still held out.

On the morning of the 16th the work of advancing recommenced. The magazine wall was breached, and H. M. 61st, the 4th Punjabees, and the Beloochees poured out from under cover of the College wall to the assault, which was gallantly led by Lieutenant-Colonel C. G. Deacon, of the 61st. The breach proved to be not so easy as was expected; it was carried, however, with little loss, and the magazine cleared out at the point

* In despair of restraining the men so long as the temptation was before them, General Wilson ordered that every bottle of beer, wine, or spirits in the shops or go-downs should be broken. The number destroyed was almost *fabulous.* The loss to the sick and wounded was to be deplored, but thus only was it possible to keep the army within bounds, and to maintain any order.

of the bayonet, and Englishmen once more moved among the ruins which marked the scene of Willoughby's heroism. Kissengunge, too, was abandoned on the same day by the rebels, and was occupied by a small body of Goorkhas.

On the 17th a further advance was made; the old "Delhi Bank House," standing in a large well-wooded enclosure which opened into the Chandnee Chouk, from which a very heavy fire had been kept up on Skinner's House and the advanced positions, was carried, though not without heavy loss. Here, at a great hazard—for at the gateway into the Chandnee Chouk the rebels had run in a gun, and plied the building with round-shot—a mortar-battery was planted, which played, as was afterwards proved, with deadly effect on the palace.

The 18th saw further progress—the line of communication along the canal bank, between the magazine and the Cabul Gate completed. But the Burun Bastion and Lahore Gate still held out, and kept up a heavy fire on the advanced positions.

The 19th, however, dawned more auspiciously. By a surprise the Burun Bastion was carried, leaving only the Lahore Gate to complete our success on this side. It was clear, too, that the rebels were losing heart; their resistance was becoming more and more weak, their advanced picquets were being withdrawn further and further, and crowds of sepoys and townspeople were seen pouring out of the Lahore Gate in quick retreat. At the other end, also, it was the same. Colonel J. Jones, with the Rifles, had pushed on from house to house, and lane to lane, until he was within musket-range of the palace; while a battery of two 24-pounders and four mortars were pounding away at its main entrance, called the *Lahore Gate* of the palace. All was ready for an assault, when (as certain indications led the General to suspect) the palace was found to be evacuated; the main gate was blown open, and instead of a renewal of the death-struggle of the 14th, only some thirty *Ghazees* (martyrs) met them, who were soon overpowered, and the tread of English troops resounded in the deserted halls and ruined corridors of the palace of the Mogul!

The 20th was Sunday, and, with the exception of the bloodless capture of the "Lahore Gate," which had been deserted, and that of the Jumma Musjid, the Kaaba of Mohammedan India, which fell into our hands without much resistance, it was a day of rest.

But the old King and all the princes had escaped, and so long as they were at large, treason and rebellion would have a hydra-headed vitality. It was a welcome sound, therefore, to General Wilson, when that gallant "Captain of Free Lances," that most dauntless of soldiers, Hodson, reported to him that the King, though urged to place himself at the head of a fresh army, and to plunge Hansi and Hissar, and the Punjab too, now denuded of troops, into rebellion, was willing to treat for a surrender to the English. The first terms —that his palace and pension should be restored to him, and he be reinstated in his former position—were too preposterous to be entertained; but at length he moderated his demands, and asked for a guarantee of his own life, and those of his favourite wife Zeenat Mahal and her son Jumma Bukht. General Wilson at once, on his own responsibility—for time did not admit of reference—gave this pledge. On went Hodson, with some fifty of the bravest and most trusty of his own regiment, for Humaon's Tomb, about five miles off, one of the noblest of the buildings that still towered up with its glistering dome of snow-white marble in that wilderness of ruin, whither the King had sought refuge. Sending in the faithful moulvie to negotiate the terms, Hodson awaited the issue close by. Two weary hours did he wait — which seemed the longest hours of his life, in consciousness of the momentous interests at stake. At length the answer came that the terms were agreed to. He now advanced alone to the entrance of the tomb; out moved the royal prisoners in procession, and Hodson pledged his word for their safety. He demanded the arms of the King and those of the boy, and, with drawn sword in hand and revolver slung ready at his side, he posted himself by the palanquin of the King, closing in his sowars as a guard. A herd of followers had at first crowded round, and accompanied the procession some distance; but as it drew near to the city they slunk off and left their old puppet-King a prisoner in the hands of the single Saxon. As the Lahore Gate opened to admit the cortège, and the word flew along, "The King of Delhi," the guard sprang forward, and were only restrained from giving vent to their feelings of exultation in an English cheer by the assurance from Hodson that the King would consider it as an honour paid to himself. On they passed; down the Chandnee Chouk, that street where, only a few years ago, at the presence of the "PADSHAH," as he was carried on some public day to perform his devotions in solemn state in the Musjid, every native would have bowed down in abject obeisance, and even an Englishman might not raise his *umbrella** as he passed; now the old man was carried along a prisoner, shorn of power and pomp, the few idlers pressing on unceremoniously to get a sight of him, the proud Pathan and Sikh exulting in his fall. On they passed; the Lahore Gate of the palace swung open to receive him who was only again to pass out through that massive portal a convicted rebel and murderer, to drag on a miserable existence in lifelong exile. On passed the old man; every turn within those palace-walls could tell its tale of blood: close by, on the left at the foot of the stairs, had fallen the man whom he professed to honour as the representative of that Government to which he owed his all—Simon Fraser, the kind, courteous, Christian gentleman; the tulwar gash beneath which he fell still marked on the wall. On again: the corridor is passed, and the square, then appears the tank, the stone where so many women and children, victims of violated faith, were

* The umbrella is always a sign and privilege of *rank* in Eastern countries. The reader of Xenophon's *Anabasis* will remember the origin of the title *Satrap* among the Persians, literally "*an umbrella-carrier*," one entitled to carry an umbrella, hence used to designate "a man of rank, a prince."

massacred in cold blood, and no hand of his raised to stay the fiendish slaughter. On further: the Dewan Khas, the very hall probably in which, three centuries before, the great Akhbar received in solemn state and welcomed Sir Thomas Rae, England's ambassador—where of late rebel chiefs had sat in council against England's rule—there now sat England's representative, as lord paramount, under England's banner floating overhead, to receive "the last of the Moguls," and consign him to the well-merited ignominy of a prison within the palace of his fathers! Such was his welcome home!

The next day saw a further ruin of the house of Timour. Two of the King's sons, and a grandson,* learning that the King had surrendered under guarantee of his life, were encouraged to hope that the clemency, dictated, as they thought, by a sense of weakness, would extend to them. They were also sheltering in an old tomb, and Hodson was again the fortunate captor: their surrender was wholly unconditional; the only assurance asked for and given by Hodson was that the old King was still alive. Once master of their persons, he deprived them of all arms and ornaments, and made them sit in a small native vehicle, and, surrounding them with his trusty sowars, moved off towards the city. They proceeded a considerable distance without interruption, when a crowd of natives who followed began to close up, and Hodson's suspicions were aroused that an attempt at a rescue would be made, so he shot

* Mirza Moghul, the commander-in-chief of the rebel forces, Mirza Khejoo Sultan, and Mirza Aboo Buker, son of the late heir-apparent.

down the three *shahzadas* in the car, and then hastened on to the city. On reaching the Kotwallee the procession drew up, and the lifeless bodies were thrown out on the *chabutra** in front. It was a dire retribution! On the very spot where, four months before, English women and children had suffered every form of indignity and death, there now lay, exposed to the scoff and scorn of the avenging army, three scions of the royal house who had been chief among the fiends of Delhi! To the Sikhs, who crowded round, that scene appeared in all the solemnity of a fulfilled prophecy. Here, generations before, one of their own *Gooroos* had fallen, the victim of Akhbar's relentless hate, and their race had ever since treasured up the hope that on that self-same spot condign vengeance would one day fall on the imperial house, until the hope had grown into a prophecy; and in that scene they now saw the hope realised, the prediction fulfilled. Their national Nemesis was appeased!

But we must turn from Hodson and his exploits to a far different scene.

It has often been the misfortune of England to have the lustre of her brightest achievement dimmed by the death of the victor: Wolfe fell at Quebec—Abercrombie at Acre—Nelson at Trafalgar—and now, no unworthy comparison, Nicholson at Delhi. The fame of John Nicholson — the choice of the Lawrences —had perhaps hitherto scarcely reached beyond the Peshawur frontier, at furthest the Punjab. But he

* Raised terrace.

was so well appreciated there that men who knew, admired, and loved him, augured for him a bright career of honour, should he ever have a field worthy of his master-mind.* In curbing and taming the fierce spirits of a wild frontier, he displayed powers capable of the highest emprise—powers which, should the opportunity offer, would place him scarcely second among Indian generals. The day did come; and Trimmoo Ghat, Nujjufghur, and Delhi, showed that he had been rightly judged. His course—brief, brilliant, meteor-like—fulfilled all that had been hoped of him, and then closed in glory.

From the first, little hope was entertained of him when once the wound was carefully examined; indeed, considering the course the ball had taken, the vital regions it had traversed, it was only wonderful he survived so long. He was, however, spared to know that *all was well*—Delhi occupied, the King a prisoner, the princes killed—and then he could say, with Wolfe at Quebec, "I die contented." Nor had those days of suffering been unprofitable; his mind was active as ever; and though, from the nature of the wound, it was agony to him to speak, his pencilled notes passed about, and his wish—though his voice no longer—was

* The following anecdote, which the author heard Edwardes himself relate, will illustrate this:—In the beginning of 1857, Colonel Edwardes was asked by Lord Canning, at Calcutta, to state his real opinion of Colonel Nicholson's character as a public servant. After entering at some length into his high qualities, Colonel Edwardes wound up his account with these words—"If ever there is a desperate deed to be done in India, John Nicholson is the man to do it." Before the year was over, the necessity arose—*a desperate deed* had to be done. John Nicholson did it—and fell in the act.

ever listened to in council. So widespread and deep was the interest which centred in him—not in camp only, but throughout the Punjab—that with each day's bulletin of the progress of the troops was flashed up a report of his state. After lingering nine days, he sank on the 23d, at the early age of thirty-five years. The next day his remains were followed to their resting-place in the new cemetery, close to the spot where he formed up the columns for the assault on the 14th, by sorrowing hundreds; chiefest among those present, his long-tried friend and brother-in-arms, Neville Chamberlain; while all the Punjab felt the shock of grief,* and hearts bled at the whispered tidings, "Nicholson is gone." His was "a name," as Sir John Lawrence well said in his official report, "which can never be forgotten in the Punjab."

* The following public acknowledgment of his worth will convey, though feebly, some idea of the public sorrow felt at his loss; private grief is too sacred to be individualised:—

Extract Division Orders issued by Brigadier-General Cotton, commanding Peshawur Division:—

"DIVISION HEADQUARTERS, PESHAWUR, *24th Sept.* 1857.

"With heartfelt and unaffected sorrow, Brigadier-General Cotton announces to the troops under his command the death, at Delhi, on the evening of the 23d instant, of Brigadier-General John Nicholson.

"Bold, resolute, and determined, this daring soldier and inestimable man fell mortally wounded when gallantly leading a column of attack at the assault of Delhi on the 14th inst.

"England has lost one of her noblest sons, the army one of its brightest ornaments, and a large circle of acquaintance a friend warm-hearted, generous, and true.

"All will now bewail his irreparable loss."

It is interesting to know that in the *Gazette* which contained the list of honours conferred by her Majesty on the heroes of Delhi, it was expressly mentioned that among the foremost there would have been the name John Nicholson, had he been spared to receive them.

"Anxiety and suspense," wrote Colonel Edwardes, "about Delhi, reached its climax on the 14th September, the day fixed for the storm; and when the telegraph at last announced that desperate feat of arms, and General Nicholson dangerously wounded, it did not sound like victory. And day by day, as gate after gate and quarter after quarter of the rebel city was mastered by that band of heroes, the question still was, *Is Nicholson any better?* On the 20th, Delhi was completely in our possession, and every English heart thanked God for it. There seemed a hope, too, that Nicholson might live. On the 23d that hope was extinguished; and with a grief unfeigned, and deep, and stern, and worthy of the man, the news was whispered, *Nicholson is dead.*" *

Five-and-twenty years before, Dr Darling, the schoolmaster of Dungannon, had declared that John Nicholson, then a small boy, would one day make himself heard of in the world; and on the page of history the name of John Nicholson will ever be interwoven with the records of the fall of Delhi. Ten years after, the Dungannon schoolboy had grown into a stripling soldier, and was giving promise of a career of chivalry by deeds of prowess within the walls of Ghuznee. For the bitter tears he then wept, when forced to give up his sword to the overwhelming foe,† he now received the tears of a sorrowing army.

* Edwardes's Official Report, published in the *Punjab Mutiny Report*, par. 168.

† It is pleasant to record any act of individual heroism:—"Nicholson, then quite a stripling, when the enemy entered Ghuznee, drove

A plain massive slab, on which the simple tale is told that he led the assault and fell in the moment of victory, worthily marks his grave.

Delhi was now wholly in our hands: the Palace, the post of honour, held by the gallant Rifles and heroic Goorkhas, under Colonel J. Jones, with the title of "Commandant of the Palace," an honour well won and gracefully accorded by General Wilson;* the Jumma Musjid occupied by Coke's Rifles; other corps distributed over the various minor buildings; the Lahore and Cashmere Gates alone remained open, and even through them not a native entered without a pass; all the rest were closed.†

The services of the army were thus worthily acknowledged by Sir John Lawrence, who had himself formed, supplied, and finally pushed on the army to victory:—

"All honour to the noble army which, under command of Major-General Wilson, has effected the most important conquest, by which the widespread rebellion of the mutinous Bengal army has received a complete defeat in Upper India. The days of Clive and Lake are again revived among us. Neither the devastation

them thrice back beyond the walls, at the point of the bayonet, before he would listen to the order given him to make his company lay down their arms: he at length obeyed, and gave up his sword with bitter tears, and accompanied his comrades to an almost hopeless imprisonment."—KAYE'S *Affghanistan.*

* See ROTTON'S *Siege*, p. 316. It proved, however, shortlived and nominal, for it was censured and ignored by the Supreme Government.

† For General Wilson's official despatch of the assault, see Appendix P.

of that terrible scourge the cholera, nor the deadly stroke of an Indian summer's sun, which have so grievously thinned the ranks of our small army during the past three months, the harassing and almost incessant duties of the camp—the ever-recurring combats with a highly-trained and veteran enemy, who outnumbered us by thousands in men, and by hundreds in guns of all calibres—the stubborn and desperate resistance offered by the mutineers during and since the assault on the 14th instant—nothing has abated the ardour of our troops, European and native, nor quelled that indomitable courage and persevering energy which take no denial, and will brook nothing short of success.

"It will be for a grateful Government to acknowledge as they deserve the services of Major-General Wilson and his army to the British Empire in India; but the Chief Commissioner cannot refrain from offering them the warm tribute of his heartfelt admiration.

"Sir John Lawrence requests that a royal salute may be fired at all the principal stations in the Punjab in honour of the capture of Delhi."

On the Sunday after the complete occupation of the city, Divine service was held in the Dewan Khas; the throne-room of the Moguls re-echoed the words of our sublime Liturgy in thanksgiving for a merciful deliverance and a final triumph; and from lips and hearts ascended the acknowledgment—

"Not unto us, O Lord, not unto us, but unto Thy name be the praise!"

CHAPTER XVIII.

THE GOGAIRA INSURRECTION, MURREE.

DELHI taken, it was hoped all was safe: but a fresh danger threatened. The Punjab, drained of troops to the lowest degree to achieve that capture, seemed doomed to fall in the very moment of success. The chord so long strained, and now strained to the utmost, snapped.

Mooltan, being some 200 miles off the line of telegraph, was among the last places in the Punjab to learn what had been passing at Delhi. It was late on the 15th of September before the first vague yet welcome tidings reached, that "the city had been assaulted." The next day the post-office was thronged with officers, eager, impatient for further news—but none came: mid-day passed, evening glided into night, yet no post arrived; the next morning the same. Expectation and anxiety were at their height. What could have occurred to cause the delay? Had the army proved too weak? Had the assault failed? Had the troops been repulsed? Or had the Punjab, after all, risen? When, on the evening of the second day, the delay was accounted for by the intelligence that the Dâk had been stopped and robbed at Gogaira, between Lahore and Mooltan, it was a relief, a positive relief, to find that, after all, the danger was at their own door, and only a petty rising of some villagers along the main road; still leaving room to hope that all was progressing well at Delhi, and the rest of the Punjab remaining quiet. But each succeeding day brought fuller tidings, and worse; the petty rising of a few villagers grew into the insurrection of a district; the whole country around was in arms!

Before following out the steps which were so promptly and so well taken for the suppression of this outbreak, it is important to examine the causes from which it sprang, and the real amount of danger involved in it.

The country between Lahore and Mooltan, forming the centre of the Baree Doab, is little better than a wilderness. Over its vast arid level—now strewn with fragments of brick and pottery, which carry back the mind to days when those tracts teemed with busy multitudes—broken only by mounds, the sites of once flourishing cities—now straggle small bodies of Jats, whose avowed occupation is that of shepherds, tending herds of cattle, which find pasturage on the scant herbage, or camels that crop the foliage of the stunted brushwood. Of these races some would seem to be descended from the earliest conquerors of the soil, whose Hindoo forefathers perhaps lorded it in the cities over the ruined sites of which they now wander. Such, for instance, are the Lungreals, Khurruls, and Kathias. Others again there are who have clearly immigrated at no very remote period from the surrounding districts; here are

Bhuttees and Belooches, from Bhutteeana and Scinde. All now, whatever their original creed, are followers of the Prophet, but make any creed at all wholly secondary to their predatory habits. The chiefs of the several clans have generally established themselves in the more fertile tracts which border the rivers, while the mass are scattered over the *Barh* or central flat.

These tribes had been cattle-stealers and thieves from time immemorial; but being of no political importance, the Sikhs, after two unsuccessful attempts to conquer them, took only the precaution of having armed escorts when passing through the district, and allowed them to remain in almost undisturbed indulgence of their predatory propensities, especially as these rarely extended beyond their own immediate neighbours; thus they were generally left to settle their raids and their thefts, and to fight out their quarrels among themselves. But at the annexation the British Government could not rest content to connive at so lawless and dangerous a state of things, especially in a district commanding a line of road of such commercial importance as that between Lahore and Mooltan, connecting, as it did, the seat of local government, and the wealthiest and most productive portions of the new territory, with the grand outlet for their traffic, the Indus and Bombay. The predatory tastes of these tribes were now checked by laws vigorously enforced, involving punishment and restitution; and under the influence of these stringent measures, the road from Lahore to Mooltan had become as safe as any in Bengal.

So great a change had thus been effected that many tribes had almost abandoned their hereditary raids, and settled down into peaceful herdsmen; many of the chiefs had become men of wealth and substance; and the stake they thus had in the country was at this time considered as in some measure a guarantee for their fidelity to Government, and their co-operation in the maintenance of order. But still there were other chiefs, who, with their clans, mourned over the departed days of raids, fretted under the tight-fitting yoke of English rule, dreaming, it may be, in their Mohammedan fanaticism, of a restored Mohammedan supremacy. These tribes had, throughout these troublous times, been regarded with anxiety, and been rigidly watched. However, four months had passed over, and, with the exception of the abortive *emeute* in the Gogaira Jail in July, all had been quiet. The example of some of the better disposed of the chiefs near Mooltan, the triumphant disarming of the sepoys there, the constant passage of the reinforcements through the district—these, and the precautionary measures of Government, had helped to keep them under; and it was now hoped that, with Delhi once in our hands, the storm had been weathered.

But influences had been at work which it was impossible for Government, with all its vigilance, to prevent or counteract. The chief of the Khurrul tribe, by name Ahmed Khan, was a traitor at heart; he had been in constant communication with the rebels of Delhi and Hansi, and (as he boasted) with the King of

Delhi himself. Then the outbreak at Agra had let loose all the convicts of that jail, which, being the central one for the North-west Provinces, swarmed with the most desperate characters of Northern India, having among them a fair proportion from the Mooltan and Gogaira districts. These were no sooner free than they had hastened up to their homes with glowing tales of success, exaggerated accounts of the discomfiture and total extermination of the English below Delhi, and of their hardly-maintained position there. These men were now lurking about their old haunts, or lost in the dense jungles of the Barh, where English power was too much occupied, or too weak, to reach them, sowing broadcast the seeds of disaffection, and appealing to their brethren to rise and put an end (as they said had been done below) to the English rule.* These, and similar appeals from other quarters, were irresistible. The whole clan of Khurruls, with Ahmed Khan at their head, sounded the tocsin of rebellion, and the disaffected from every quarter flocked in to his standard ; and now the whole country was in commotion.

On the first tidings of the outbreak reaching Mooltan, on the 17th, Major Hamilton, the Commissioner, despatched some seventy sowars of the 1st Irregular Cavalry, with Captain Fraser, the Deputy-Commis-

* The 9th and a wing of the 17th Irregular Cavalry had a few days before passed through Gogaira and the Khurrul district, and it is not unlikely that the disaffected among them had some share in rousing the country by false reports of the state of things at Delhi, and the assurance that the "Badshah" himself was close at hand on a triumphal "progress" through the country.

sioner,* to hold Tolumba, and clear the road towards Lahore. On the following day came the intelligence that the dâk horses had all been taken off the road, the *Thanahs* attacked, the police disarmed and maltreated; and, above all, that Kumalia, a large town on the opposite side of the Ravee, the granary of the district, had been sacked.

Mooltan was in no condition to spare a force of sufficient strength to coerce men who had inaugurated their outbreak with such daring. Of the wing of the 1st Bombay Fusiliers, scarcely 300 in all were fit for service. Two companies were needed to hold the fort, and the rest to overawe the two disarmed Hindostanee regiments. Of the new Punjab infantry regiments, as yet only a mass of new recruits, scarcely one was fit to handle a musket; so two squadrons of the 1st Irregular Cavalry, with Captain Tronson's police, which from the constant demands of the district were now reduced to a mere handful, was the whole strength of the brigade.

However, the outbreak must be suppressed; and Major Chamberlain rose from a sick-bed to reinforce Captain Fraser with some more of his cavalry. Having united their little forces, strengthened, too, by the accession of two volunteers—Mr Page, a civil engineer, and Mr Taylor of the postal department, both of whom found their occupation gone by the outbreak—and also by a small party of Gordon's Sikhs, who were passing along *en route* to Umritsur, they now pressed

* It was the sickly season, and not an officer of the regiment was fit for duty.

on, but with the utmost caution, for drums were heard beating in all parts of the adjoining jungle, and spies reported large gatherings there, varying from 3000 to 5000, but the grass was so high and thick that not a man could be seen.

On the afternoon of the 23d they reached Cheechawutnee, which, they found, had been vacated by the rebels only an hour before. As evening was closing in, a body of rebels, mounted and on foot, came out of the jungle, and Chamberlain at once attacked them, though probably numbering five to one, and soon drove them back to the cover of the jungle again, with some loss.* Chamberlain now took possession of the serai, and also of a small two-storied tower close by, which was in fact "the key" to the serai. Night had scarcely closed in when they were attacked by the rebels in force, the village and the garden-walls in the neighbourhood furnishing shelter, from which the sharpshooters plied the serai and tower with almost incessant musketry. Even the women took their part, moving along the tops of the houses with their skirts stretched out, so as to cover the matchlockmen as they crept about from point to point. A sortie in any force was out of the question: † it must have lost men, and there were only about 120 sabres in all, and a few Sikhs. To

* The rebels are supposed to have lost from fifty to sixty men, while of the Irregular Cavalry there were nine casualties.

† One sortie was, however, made, which Mr Page gallantly led, to destroy a house close by, from which a very galling fire was being poured in. Of both his volunteers—Mr Page and Mr Taylor—Major Chamberlain speaks in the highest terms. "Fine, brave fellows," he says; "better men for hard work could not be desired."

retreat, even if they could have reached Mooltan alive, would only have been to give courage to the rebels, and to spread the rebellion still further. So Chamberlain resolved to make the serai and tower his stronghold till he should be relieved, and sent off a messenger to Mooltan reporting the state of things.* The rebels were hourly increasing in number; their fire, too, was telling, for the serai and fort furnished no cover; if a man showed himself for one minute, he was almost sure to be knocked over. In this emergency, an impromptu parapet was run up by piling the baggage-saddles of the ponies, and even the cavalry saddles, tents, bedding, everything that could be made available, on the walls, and behind this loopholed breastwork the men were able to ply the rebels more effectively, and with less risk to themselves. Thus passed another night and day; the rebel force increasing in numbers and in insolent daring. They shouted out during that night that they had killed Mr Leopold Berkeley, of Gogaira, which, alas! proved too true.

Mr L. Berkeley, a fine, brave young fellow, was at this time extra Assistant-Commissioner at Gogaira; he at once sallied out with a few police, horse and foot, bent on clearing the road, and in his first encounter repulsed the insurgents with some loss. The next day they came up in increased force in the neighbourhood of Mahomedpore, and although warned

* The messenger attempted to go out that night, but was detected, and barely got back to the serai alive; however, he contrived to get away before morning.

that he could not make head against such overwhelming numbers, on he went, resolved in making the attempt.* His young zeal was soon drawn into an ambush; he found himself in a swamp through which they had lured him to the attack; his foot-police fought well, but his horsemen bolted: he was soon surrounded, and literally hacked to pieces, but not before he had brought down three or four of the rebels with his own hand.

Captain Elphinstone, in the same district, had also a gallant and successful encounter with another party, the Khurruls, of which the following account is taken from the Official Report:—"Captain Elphinstone, the Deputy-Commissioner of Gogaira, having received accurate information on the 20th, that Ahmed Khan, Khurrul, and his men, had taken refuge about twelve miles distant from that station, a party of the Punjab police, horse and foot, under Captain S. Black, a detachment of Captain Wales's Sikh Cavalry under Lieutenant the Hon. F. Chichester, and of the Gogaira levy under Lieutenant Mitchell, were forthwith ordered against him; and the result, after a somewhat severe fight, was, that the Khurruls were cut up, Ahmed Khan himself and his son being among the killed.

"Ahmed Khan and his followers fought stoutly; and Captain Black and Lieutenant Chichester were surrounded more than once during the mêlée, the country being by no means favourable for the action of cavalry.

* So confident was he of success, that he took pencil and paper in his pocket that he might send off a report of the adventure from the field. In him Government lost a most valuable servant.

Sirdar Nehal Singh, Chachee (orderly officer to the Chief Commissioner), whose gallantry was conspicuous, was wounded in the leg by a matchlock ball."

To return to the Cheechawutnee serai. When they found force would not carry it, the rebels betook them to treachery. The Woordie Major of the 1st Irregular Cavalry has been already mentioned. It will be remembered that even the traitors of the 62d and 69th N. I. at Mooltan admitted that he had kept his regiment stanch, and thus saved Mooltan. The rebels now attacked him with offers of anything—everything—if he would only give up the five *Feringhees*, and himself take command among them. His reply was worthy of his previous conduct, and of the trust so implicitly placed in him by Major Chamberlain, that the only means of obtaining possession of the persons of the officers was over the bodies of himself and the rest of the garrison.

On the 25th a sudden stir was observed amongst the rebels; there was a move round the serai towards the river. This was explained by a spy as being caused by news having come in to the camp that a large force of all arms was advancing from Lahore, and had reached Hurruppa: but it was also hinted by the spy that the move might be a *ruse* to induce the little garrison to move out, when a rush would have been made on the serai and tower; a hint which was not lost on Chamberlain. That evening the whole body of rebels marched off, with the view, it is said, of confronting the succouring force at Hurruppa. With the chance of the report being true, Major Chamberlain sent off a messenger, with a note sown in the sole of his shoe, and later in the day a small boy with another note, to apprise the officer commanding of his dilemma.* Early next morning the sound of heavy guns in that direction fell like music on the ears of the little garrison, and by mid-day the column had encamped close to the serai. Two days after, further succours came in from Mooltan.

We must here break the thread of the narrative to account for the appearance of these relieving forces.

On the 16th of September no Mooltan dâk reached Lahore, nor on the following day; and, to add to the intense anxiety at the non-arrival of the mail, came in that afternoon the announcement that the whole Gogaira district was in arms. Sir John Lawrence was at Lahore. He fully appreciated the momentousness of the danger. Though he had risked everything for the capture of Delhi, and Delhi had now fallen, all might still be lost if that spirit of unrest which was astir throughout the Punjab were once allowed to gain head. Let the coal-damp ignite at a single fissure, and what could save the whole mine from exploding?

Immediately he ordered off a squadron of newly-raised Punjab cavalry to the rescue. No rest did he get that night till it was fairly on the move. That night they started from Anarkullee, and by forced marches were with Chamberlain within six-and-thirty

* The first note miscarried; the second reached Colonel Paton about midnight, and decided him on advancing to the rescue; otherwise the next morning would have seen the Lahore column on its way back, *in utter ignorance of Chamberlain's difficulty!*

hours. Next night saw a column (consisting of three horse-artillery guns, one squadron of Lahore Light-horse, one company of H. M. 81st Foot, and two companies of a new Punjab levy) move out from Mean-Meer under Colonel Paton.

It reached Hurruppa without any encounter; but here the rebels had thrown themselves across the road to oppose its advance—encouraged, it appears, by the idea that, because they saw no *red-coats,* there were only Punjab levies; but to their cost they soon found that Englishmen were Englishmen still, though dressed in *khakee.**

Succours also were coming in from the opposite quarter. Chamberlain's messenger reached Mooltan on the 25th, and at once Brigadier Farquharson started off a force to his release, consisting of two horse-artillery guns with their volunteer gunners, 250 newly-raised Punjabees, and some police, with 100 more sabres of the 1st Irregular Cavalry under Captain Dennis. Thus on the 28th, by the junction of these two columns, the force at Cheechawutnee consisted of five horse-artillery guns, about 220 1st Irregular Cavalry, one squadron of light-horse, one company of European

* At the time of the mutiny a change was being introduced in the dress of the European infantry. The long-established "red cloth coat," which gave to them the distinctive name among natives of "*lāll coorte wallahs*" (red-coated fellows) was giving way to the cooler, cleaner jackets of drill dyed drab, previously used in the Guides and the Punjab Police Corps, now everywhere known as *khakee* (earth-coloured), the value of which were so soon to be experienced in facilitating the secrecy of movements; for a red jacket would be at once detected where a suit of khakee passed unobserved.

infantry, and about 400 Punjab infantry; a force quite sufficient to awe back the rebels into their jungles.

Meanwhile other steps were also being taken to check the spread of the infection in the district. Captain Hockin was at Leia with his wing of the 17th Irregular Cavalry when he heard of the outbreak: he at once volunteered to move his men along the right bank of the Ravee, with the twofold object of cutting off any of the rebels who might attempt to cross the river and raise the Rechna Doab (which was as yet quiet), and also to effect a junction with Chamberlain if necessary. From the Jhung side Captain Hawes, the Deputy-Commissioner, was bringing up all the police he could safely detach, to arrest the spread of the insurrection in that quarter; while Captain Tronson, accompanied by Major Voyle, the Deputy-Commissioner of Mooltan, took 100 of his mounted police along the right bank of the Sutlej, to cut off all communication with the country of that most dangerous of our neighbours, *our nominal ally*, the Nawab of Bhawulpore. An appeal was also made to the loyalty of all the well-disposed chiefs around, and readily responded to.

Thus to the utmost were the available resources at every point brought to bear on the rebels; and the net was slowly closing in around them.

The primary duty, however, of the force now concentrated at Cheechawutnee was to clear the road and re-open communication between Mooltan and Lahore, and then to punish the rebels. To effect this, the column under Colonel Paton took charge of the road on the Lahore side as far Gogaira (the insurrection not having extended beyond this), while Major Chamberlain moved his portion towards Mooltan, arranging for the defence of the different serais along the line, and leaving a small garrison in each. While thus engaged, tidings came in of distress at Kumalia. This important town had been at first sacked by the insurgents, but subsequently reoccupied by Mr M'Mahon, the Extra-Assistant-Commissioner of the district, with a few Belooch recruits and some armed villagers. But the position he chose was so unfortunate and utterly untenable that he was in constant dread of being attacked, and applied for succour. Chamberlain moved across the Ravee to his rescue; but on his way heard that Mr M'Mahon had already retired on Jhung in the opposite direction, and Kumalia was once more in the hands of the insurgents. However, he pushed on, and after great difficulties in crossing the Ravee reached Kumalia, which he found again evacuated by the rebels and in flames. The whole town presented a scene of wanton desolation; in addition to the general wreck of property of all sorts, the streets were literally strewn with the shreds of the *bunniahs'* * account-books, which the rebel villagers had torn to pieces to destroy all record of their debts. It was indeed "acquittance in full" for all the extortion and robbery practised on them for years by this most avaricious class of money-makers. It was a dire retribution on men who had gloated over and fattened on the spoil which the simplicity or the

* *Bunniahs* are petty tradesmen and shopkeepers.

necessities of their neighbours had placed in their hands—and one they little dreamt of, or the wealthy men would never have co-operated with the leaders in the insurrection; they would have thought twice before they risked all on such a venture; and, when too late, they learned to cry out, "Save me from my friends!"

A word about these leaders. The foremost among them had been the turbulent cattle-lifter, freebooter, *Ahmud Khan*, who headed the Khurrul clan; but he had already fallen. The Khatia clan was led by one *Mahomed Khan;* the others ranged themselves under leaders of lesser note; but the greatest man among them, the bravest, and most influential, was *Meer Buhawul Futwanah.* That men who owed all their wealth—and some of them were very rich—to the strict just rule of the English, should be so insane as to stake their all on such a cast, was wonderful indeed: for it was to the protection and power of the English they owed the undisturbed possession of their fertile tracts along the banks of the Ravee, rich in grain, in grass, and timber, and the safety of their hoards of money; and yet, under the blind fanaticism of their creed of blood, and under some imaginary grievances, they hazarded all—and lost all. Kumalia in its desolation was only a type of every other town and village along the river-banks: all alike were deserted; and the whole population had retreated to their jungle fastnesses.

To follow up the insurgent force—in the face of the natural difficulties of the country, multiplied as they were by the rainy season, which was now in full force; across swollen nullahs, through the rank dense vegetation of a gigantic jungle (the fertile source of fever, too), not a foot of which was known, and where even a mounted horseman could seldom see five yards in advance, especially with a force mainly cavalry—if not impossible, would have been perilous in the extreme. With no guides, moreover, except some chance stray villager, who was almost sure to mislead them, the force would have found itself baffled at every turn, while the jungle furnished perfect shelter to the rebels, who were familiar with every inch of the ground. So Chamberlain, acting on the principle laid down and confirmed by all Indian experience from the days of Arthur Wellesley himself, that jungle fighting was madness, with all to lose and nothing to gain, gave up the idea. Lighting on a clearing, large enough to admit of his keeping beyond musket-range of the jungle, he pitched his camp, and waited for the co-operation of a column moving down from Gogaira.

While the little force was camping here, the fidelity of the worthy Woordie Major, *Meer Burkut Alee,* was again put to the test. The insurgent leader, Buhawul Khan Futwanah, sent a letter into camp, reproaching him for being false to his faith, and at the same time offering him absolute command if he would join them.* But the bait was as little successful as before.

* Translation of the letter from Buhawul Futwanah, Sulabut Turanah, and Sarun Wyneewal, leaders of the Gogaira rebels, to Meer Burkut Alee, Woordie Major of the 1st Irregular Cavalry:—

"It is highly unbecoming and improper that you should be engaged

At this time Lieutenant Cureton joined from Jhung with a small reinforcement of about 100 cavalry and 200 infantry, but they were raw recruits, the best only half-drilled, and the rest of them perhaps had never fired a shot in their lives. However, more valuable succour was coming in from the opposite direction. Major Hamilton had rallied round him all the trusty clan chiefs of the Mooltan districts, with the Lungreals at their head, and had called in also to his aid the well-disposed chiefs on the Ravee, with their gatherings; and with this force,—valuable not so much for their numbers as for the moral effect of the presence of the chiefs—had moved down, and was on the opposite bank of the Ravee.

in any hostile operations against the faithful followers of Islam; because the holy Prophet (may praises and blessings be upon his exalted head) has forbidden and proscribed it: therefore you should believe in the promises hereby offered.

"On the oath of Islam the prophet, and the holy and blessed Koran, therefore, we tender all kinds of friendly promises, trusting to your giving them credence and joining our ranks. As we are both of us believers in Islam, so faithfully do we promise that these are no false assurances. Upon our oaths, made before God and the Prophet, we tender whatever you may desire for your comfort and happiness, and we will henceforth consider you the lord and leader of our fortunes! Therefore, accept our offer, as also expenses for feeding the numbers of men and horses you may bring with you. You can do with us exactly as you please; whatever you order will be obeyed.

"The proceedings of Mahomed Khatia and others against you at Cheechawutnee were most improper; they were false to their religion, and can never be trusted: but pray banish it from your memory. Trust in us more firmly than in the expressions herein faintly described. Being short of paper, we have not been able to send an envelope, and we further trust you will excuse the want of a more elegant writer."

(For the translation of this letter, as also for much valuable information, the author desires to tender his special acknowledgments to Major Chamberlain.)

Tidings now came in that the insurgents were in great force in the famed stronghold called *Jublee,* which lay betwixt the two forces ; and a joint attack was resolved on. Unfortunately, the communication between them was so difficult, with an intervening tract of dense tiger jungle, some seven miles long and three miles broad, about as easy to penetrate as a Burmese palisade, that it was impossible to concert plans so perfectly as to arrange a simultaneous attack, and to prevent escape. The rebels, however, pressed by Chamberlain in front, with the Ravee on their rear, and Hamilton on the opposite bank—awed by the guns, which were never before seen in that fastness, and perhaps still more by the knowledge that their neighbour chiefs were on the side of the English—finding their sanctuary no longer impregnable, and the round-shot tearing through their camp—lost heart and bolted, leaving many of their number dead, and more wounded, whom they could not carry away. And in this capture of the *Jublee* jungle the neck of insurrection was broken.

After this the rebels gradually drew off, crossed the Ravee again, and made for the Sutlej, hoping to escape into Bhawulpore. Major Chamberlain was on their track ; but, with no hope of overtaking them, he was forced to content himself with inflicting the only punishment that remained open to him. In their flight from their houses, the insurgents had driven off their herds of cattle, their main source of wealth, into the most inaccessible spots in that jungle, far out of reach, as they thought, of the English. A tracker, however, was set on, and once on the sporr or trail, he never faltered; and after some hours of wandering, now over sand, now over ground as hard as rock, now across open plain, and now through dense jungle, he tracked down the herd to its retreat, and from the *adyta* of that jungle were brought out 1500 head of cattle, besides thousands of sheep and goats, and from another quarter another haul of about 800 more head of cattle rewarded a similar search. Thus in the midst of the Punjab was re-enacted on a gigantic scale the old scene so often performed by the rival lairds of the Scottish border.

It is time to turn to events which were passing in other parts. Colonel Paton with his column, making Hurruppa his headquarters, swept the road on that side; not a rebel showed himself, and the line remained clear throughout.*

To the south, along the Sutlej, Major Voyle and Captain Tronson had been moving along over ground which the late inundations had converted into a perfect swamp. On reaching a village called Sahookee, they heard that the Khatias had moved down *en masse* after their defeat by Colonel Paton, and were meditating an attack. At night† the rebels fell on the little camp, but found them on the alert, and were met with such a

* Once only, and then only for a day, was the mail again interrupted.

† *On the same night* that Chamberlain fought them at Cheechawutnee, and poor Berkeley was killed at Gogaira!—so widespread and well concealed was this insurrection!

withering fire from the handful of police as to stagger them, and they fell back; a second time they made the attempt, and were a second time repulsed. The village itself was now attacked and carried; all the cattle seized and given to the friendly Lungreals. The rebels moved off towards Pak Pathan, with the purpose of sacking it; but Major Voyle and his party followed up to the rescue, and the place was saved. Here they were in the act of making overtures to the Nawab of Bhawulpore when the tidings of the fall of Delhi reached the ears of that worthy, and instantly turned the current of the Bhawulpore policy. With a hypocrisy in keeping with his whole career, the Nawab now ordered every insurgent, who, trusting to his promise of protection, had crossed the Sutlej, to be seized and given up to Major Voyle. Their "Alsatia" closed against them, the rebels broke up and dispersed.

Captain Hockin's party alone remains to be accounted for. They were pushing along the right bank of the Ravee when tidings arrived of a fresh danger. The 9th Irregular Cavalry were halted at Kalabagh on the Indus, and were said to have mutinied, and to be on their way to join the insurgents, but this soon appeared to be, happily, an exaggeration. It will be remembered that both these Irregular Cavalry corps had been for some time regarded with great suspicion. They had been withdrawn from Delhi and thrown out into this district, as the place where they could effect the least harm, and where, beyond the reach of infection, they might, if anywhere, remain stanch. In the 9th there had long been a feud between two of the native officers, which, though hitherto kept under, now fanned by the cunning of some disaffected traitors of the corps, burst out in all its fury. The leader of one of these regimental factions was a *Ressaldar Sirdar Bahadur, Wuzeer Khan*, one of the bravest men in the Indian army—the man who in Afghanistan had most gallantly saved the life of his commanding officer, Captain Christie.* In the regiment, also, were a small knot of desperate traitors, men from his own district of Puttiala, who had long tried in vain to win over the ressaldar. The corps was halted at Kalabagh on its way to Bunnoo, when the leader of the other faction taunted Wuzeer Khan with cowardice, "that he did not dare to put himself at the head of his Puttiala brethren." Unfortunately the taunt told. That night, while Captain Campbell, the new commandant, lay asleep in his doolie, shots† were fired at him; the traitors were up, with the ressaldar at their head. However, under cover of night, they went off without inflicting any injury, and made for the Ravee. They were at first confronted by a party of Mooltanee Horse under Mr L. Cowan and Ensign Chalmers; but the Mooltanees failed, only a ressaldar and a sowar could be brought to the charge, though Ensign Chalmers most gallantly led them on: deserted by his men, he was soon cut down and severely wounded, and the

* He originally raised the regiment which, after him, was so long known as "Christie's Horse."

† Four shots entered his doolie; two passed through over his head, and two lodged in his pillow.

sowar killed. Mr Cowan fared better; he charged through the mutineers, who were all dismounted, and escaped without a wound. But nothing could bring the men up to the attack. Leaving half of them to keep the mutineers in sight, he now fell back to a little village at hand, and despatched a messenger for Captain Hockin; who, however, was already pushing on, having started at the first tidings of the outbreak, and soon joined him. The rebels had in the meanwhile moved off to another village a few miles further. Here Hockin and his sowars came upon them, dismounted and resting under a tree. Having first called upon them to lay down their arms, he was bringing his men to the charge, when Ressaldar Wuzeer Khan stepped forward, and addressed Alee Woordie Khan, a ressaldar of the 17th, himself a noble specimen of a native officer and gentleman: "We are both ressaldars," said he, "let us see which is the best man." The rest pulled up and looked on while the two champions prepared for the fight.

Rarely could tented field in the age of tournay have witnessed a nobler "passage of arms" than took place that day, beside that ignoble village on the Ravee banks, between these two Pathans of gentle birth.*

Heaven defended the right; the loyal Alee Woordie Khan, though severely wounded himself,† brought his

* The English reader may smile in scorn at such a simile; not so he who has seen the noble frames and manly bearing of some of the Pathan chiefs of the Punjab.

† The Woordie Khan was severely wounded in the left thigh. For this act of gallantry he was made a *Sirdar Bahadur*.

rival to the ground, from which he never rose again. The attack now became general; down bore the sowars of the 17th (most of them Poorbeahs!), with Hockin at their head, and not a mutineer survived.* Thus ended this episode in the mutiny.

The Gogaira insurrection was now at an end. The bodies of troops, small though they were, which had been brought in from the different points, had been sufficient to close in the insurgents, and to prevent the disaffection spreading to the other districts; the two columns under Colonel Paton and Major Chamberlain had cleared the road, defeated the insurgents, and broken them up; Major Voyle had met them bravely; Major Hamilton had most gallantly brought up his succours; and thus, baffled at every point, the insurgents learned the cost of rebellion in the desolation of their homes and the loss of their cattle. They learned, too, that though in their jungle fastnesses they could defy the Sikhs,† the appliances of the English, and their determination, were far more formidable: they saw guns dragged along roads, and through jungles,

* The mutineers were altogether eighteen in number—the ressaldar, sixteen sowars, and one bheestie: every one of them was killed. Of the 17th not a man was killed on the field; eight were wounded, of whom one afterwards died. Mr Thomson, the extra Assistant Commissioner of Leia, who had volunteered to accompany Hockin, and charged most gallantly, was very severely wounded, having his left hand cut off, and receiving five other sword-cuts. It reflected no little credit on Captain Hockin that his influence and command were so effectual as to bring his detachment, constituted as it was, against the rebels.

† Runjeet Singh lost two small *armies* in his endeavour to bring the lawless denizens to order. They literally perished in the jungle.

and across nullahs, where guns had never attempted to come before. At length the leaders in despair threw themselves on the clemency of the Government whose power they had learned to fear. In the beginning of November, Mahomet Khan Khatia, the surviving firebrand of the insurrection (for Ahmed Khan Khurrul was dead), surrendered to Major Hamilton; Bhawal Khan Futwarrah soon followed; and the other petty leaders were only too thankful to come in under amnesty; while the poor misguided dupes returned to their villages, the victimised bunniahs to their shops, and the whole district was again quiet.*

From the same causes, danger threatened the Punjab also from another side, to which brief allusion must be made, though the gallantry displayed in the defence deserves far more full and detailed mention.

In the beginning of September, the hill sanatorium of Murree, lying to the east of Rawul Pindee, on the borders of Cashmere, was in imminent peril. Here all the wives and families of the residents in the northern stations of the Punjab, from Jhelum to Peshawur, had

* The losses incurred in this outbreak in the destruction of Government buildings, or spoliation of private property, was estimated at about 5¼ lakhs of rupees (£52,500), for which sum compensation was obtained in the following manner:—

Plundered property recovered, about 1¼ lakhs,		£12,500
Cash collected from the insurgents,	do.,	12,500
Property of insurgents confiscated, &c., 1½ lakhs,		15,000
Realised by fines, &c., 1¼ lakhs,		12,500
	Total,	£52,500

been concentrated in the first weeks of the outbreak, some hundreds in number, with only a few sickly men left from the European regiments in the neighbourhood, and two companies of Sikhs sent up by Major Becher from Huzara, as a guard. Such a position, isolated from all other European troops, surrounded by a Mohammedan population at best turbulent and predatory in habits, promised to be an easy prey. The drain made in the close of August on the Punjab stations in order to throw every available man on Delhi, had reduced it to a still more defenceless state. But Delhi still stood out, and the Mohammedan neighbours seized the opportunity to sate their fanatical revenge or their greed for plunder, and by a most formidable combination rose simultaneously on every side, and, crowding up the nearer hill-sides, threatened the destruction of the station. Nor were there only foes without, there were traitors within; several of the Mussulman table-servants were in league with the hillmen, and for some hours the danger to Murree was imminent.* But happily Murree was blessed with a few brave men and true, either sent up there on sick leave, or attached to the Government offices located there. There was a quick rallying of volunteers of all classes; and with Major Luard of the 55th N. I., and Captain H. C. Johnstone of the 5th N. I. (in charge of the Derajat Revenue Survey), at their head, a prompt

* The fidelity of one of Lady Lawrence's personal attendants, named Hakim Khan, himself an influential man of one of the tribes that had risen, and the sagacity of the local officers, were the means, under God, of saving Murree.—*Punjab Mutiny Report*, para. 88.

organisation was at once arranged;* the ladies and children collected in the barrack square; a cordon of sentries surrounded the station, and the three weakest points were held in some force; so the Dhoonds (the distinctive name of these disaffected hillmen), stealing up the hill-sides in the dead of the night, bent only on butchery and plunder, found the whole station waiting for them. So cool and fearless an attitude did the little garrison assume, that the Dhoonds thought discretion the better part of valour; and, after a few hours of skirmishing, slunk off, with the loss of two or three of their number, who, less cowardly than the rest, had trusted themselves within musket-range; and quiet was again restored.

"After the repulse of the Dhoonds, it was found that the conspiracy affected many more clans and a much wider extent of country than had been suspected. It reached far into Huzara and nearly down to Rawul Pindee; and, excepting the Khurrul insurrection in Mooltan, was by far the most extensive rebellion that has occurred in the Punjab during the year. Treachery was added to violence. Two Hindostanee native doctors in Government employ, educated at Government

* Succours also were summoned up from Huzara. At the urgent solicitation of Mr Thornton, the Commissioner, Major Beecher, despatched from Abbottabad every man he could spare; but before they could arrive the danger had passed over, having themselves been in imminent peril *en route*. They had to cross a most difficult country full of morasses and defiles. The Khurrals laid an ambush to cut them off, but Providence saved them. The road on which the trap was laid became impassable from the rains. The force turned off, and not till it had passed the spot, did it learn the greatness of the peril from which it had beeen delivered.—*Mutiny Report.*

institutions, and then practising in Murree, were found guilty of being sharers in the plot. They were both executed There seems no doubt that the hillmen reckoned much on the support and directions they were to receive from their Hindostanee friends in the station, and several of the domestic servants were seized and punished for complicity."

CHAPTER XIX.

QUIET RETURNING—THE TRIALS OF THE KING OF DELHI, THE NAWAB OF JHUJJUR, AND THE RAJAH OF BULLUBGHUR—THE REWARDS OF THE RAJAHS OF PUTTIALA, JHEEND, NABBA, AND KUPPOORTHULLA—THE PRINCIPLE OF COMPENSATION CARRIED OUT THROUGH THE PUNJAB—THE DISBANDING OR RE-ARMING OF THE REMAINING POORBEAH REGIMENTS.

WITH Delhi in our hands, Gogaira restored to order, and Murree safe, the Punjab government began to regain their footing. Not even in the mid-stream of the Poorbeah mutiny, in May and June, had they been in so critical a position as during the last few weeks, steering their course between the shoals of Sikh rebellion and the quicksands of Mohammedan outbreak. At length they began to "feel the ground," and to find it firm ; and now they trode more safely, and could take a calmer, wider survey, of the dangers they had passed through—of the crisis, and its consequences.

Arch-traitors there were to be punished ; princely allies to be rewarded and honoured ; loyal sufferers to be compensated, and losses to be made good ; and some 15,000 disarmed Hindostanee soldiers yet to be disposed of, before safety could be insured. Such was the work before them. And with the restoration of quiet this work of retribution began.

Qui cito dat bis dat is a rule fully appreciated by an Asiatic; he understands the short shrift and a cannon's mouth, or a halter, for mutiny, and a dive into a bag of rupees for good service, better than protracted formal trials and long-delayed presents; and such had been the order of the day while Delhi stood out, and treason was rife. But there were traitors whose position and the magnitude of whose crimes raised them beyond the reach of such summary martial law, as also there were allies whose noble fidelity claimed honours and rewards which only the Supreme Government could confer.

Foremost among the traitors, of course, stood the old King of Delhi himself. He had surrendered on the solemn pledge given by Hodson, on the authority of General Wilson, that his own life and that of his Queen Zeenat Mahal, and her son Jumma Bukht, should be safe; but justice demanded that, though his life had been guaranteed, some punishment, only short of a capital one, should be inflicted on him, provided it could be proved that he had been no involuntary tool—no incapable, unresisting dupe—in the hands of designing fanatics, in the work of rebellion and bloodshed during those four months of blood.

On the 27th January 1858 the solemn trial began. Before a special military commission—presided over by Colonel Dawes of the Bengal Artillery, "an officer of high character and attainments," and composed of members worthy to represent with him English honour and justice—appeared the old King, charged with the foul crimes of murder and rebellion. There sat the last of the Moguls, on a mean *charpoy* (native bed), before his English judges, with the assumed air of idiocy or imbecility, in inane silence, only broken by an occasional irrelevant question or meaningless remark. Day after day, with unwearied patience, did the court, in its earnest desire to deal out justice, listen to the tedious evidence which sought in vain to prove the old man innocent, or rather irresponsible for the atrocities of his sons and the troops. It may be he was not guilty of the blood of Mr Fraser, Captain Douglas, Mr and Miss Jennings, and Miss Clifford, sacrificed at his own palace-gate on that ever-memorable 10th of May, or of the lives of the many victims, chiefly helpless women and children, who were that day cut down in Dariao Gunge and along the sands on the river-bank beside his palace walls; but the blood of those forty-nine poor victims who, a week after, having surrendered on the pledge of safety, were hacked down by his fiendish sons and their bloodthirsty minions at the tank in his garden, within sight and hearing of the windows of his own private apartments, called aloud for vengeance. Then, too, the scaling-ladders supplied from the palace to help the crowd over the walls of the gallantly-defended magazine; the aid so readily given to that monster whom he delighted to honour, Muhammad Bukht Khan, late subahdar of artillery, and now made chief commissary of ordnance, and virtually commander-in-chief; the appeals to the native chiefs around, in so many instances, such as Jhujjur and Bullubghur, too successful; the ready welcome to all mutinous regiments from every quarter, making Delhi the focus of rebellion; and the results of all this, the blood which flowed on every side, the hundreds of brave and once-confiding Englishmen who found a grave in that camp, and the bleached bones of once faithful sepoys, lured by him from their allegiance, which strewed the hillside: all this was foul treachery and rebellion from a pensioned subject against the British Government.

"*Guilty of all and every part of the charges brought against him,*"* was the verdict of that court. *Death* could alone have been the sentence, but for that pledge which nothing but the sternest necessity of the hour could have justified. Under it the mitigated sentence of transportation for life was passed and confirmed;

* The following were the charges preferred against the King of Delhi:—

First—For that he, being a pensioner of the British Government in India, did at Delhi, at various times between the 10th of May and 1st October 1857, encourage, aid, and abet Muhammad Bakht Khan, subahdar of the regiment of artillery, and divers others, native commissioned officers and soldiers unknown, of the East India Company's army, in the crimes of mutiny and rebellion against the State.

Second—For having at Delhi, at various times between the 10th of May and 1st October 1857, encouraged, aided, and abetted Mirza Moghal, his own son, a subject of the British Government in India, and others unknown, inhabitants of Delhi, and of the North-west Provinces of India, also subjects of the said British Government, to rebel and wage war against the State.

Third—For that he, being a subject of the British Government in India, and not regarding the duty of his allegiance, did at Delhi, the 11th May 1857, or thereabouts, as a false traitor against the State, proclaim and declare himself the reigning king and sovereign of India, and did then and there traitorously seize and take unlawful possession of the city of Delhi; and did, moreover, at various times between the 10th of May and 1st October 1857, as such false traitor aforesaid, treasonably conspire, consult, and agree with Mirza Moghal, his own and after lingering on for some months in durance vile in a pent-up corner of the once costly and magnificent palace of his fathers, the last King of Delhi was sent off, accompanied by his wife, Zeenat Mahal, who shared his fate, and "the intelligent youth"* their son, Jumma Bukht, in all the ignominy of broken faith and fallen pomp, to drag out a few years more of miserable existence in banishment.

Thus passed away Mohamed Bahadoor Shah, the pensioned puppet-king of Delhi and the last of the Moguls, a convicted traitor, rebel, and murderer; and with him all honours, dignities, and privileges enjoyed by the house of Delhi have ceased for ever.

To the trial of the King of Delhi a precedence has

son, and with Muhammad Bakht Khan, subahdar of the regiment of artillery, and divers others, false traitors unknown, to raise, levy, and make insurrection, rebellion, and war against the State; and, further, to fulfil and perfect his treasonable design of overthrowing and destroying the British Government in India, did assemble armed forces at Delhi, and send them forth to fight and wage war against the said British Government.

Fourth—For that he, at Delhi, on the 16th of May 1857, or thereabouts, did, within the precincts of the palace at Delhi, feloniously cause, and become accessory to, the murder of forty-nine persons, chiefly women and children, of European and mixed European descent; and did, moreover, between the 10th of May and 1st October 1857, encourage and abet divers soldiers and others in murdering European officers and other English subjects, including women and children, both by giving and promising such murderers service, advancement, and distinction; and further, that he issued orders to different native rulers having local authority in India, to slay and murder Christians and English people whenever and wherever found on their territories; the whole or any part of such conduct being a heinous offence under Act XVI. of 1857 of the Legislative Council in India.

* So described by Colonel Hogge, of the Bengal Artillery, who used to take him out on an elephant for a daily "airing" during the time of his confinement at Delhi.

been given which his position demanded over the other traitor chiefs on whom the day of retribution had come, though the trials of the Nawab of Jhujjur and Rajah of Bullubghur had, in point of time, preceded it. These only lesser traitors in power rather than in will had already expiated their treason on the gallows.

The former of these was the first to suffer; his treachery was the most flagrant. His family had been *made* by the English. Just half a century before, a vast territory, consisting of Jhujjur, Badlee, Kanaud, Narnoul, and other districts, the whole producing a revenue of above twelve lakhs of rupees, had been granted to him by the British Government, the only service required of him in return being to furnish a given number of sowars to the civil authorities of the neighbourhood. Yet what was the conduct of the grandson of that Government nominee? It may be accepted as a generally safe rule, that the servant reflects the spirit of his master. Now Jhujjur sowars proved false at every point. A small body of them were in attendance upon Mr Simon Fraser at the Calcutta gate when he endeavoured to resist the entrance of the 3d Cavalry troopers, but not one of them supported him, nor, when he was wounded, attempted to rescue him; so with those who were attached to Sir Thomas Metcalfe's escort, when called on to do their duty not a man stirred. At Goorgaon, about five-and-twenty miles from Jhujjur, Mr Ford, the magistrate, noticing the seditious spirit in the town, sent to the Nawab for help; a few sowars straggled out, but they insolently refused to obey orders, and actually incited sedition. At Rohtuk also, Mr Lock, the magistrate, applied to the Nawab for succour, which was point-blank refused; and when, a few days after, a body of these sowars did come out, it was only to help in plundering the treasury and destroying the station. Not, however, that their treachery alone would have implicated the Nawab; nor was it needed even to strengthen the case against him; his own conduct clearly showed himself to be from the first a traitor at heart. The evidence of Sir Thomas Metcalfe alone was sufficient to hang him. Sir Thomas Metcalfe had peculiar claims on him; his uncle, Sir Charles, as Resident, had more than once befriended the Nawab in former years, and his father, Sir Theophilus, had more lately, as Commissioner of Delhi, conferred many favours on him, and for himself the Nawab had avowed eternal friendship. Yet, when Sir Thomas Metcalfe, after having lain concealed for some days in Delhi, escaped to the fort of Nanoud, and entreated shelter and assistance, neither shelter nor help were there for him. The Nawab refused to see him, and, driving him away without escort, guide, or arms, warned him to leave the territory immediately, having taken away, too, his own horse, on which he had escaped, and substituted for it a miserable bazaar pony. Thus threatened, his steps dogged through the country, Sir Thomas struggled on under a mid-day sun, and hardly escaped with his life to Kurnal. But proofs even stronger of his treason were forthcoming; the Nawab himself was *at Delhi* on the 11th of May, yet not a single effort did he make to restrain either his own men or the populace. He was the avowed friend of the English Government, yet in his constant communications with the various civil officers around, not a word of warning ever escaped him that danger was at hand; but with the characteristic ingratitude and thirst for power of Indian chiefs, he took his place beside the traitor King of Delhi, sent troops into the city to fight the English, by his vakeel presented *nuzzars* to the King in durbar, maintained a regular correspondence with him, with loudest professions of fidelity and sympathy; and in everything (except in his reluctance to comply with the King's exorbitant demands on him for money) supported the cause of the rebels. When brought on his trial (in the end of December), his miserable defence was, that during the whole mutiny he had acted under compulsion, that he was merely a tool in the hands of his own soldiers, that he had applied to the English for assistance and advice,* but none had been given, and so he had been forced to join the King: but that no European lives had been sacrificed in his territory (while some had been protected), and that the treatment of Sir Thomas Metcalfe was without his knowledge. Such a defence could avail him little; he was found guilty, and sentenced to be hanged, and all his property confiscated to the State.

* This is so far true that he wrote to Mr Greathed, to ask his advice; but it was when the prospects of the English were brightening, and the demands of the King for money were more pressing; his object doubtless being to act the double traitor, and so to play his cards as to win with the winning side.

Bitterly did he bewail his treachery to Government, under which, he said, he had ever lived so happily and prosperously. The sentence was carried out two days after, opposite the Delhi Kotwallee; every precaution being taken, by a large body of Rifles and other regiments lining the Chandnee Chouk, to prevent any attempt at a rescue.

He was soon followed to the gallows by another chief, who, like himself, had avowed his treason from the outset, though endeavouring also to play the double game; this was Nahur Singh, the Rajah of Bullubghur. Something might, perhaps, be pleaded in favour of the difficulties of his position; his estate lay within twenty miles of Delhi, on the Agra road, and he was surrounded by traitors and a turbulent population on every side, and was consequently (he said) swept by the force of the tide into the rebellion; but, on the other hand, the line he from the first adopted admitted of no such palliation. It is true, he facilitated the escape of some Europeans in his territory, and in the month of June addressed the Agra government for help and advice; but instead of hinting to any English official the impending danger, of which he must have been cognisant, or, after the battle of the Hindun and Badlee-Serai (which showed him that the cause of the English was by no means hopeless), attempting to escape with his family across the Jumna, he raised troops for the King, helped him with money and provisions, and actually invaded the British territory and seized Pulwul. When Delhi fell and all was lost, he gave himself up, hoping (like other cravens who fared better at a later period) to save his miserable life by making other lives the price of his own. But such compromises did not accord with the fearless even-handed policy of the Punjab government. Sentence of death was passed, and before it could be reversed, he was hanged, on the 9th of January, and all his estates forfeited.

The fate of the chiefs of Dadree and Runeea has been already noticed; under the stern administration of the Judicial Commissioner they had already paid the penalty of their treason with their lives.

It is refreshing to turn from treachery and its punishment to loyalty and its reward. Of those who proved faithful among our native allies, the Maharajah of Puttiala takes the first place, both in rank and the services he rendered. It has been already explained that, from the position he held as the acknowledged head, not only of the Malwa Sikhs in the Cis-Sutlej states, but also of the rajahs and petty chiefs in the adjacent hills, everything depended on the attitude he assumed. Had he delayed or wavered, or, having once embarked in the cause of Government, had he showed signs of hesitation, or even indifference, the whole country around must have gone. A single loyal rajah here or there might have struggled to our support, but, overpowered by the influences of the neighbouring courts, he could at best have rendered only feeble service. But with their chief pledged to the cause of Government, prompt to attend to the first summons, hurrying to the interview with Mr Forsyth, placing himself, men, and money in Mr Barnes's hands, throwing himself into the troubled district of Thaneisur before it had time to rise, or we time or means to occupy it in force, and from that day bearing on a straightforward manly course—even eager to take his place in the army before Delhi—with such an example, all others followed; they were drawn into his wake. He stood forth in his own person a high orthodox Hindoo,* to give the lie to the imputations against Government about the greased cartridges, the adulteration of flour with bone, and other subtle devices, to break the caste of his co-religionists. His support alone, so prompt and unwavering (as has been well said), was worth a brigade of European troops; to say nothing of the troops that he himself, at his own expense, threw over the whole country at Umballa, Saharunpore, Kurnal, even to Rohtuk and Hissar; or the further proof of his devotion and confidence in sending in five lakhs of rupees, and a willingness to add another similar sum, if needed, to the Punjab loan. Such noble alliance could not fail of its reward.

General Wilson, in his despatch on the assault of Delhi (dated September 22d), bore testimony to "the loyal services and great assistance" rendered by the Maharajah. So, too, the Governor-General (G. O., Nov. 5th, 1857) declared that this loyal and constant co-operation merited "the marked thanks of Govern-

* A Sikh is, generically speaking, a *Hindoo*.

ment;" and added, "These true-hearted chiefs, faithful to engagements, have shown trust in the power, honour, and friendship of the British Government, and they will not repent it."

And when the day of reckoning came, the pledge was well kept. Narnoud, a tract of land out of the confiscated territories of the traitor Nawab of Jhujjur, valued at above two lakhs of rupees a-year, was conferred on the Maharajah and his heirs in perpetuity, "on condition of good behaviour and of service, military and political, at any time or quarrel, danger or disturbance."* Added to this what, though comparatively insignificant in value, was perhaps more prized by the chief himself, was the restoration of the family estate of Bhuddour, which adjoined his own possessions, and had been recently brought under British rule—this gave him back the Bhuddour sirdars to grace his retinue in durbars—also the princely palace in Delhi that had belonged to the favourite wife of the old King, Zeenat Mahal; while great addition was made to his titles.†

* From a summarised account of the rewards given to our faithful allies published by the Punjab Government in the *Lahore Chronicle.*

† Furzund Khans Munsoor Zuman, Ameerool Onvrae; Maharajah Dhurraj Rajaishur Sree Maharajah, Rajgan, Nirunder Sing Mahundur Bahadoor. Which may be translated as follows:—Special son, conqueror of the world, chief of the chiefs, Maharajah Dhurraj Rajaishur Sree Maharajah of Rajahs Nirunder Sing Mahundur Bahadoor.

خطاب عطيّه حال بسركار پٹياله

فرزند خاص منصور زمان امير الامرا مهاراجه دبراج راجيشر سري
مهاراجه راجگان نراندر سنگه مهيندر بهادر

Next in importance to the Puttiala chief, was his kinsman of Jheend, and only second to him in the aid rendered during the momentous crisis of 1857.

Happy for England the day that saw the Jheend patrimony restored to the Phoolkean line instead of being annexed by Government! Happy the day when, on the death of the childless Sungeet Sing, in 1834, the claim of a remote kinsman was acknowledged, and Surroop Sing, instead of living on, a discontented, disaffected witness of his ancestral estate absorbed by the Government, and ready to turn the rebel should the opportunity offer, was converted into a grateful feudatory, and proved a trusty ally in the hour of need.

The Jheend Rajah had not waited for his Puttiala kinsman to avow himself. Instantly he heard from Delhi of the outbreak and massacre, without waiting for a summons from Government to fulfil the conditions of his protected fief, he sent off a messenger to Umballa for instructions, and in the meanwhile collecting all his troops, moved towards the line of road where the danger threatened; here Mr Barnes's request reached him, and he pushed on to hold Kurnal and the main-road. With his gallant little force, scarcely numbering 800 men, he was henceforth ever in the front of the struggle. He moved down in advance of the avenging army to clear the road and to collect provisions. Accompanied by Captain M'Andrew, who had been deputed from Umballa, he seized in succession each post on the road, and was draining his own territory to supply the wants of the army when the ordinary resources of the commissariat were crippled by the suddenness of the outbreak. His was a noble instance—alas, too rare!—of unfaltering loyalty. There had been no delay in choosing his side, and there was no timidity or lukewarmness in supporting it; unflinchingly, fearlessly, regardless of promises and threats alike from the rebels, and the desperate position of the English, he committed himself to stand or fall with us; and at all hazards he kept his pledge. He first secured the bridge of boats over the Jumna at Baghput, by which alone communication could be held with Meerut; his troops took part in the engagement at Badlee-Serai; and from that day he was ever in the midst of the struggle before Delhi, the only chief present in person. Though his main duty lay in guarding the rear, and protecting the line of posts toward Kurnal, his manly form might often be seen among his men posted on the ridge; here now and again he would dismount, and, with his saddle for a rest, prove his skill with the rifle on some Pandy whose rare courage might tempt him beyond cover. He staked his all on the final success of Government, and in the hour of that success (to echo the words of Lord Canning) "he did not repent the trust he had placed in its power, honour, and friendship."

In reward for services so nobly rendered he received a large increase of territory adjoining his own, taken from the forfeited lands of the Dadree traitor, to the value of above a lakh of rupees—a vast accession to one whose whole revenues had previously amounted to only about two lakhs. He also received in the Koolârun

Pergunnah of the Thaneisur district several villages, valued at 14,500 rupees yearly revenue; and in Delhi itself the confiscated house of the rebel Shahzada Aboo Bukir; with further honours, of no little importance in the eyes of a native, in the increase in the number of guns to form his salute, and of trays to be presented to him on grand durbar days; his title* also was considerably increased. And it may be well hoped that the honours with which he was rewarded have made him a still more stanch and lasting ally.

The Rajah of Nabba, from the position of his territory, occupied a less prominent part in the disturbances of that time; yet was he as ready to throw himself into the scale, with what weight he might carry, as his more influential neighbours of Puttiala and Jheend. Loodiana, a town of turbulent, discontented fanatics, was kept under by his presence. Mr Ricketts, the civil officer of the district, ever bore ready testimony to his youthful zeal and influence. He supplied an escort for the siege-train from Philour; it was with his artillery that Ricketts and Williams so gallantly contested the Lussara Ghat with the Jullundhur mutineers; he was ever ready to supply carriage for stores when called

* Furzund Dilbund, Raskhool Aitkae, Raja Surroop Sing Walee Jheend. Translated thus:—Most cherished son, of true faith, Surroop Sing Walee Jheend.

خطاب عطيّه حال بسركار جيند

فرزند دل‌بند راسخ الاعتقاد راجه سروپ سنگه بهادر والي جيند

upon ; promptly was every fugitive mutineer who stole away into his territory caught and given over to Government. Indeed, according to his means—nay, perhaps even beyond his means—did the young Rajah of Nabba support the cause of the British. His reward, like that of the other chiefs, consisted in the accession of territory ; the two important districts of Bhawul and Kantee, taken from the Jhujjur chief's territory, to the value of about a lakh of rupees a-year, were conferred on him, with other corresponding honours of etiquette, and an addition to his title.*

The conduct of the boy-prince of Nabba, and the manner in which it has been rewarded by Government, will teach a lesson to the native princes of India. The old Rajah, Deo-In-Singh, deposed in 1846 for treason, left to his son a kingdom shorn of a quarter of its revenue and much of its power, and now draws on a degraded and dishonoured, though pensioned manhood, while his youthful son, by well-proved loyalty, has won back for his house an accession of revenue nearly equal to what his father's treachery forfeited, with an increase of honour and importance which never before attached to the Nabba house.

* Furzund Urjemund Uqueedut, Pawunt Berar Bunse Sir-more Rajah Bhurpoor Sing Malindur Bahadoor. Translated thus:—Noble son of good faith, Pawunt Berar Bunse Sir-more Rajah Bhurpoor Sing Malindur Bahadoor.

خطاب عطیّہ حال بسرکار نابہہ

فرزند ارجمند عقیدت پیوند بڑار بنس سرمور مالوندر راجہ بھرپور
سنگہ بہادر

The policy which dictated the selection of the portions of territory given as rewards to these loyal chiefs, is thus concisely explained in the demi-official document already quoted :—

"The territories granted at the suggestion of the Chief Commissioner of the Punjab have been most judiciously selected from the Jhujjur district. By giving the Maharajah of Puttiala a *locus standi* in that portion of the country, a friendly Hindoo power is placed in the midst of a turbulent Mohammedan population, and a barrier is interposed towards the independent states of Ulwur and Jeypoor with its feudatories of Shekawattee and Ketru, the population of which proved themselves unfriendly during the late crisis. To protect the Jhujjur border would require a strong frontier police, backed by a large military force, and this task will now be undertaken by Puttiala. The divisions of Bhawul and Kantee, granted to the Nabba Rajah, are adjacent to that of Narnoul granted to the Maharajah of Puttiala; and thus we have two stanch adherents on the border of our territories on whom we can place strict reliance."

But there were other chiefs who, though far lower in rank and importance than the three above mentioned, deserve notice as having shown their loyalty, and obtained its reward.

First among them we must place the Nawab of Kurnal, whose conduct is the more remarkable, as he stands out alone in loyalty among the Mohammedan chiefs of the district. Jhujjur, Dadree, Runeea, and others, played the traitor while the Nawab of Kurnal remained true; and that with perhaps greater temptations to join the traitors, and greater opportunities of wreaking vengeance on the English. Although on the 12th of May he saw the fugitives from Delhi of every rank and class—the brigadier and the magistrate, no less than private individuals and women and children—pouring in powerless, he did not, like the traitor of Jhujjur, close his gates against them, or, like him of Runeea, hound on his myrmidons to the spoil; but, defiant of consequences to himself, should the days of English rule be really over, he boldly cast in his lot with us.* He furnished shelter, food, and even money, to the exhausted refugees—supplied means of conveyance to pass them on to Umballa—threw out his own sowars to patrol the roads—raised a levy from the district, and, with consistent and unwavering loyalty, stood by the English throughout. As the army came streaming down towards Delhi, the prospects of the English of course brightened in the eyes of the Nawab; but days of trouble and danger came again. The position of their army before Delhi during that memorable month of July raised many a misgiving in the hearts of brave men; none could know its precarious condition better than Ahmud Alli Khan, yet he never wavered or relaxed; nay, according to his little means (for his whole revenue was only some 20,000 rupees a-year) he seemed to increase his efforts. When the Ranghurs were threatening to rise, he sent off one of his two guns and some infantry to support Captain Hughes's

* See vol. i. p. 209, note.

little force of Punjab Cavalry, and in the capture of the rebellious village of Bulleh, Captain Hughes declared that he owed his success mainly to the Kurnal succours.* This signal fidelty of the Nawab was rewarded by the remission of the sum of 5000 rupees a-year, which the Nawab had always paid as quitrent to Government, and a present of 10,000 rupees, "to be conferred on him in open durbar, as a reward for his distinguished loyalty, and for the eminent services rendered by him during the rebellion."

"At a time"—such is the language of the Supreme Government when speaking of this particular case—"at a time when treachery was so common among native chieftains, it is very gratifying to know that there were still a few faithful, who, through all adversities and amidst all temptations, remained stanch and true to Government, and who now, when the prestige of the British Government is again re-established, will receive from that Government rewards and honours for their fidelity."

Nor must the services of the Rajah of Furreedkote be omitted. They are thus officially acknowledged:—"Though no conspicuous services were rendered by the Rajah, yet he showed himself loyal and eager in our cause; he hastened to Ferozepore at the first news of the mutiny at that station, and his troops guarded the ferries as high as Hureekee. He sent a few men with General Van Courtlandt, and seized several fugitive sepoys escaping through the territory. His troops also

* See *supra*, page 143.

accompanied Major Marsden, when that officer went to Seytokee in the Nabba territory to quell an insurrection raised by a fanatic Gooroo, who was killed on the occasion; and Major Marsden speaks highly of the alacrity and zeal displayed by the Rajah and his men."*

In acknowledgment of these services, he was delivered from the duty of furnishing his contingent of sowars to the Ferozepore Commissioner, and received an increase of honours and title.

And last of all were the smaller Jageerdars, or petty rajahs, as they are called, who have been already mentioned as occupying the lands along the base of the range of the Himalaya Hills to the Jumna, and for some distance along its banks; these men were chiefly of pure Manjha origin, and found their way into the Malwa country for conquest and plunder during the declining years of the Mogul empire. Since the occupation of this country by the English, these Jageerdars have been called upon to pay an assessment of some 12 per cent upon their estates, instead of the old feudal obligation of service, which was not suited to our system, and regarded as fraught with danger. Though individually of little importance or power, these chiefs formed, collectively, an influential body; and, happily for us, when the call was made upon them in the end of May to supply contingents in lieu of money payment, they promptly responded; and although little could be expected of them in actual service, they effected a negative good as local police; they presented,

* He also contributed 35,000 rupees to the Punjab 6 per cent loan.

as it were, a non-conducting medium to the turbulent population beyond; and to this extent their services claimed recognition. The Government commended them for having at least kept their own estates quiet, and as a reward remitted the whole assessment for that year, 1857, and granted a permanent reduction of one half—a reward which appears to have given full satisfaction to men whose consciences no doubt told them they had not been *very* active on the part of Government.

Nor was the loyalty of native chiefs and sirdars confined to these protected states south of the Sutlej. The Jullundhur Doab also produced its rajah, as eager in his service and self-devotion as his more wealthy and influential Phoolkeean neighbours. Indeed, it becomes a matter of regret that the young chief of Kuppoorthulla, considering the noble manner in which he bore himself, had not a far wider field, and more ample means of rendering that assistance which his heart would have dictated. He only lacked the opportunity and the power to equal the most zealous of his brethren.

But a century had seen sad decline in the power of the house of Allowallea. The descendant of "Jursa the Kalal" was now the chief of a territory scarcely larger than that of the smallest of the Phoolkeean chiefs, the Rajah of Nabba. Yet, nevertheless, with much, too, in the past history of his house calculated to moderate his sympathy with the English Government, he from the first outbreak gave himself, so far as personal influence and his limited means allowed, to the cause of Government; nobly were the calls made from time to time on him responded to. Although a money payment had been substituted for the original contingent required of his family (at a time when the heavy demands upon his reduced revenue were pressing heavily upon him), he placed men, and even money which he borrowed, at the disposal of the Jullundhur authorities; furnished guards, patrols, escorts; and, what was perhaps more valuable than all, he himself came into Jullundhur, that his presence might give confidence to the timid, while it would keep under the turbulent; for although the population were on the whole peaceful and contented, there were malcontents and traitors among them; and mutinous sepoys were constantly finding their way in, hoping to light the flame of rebellion.*

In the denuded state of the district, every available European being withdrawn to Delhi, the preservation of peace in the Cis-Sutlej States was mainly due to the active, hearty co-operation of the Rajah.†

In acknowledgment of his services, Government remitted the entire tribute for the year 1857, and reduced the yearly amount in future from nearly 1½ lakhs (above £13,000) to a quarter of a lakh (£2500),

* At a later period, March 1858, when a general disarming of the Punjab was ordered, the Kuppoorthulla Rajah, with great alacrity, issued the order that his people should be disarmed.

† It will be the grateful task of some other to recount the more distinguished, though perhaps scarcely more valuable, aid which this almost Christian chief, the Kuppoorthulla Rajah, subsequently tendered in the Oude campaign, under the auspices of his old Punjab friend Mr Montgomery: for all this, further honours in that form most coveted by Indian chiefs, the bestowal of large territory, have been conferred on him.

and presented him with a khillut, valued at 15,000 rupees, with an addition to his title.*

These were the most influential of the native allies. Lahore and Peshawur had also their Sikh sirdars, and their jageerdars, who, though not of sufficient note or importance to demand individual mention, according to their means tendered ready service to Government, and were in every case liberally rewarded.

Thus the demands of justice and policy alike were met. The reward of loyalty was as liberal and prompt as the punishment of treachery was summary and condign. May the good faith of Government, as then proved to be so safe in the hands of the Punjab authorities, have re-established its temporarily imperilled prestige in the minds of our native subjects! May it teach them still to feel that, even in the hour of danger, it is as safe to trust the promise as it is perilous to hazard the wrath of England!

But other claims of a different nature had to be considered. The English residents had in many stations been great losers. In the readiness to acknowledge the services of the native ally and feudatories, the losses of the English subject were not to be overlooked. Now it had ever been a grand principle in "the land of the five rivers," that the province should pay its own expenses, that the expenditure, the cost of civil and military establishments, &c., should be covered

* His younger brother, Kooer Bikramah, who had nobly seconded him, received the title of *Bahadoor*, and a khillut of 5000 rupees.

by the revenue. This principle was now to receive a new application. If the Punjabees would indulge in rebellion, they should at least pay for the indulgence. The Gogaira district, as we have seen, was taxed to reimburse all losses, whether to public buildings or private property, European or native. A similar restitution was to be enforced on every other insurgent district in which any outbreak occurred; Loodiana, Jullundhur, Sealkote, even Delhi itself, with Rohtuk Hissar, and Hansi, were called on to provide compensation for all injuries which their rebellion had inflicted. The rights of the British Government and its subjects were to be vindicated, and that in the widest sense; "European British subjects, European foreigners, native Christians, and natives of the country who had thrown in their lot with us, and suffered in consequence of signal fidelity," were all to receive compensation for all the losses sustained.

"The Chief Commissioner is resolved that every community, section of community, or individual, who may have plundered or destroyed property, *real* or *personal*, belonging to any of the above-mentioned parties, shall be made to pay the value of the same, to the utmost of his or their means, and within the earliest reasonable period. Provided always that the exaction of this specific compensation shall be exclusive and irrespective of penal fines, or other legal penalties to which the offenders may be subject.

"It will therefore be the duty of the local authorities to ascertain summarily and estimate fairly the value of the property plundered or destroyed under whatsoever circumstances. Thus the parties who plundered or did mischief having been detected, awards for specific sums will be declared against them, such awards being regulated exactly by the amount of the damages done, so that in this respect plunder and retribution may be in precise proportion."*

While leaving the mode of realising the amount chiefly to the discretion of the local civil officers, Sir John Lawrence pointed out, as a general rule, that in towns it should be levied by a house-tax, while in villages the same plan might be adopted so far as it would effect the object; where it failed, the rate was to be fixed on the land; and in failure of both, to raise the necessary amount the sale of the property might be resorted to. At all events, so far as possible, the amount *was to be raised.* All classes, high and low, should pay the penalty of their folly, and make good the losses caused by their rebellion.

All who had been sufferers were called on to send in their claims, due care being taken to guard against exaggerations or mistaken estimates.

The principle of thus exacting compensation was first introduced by that energetic officer, Mr George Ricketts of Loodiana. "It met my cordial approval," wrote Mr Montgomery in his official report, "and has been sanctioned by the Chief Commissioner. I consider it one of the most masterly strokes of policy of

* Extract from letter, dated 5th March 1858, to all officers in civil employ in the Punjab.

the whole Punjab. The principle is well understood by the people, that when any members of a community disgrace themselves by violent encroachments on the rights of others, the whole community to which they belong atones for their guilt by pecuniary compensation to the sufferers, and by a fine to Government for its outraged authority. In this case it produced the most strikingly beneficial effects. It quieted not only Loodiana, but all the six market-towns of the district. It inspired a salutary dread of Government, which was so manifestly inclined to hold its own, and care for neither prince, peasant, nor mutineer. Compensation was made to all the sufferers to the full extent of their losses, leaving a small balance which will nearly cover the loss to Government property."

At Sealkote, Jullundhur, Gogaira, the principle had been applied to the fullest extent, and before a twelvemonth had passed every public loss had been made good, and every private claim investigated and satisfied. It was the full intention of Sir John Lawrence, as already mentioned, to enforce this principle even on the blood-stained district of Delhi itself; but his independence of action had now ceased, communication with Calcutta was re-opened, the Supreme Government interposed its veto, and the district of Delhi escaped. This was one of the bold acts of the Punjab Government which found little favour in the Calcutta Council Chamber. Even the atrocities of Meerut were condoned by a fine scarcely heavier than that imposed for the escapade at Loodiana, while Cawnpore and suchlike districts escaped almost scot-free. The future historian of India will probably indulge in a disquisition on the probabilities of the beneficial effect of this principle, had it been universally applied. Certainly such a course would have robbed Sir Charles Trevelyan of that powerful argument against the new financial scheme, that the faithful should pay equally with the traitors—the man who was ready to give his all in support of Government should be heavily taxed to make up the deficiencies caused by the rebel.

One other measure of the Punjab administration remains to be considered. There were still some 15,000 suspected disarmed Poorbeahs; and what was to be done with them? Rarely has the ingenuity and zeal of volunteer legislators been more sorely taxed than in the present instance, in suggesting some escape for the Punjab Government from the dilemma into which their system of disarming, inaugurated by Brigadier S. Corbett at Lahore, had involved them. Propositions of every sort, and of every degree of clemency or severity, were thrust forward by amateur legislators and candidates for Government favour. There were old officers of the native army, still fondly nursing up their former love for their *babas*, and declaring their conviction that the poor sepoys only mutinied because they were *driven into* it by mistrust and suspicion. These champions of the sepoy loudly declared that it would be only an *amende honorable* to their insulted loyalty for having been deprived of their arms—only just in time, in many instances, to prevent their using them against loving and confiding masters—that all who had not committed themselves by any open act of mutiny and violence should receive back their arms, and be restored to all former privileges, with perhaps promotion, if not the "Order of Merit," to soothe their wounded feelings! On the other hand were men fresh from England, in utter ignorance of all connected with India and its sepoy army, beyond the fact that that army had mutinied and committed fiendish atrocities, and that they were sent out to punish them, and to recover the country; nothing would satisfy the ardour and vengeance of these but a general indiscriminate massacre of all suspected and disarmed regiments. Then, again, there were others of more moderate views, who recommended a less wholesale slaughter, and would have every tenth man hung, and all the rest transported for life, the only fear being lest the Andamans should be over-populated: while others, in their support of the administration of justice in all its solemn and slow forms, urged that every sepoy should have the benefit of separate trial; that all who could be proved guilty should suffer death, and all others should be regarded as innocent, and be forthwith restored to the service—little thinking what years it would take to investigate the individual cases of some 28,000 men (for there were at least that number in the whole Presidency), and what testimony would be forthcoming.

Thus was invention at its wit's end to devise some plan by which the Punjab might be relieved of its incubus of disarmed Poorbeahs. In due time, however, it was announced that a solution of the difficulty had been arrived at;* and then men wondered that the idea had never struck them: it was so effectual and so simple withal.

All the disarmed Hindostanee regiments in the Punjab, with two or three exceptions, were to be disbanded and sent off to their own homes; first those, the majority of the whole army, who came from Oude (for that country had been by this time† brought into a somewhat peaceful state, and was, moreover, strongly garrisoned by Europeans and Poorbeah-hating Punjabees), and afterwards the Bhojporees, who formed a very small proportion, were to pass down as soon as Behar and that district should be reduced to order.

The plan was simply this: twenty men a-day from each station were to be sent off, without arms, under a small armed police escort, and to proceed, stage by stage, till they reached the border of their own country, and then to be left free to follow their own course homewards, with the warning that instant death would be the result of any attempt at outbreak or escape. Three different routes were laid down to expedite their dispersement, and at the same time to avoid their collecting at any one point in force; those from Umritsur going through Jullundhur, Loodiana, and Umballa to Delhi; those from Lahore by Ferozepore, Loodiana, Saharumpore, and Meerut; while those from Mooltan

* A demi-official statement of the plan to be adopted in the Punjab appeared in the Indian papers, with the view to relieve public anxiety.

† *August* 1858, when the plan was carried out.

were to branch off by Sirsa and Hansi. By this arrangement sixty men a-day would be passing down by three distinct routes—each party of twenty men, with ten miles between, and police along the whole road, so that combination would be impossible—three streams flowing in separate channels, never uniting their waters, never stopping, but rolling on day by day till the Punjab should be drained. For the regiments farther north, as at Rawul Pindee, and in the Peshawur valley, another plan was to be adopted: they were to be brought down in detachments under strong escorts of formidable Gizailchees, Mooltanees, and other frontier "barbarians," until they reached Umballa, where the process of dissolving by twenty a-day would begin; the lower stations being emptied out before the men from the Peshawur division arrived.

This plan was most successfully carried out.* A

* With only one exception. The 62d and 69th N. I. were still at Mooltan, where they had only been kept under by the presence of a wing of the 1st Bombay Fusiliers and some Royal Artillery, and also by the moral check of the 1st Punjab Irregular Cavalry; but these had lately moved to Jullundhur. The very day before the order came for their disbandment, as if their consciences feared a far more severe and juster fate, which they hoped to anticipate, they wound up their career of treachery by a desperate onslaught, armed with clubs, charpoy-legs, stones, &c., on the guns and European guards. So sudden was the attack that they seemed to have the upper hand, but it was only momentary. The guns were soon recovered; the Fusiliers turned out in force; the grape swept through their crowds, and the musketry told fatally; and after a severe resistance — having, however, killed one officer and several men—they beat a retreat, and made for the Sutlej, hoping to find shelter in Bhawulpore. But what with the swollen stream, which swept them down in crowds, and the police whom the district officers had from every side thrown on their rear, very few crossed over or escaped. A few days after, they were brought in by hundreds to Mooltan for trial. The ringleaders suffered death,

few weeks saw the Punjab relieved of what had been for many months a cause of anxiety and alarm. A few weeks, and 15,000 Poorbeah soldiers had passed away. Travellers on the Grand Trunk Road would meet each day's detachment as it moved on—some looking defiance in their powerlessness, others seeming light-hearted and happy: all peaceful and orderly. The Chandee Chouk of Delhi saw each day's party pass along; and here, perhaps more than anywhere, their hearts failed them: they who a while before had revelled in dreams of triumph, when the restored *raj* of their own "Badshah" should give them *here* an elysium of independence and glory over the ruins of the Feringhee rule, now passed through, disarmed, disbanded, guarded, crestfallen, detected traitors to the paternal Government whose salt they had eaten for so many years.

Nor did their return to Oude hold out any brighter hopes. They might now revisit those homes from which the calls to vindicate the purity of their caste had some months before so successfully aroused their fanatic fury; but rebellion, so long loud-tongued and defiant, had now hidden its diminished head; and where had formerly been small detachments of a single European regiment, and thousands of their own Poorbeah *bhaibunds,* now 16,000 European soldiers and above 15,000 Punjabees were holding

and the rest transportation or imprisonment. Thus did the Mooltan traitors, by a more summary, and, as it proved, complete process, relieve the Punjab of their presence.

down with iron grasp a disarmed populace. Among such the disbanded sepoys, coming to their home one by one, without money or arms, could do little but relapse into their original condition of peaceful agricultural labourers; after a time, perhaps, to re-enlist into the service which they had once disgraced, but which was now so changed from its old Poorbeah monopoly, that were they still traitors and mutineers in heart, they could never again hope, in such a heterogeneous mass—Sikh, Punjabee, Afghan, Mooltanee, Goorkha—to organise conspiracy or kindle the flame of mutiny and rebellion. Such was the fate designed for the remains of Bengal's once-vaunted sepoy army.

There were to be a few exceptions. There were some regiments, who, though precaution demanded that they should be disarmed, had yet borne themselves so well, that, as an acknowledgment of their better conduct, and perhaps still more to show that Government did not war against Hindostanees indiscriminately, and as a body exclude them from the ranks of the army, but was still willing (as, indeed, both policy and necessity demanded) to admit them again into the service—to these it was resolved to restore their arms, in token of continued confidence. These favourable exceptions were the 33d N. I., who had been brought in from Hoosheyarpore, and disarmed by Nicholson at Philour in the end of June; the 59th N. I., who were disarmed a few days after at Umritsur; and the 58th, who, at Rawul Pindee, in the beginning of that month, despite the temporary panic and flight, had laid down their arms; and the right wing of 4th N. I., at Hoosheyarpore.

In each case their arms were given back in general parade, with an address to the men, calling on them to prove themselves worthy of the confidence still placed in them.

But the 4th N. I. deserve more special notice. It will be remembered that this regiment was, at the time of the outbreak, divided in wings between the fort of Kangra and the station of Noorpore: the left wing at Kangra had been quietly dispossessed of their arms, and relieved of some of the fort guards by Younghusband's *Shere dils;* the right wing had promptly given up their arms at the order of Major Wilkie. Since that time, both wings had been kept separate—the one remaining at Noorpore, the other being moved into Hoosheyarpore. Months passed, and the whole regiment continued to be most orderly: so much so, that the 4th N. I. were always pointed out as the first corps—if *any* were to be again so far trusted—who should have their arms restored with honour. But time was to prove how little one wing at least was worthy of such trust.

The night of the 5th of May 1858 was to have seen the station of Hoosheyarpore given up to fire and sword! Scarcely two hours before gunfire, at nine o'clock—the time fixed on for the massacre—Lieutenant Currie, the adjutant, while riding quietly to the mess-house, received a warning from one of his servants, who was watching for him, that he had just discovered a conspiracy which involved the life of every European in the station.* No time was lost. The safety of the ladies was provided for by collecting them all into a central bungalow: Major Paterson, commanding the wing, applied to Mr Simpson, the Deputy-Commissioner, for help; a strong body of police were brought in, while 200 Sikhs of a new levy mustered, and moved down to the lines. Here a roll-call was sounded—all hands turned out, and only two or three men were missing. The whole regiment was now formed on parade, and surrounded by police and Sikhs; and a general search commenced. Tulwars were found concealed in the lines; many more, and some matchlocks, in a dry nullah close by; the *mistree* (blacksmith) was seized, his workshop searched, bullet-moulds and newly-cast bullets found in the floor, and the fullest proof obtained that that timely notice had saved the station from a most bloodthirsty conspiracy. The wing were the next day marched off to Jullundhur under strong police escort, where a military commission was assembled, under Major Crawford Chamberlain, to investigate the case. By the end of May above 200 men of various grades—so widespread was the conspiracy—were convicted and punished; some blown away from

* He had chanced to go into the workshop of the regimental *mistree* (armourer), and found him casting bullets. On asking what it meant, he was told, "What, don't you know what is going to happen to-night? We are going to murder all the *sahib logues;* the men are told off to attack every house." The man instantly came and told his master.

guns, others shot, and the majority transported for life, or imprisoned for fourteen years.

All eyes were instantly turned with anxiety to the right wing, who were still at Noorpore, under Major Wilkie. What would they do?—and how could their officers escape? But for two years and a half the two wings had been separated, and it was known that little sympathy existed between them. So, when the right wing heard what had happened at Hoosheyarpore, they expressed the most vehement indignation, gave up their side-arms at a word from Major Wilkie, and actually *petitioned* that they might not be sent to Jullundhur, and be brought into contact with the miscreants of the left wing. They were allowed to remain at Noorpore, conducted themselves with the utmost propriety, and eventually they received back their arms with honour, having given this additional proof of their stanchness and loyalty.

Besides these corps who were thus rewarded, there were a considerable body of sepoys, above three hundred in number, from the 36th N. I. and 61st N. I. at Jullundhur, and the 3d N. I. at Philour, who had remained faithful when their regiments mutinied. Sir John Lawrence had pleaded for these men: some of them had rescued the treasure under their guard; some had preserved their officers; some protected ladies, and had given full proof of their fidelity. As an act of duty to them, Sir John Lawrence urged that they should be rearmed, and suggested their being formed into one regiment, the name of which should henceforth bear witness to their loyalty. They were consequently formed into a special irregular corps, called the *Wufadar Pultun*, or "Faithful Regiment," under Major Innes of the 61st N. I., whose life had been so nobly preserved by some of themselves at the Jullundhur outbreak.*

There remain only a few more to be accounted for.

A considerable body of stragglers from the Sealkote Brigade had found sanctuary in Jummoo. Large portions of these were, by the firm attitude assumed by Sir John Lawrence, extorted from the protection of Maharaja Rumbheer Sing; but as his word had been pledged to them that their lives should not be forfeited, they were only sentenced to transportation for life. Others remained sheltered along the lower hills, and some months after made a desperate attack on Madhapore, a small station at the head of the Baree Doab Canal, where they committed some cruel atrocities, but were repulsed and driven across the river with heavy loss by the young engineers and their workmen. The last detachment of these miscreants lingered on for some months longer, skulking in the higher ranges, madly thinking to bring down the men of *Spiti* and the *Chinese* of the border *en masse* on our hill stations. But, after discouragement and repulse everywhere, they gave up the attempt, and moved down, hoping to steal through the Terai to their own homes. But their movements had been all the while known to Major Hay, the energetic Deputy-Commissioner of Kooloo, at

* See Appendix Q.

the foot of these hills; and his successor, Mr Knox, carried out his measures vigorously, and was rewarded with success. With a mere handful of police, and aided by the Spiti men and Chinese, who had already hemmed in the rebels in a valley on the border, he succeeded in capturing the whole party, eighty-four men and five women and children, and brought them in—a distance of above a hundred miles—to Kooloo, under this slight escort, and then, under stronger guard, sent them on to Lahore for trial.

Thus an army 41,000 strong—for such was their strength in the Punjab (including Delhi) at the outbreak—had wellnigh passed away! Eight regiments had mutinied and been destroyed; twelve had escaped—some with, and some without, arms; 15,000 men were disbanded and sent off to their homes; and there remain about 6000 men to keep up the remembrance that a Poorbeah army once occupied the stations of the Punjab. Of these, two corps must ever be honourably remembered—the Kelat-i-Ghilzie Regiment, in the Peshawur forts, and, perhaps still more, the noble 21st N. I., which, during those troublous months, retained its arms and its good name: surrounded by mutinous comrades, assailed by seditious appeals and threats, it never wavered, was never suspected, and stood faithful throughout.

But the Punjabee regiments had, in the meanwhile, as already shown,* been increasing rapidly. In May 1857 they numbered some 19,000 men; within the

* Supra, page 126.

year they had risen to 46,000;* and such was the force, backing up twelve European corps (which by the end of the year were little better than skeleton regiments), and a few hundred European artillery, with the large native contingents, which enabled the Lahore Government, under Providence, to hold the Punjab, and recover Delhi.

* This calculation only refers to the *Punjab;* it does not include that vast body which, despite Sir John Lawrence's earnest warnings and remonstrances, Government continued to raise for Hindostan, and have since been obliged to reduce.

CHAPTER XX.

JUDICIAL MEASURES—POLICE—FINANCE—THE LOAN.

THE reader has been carried on from one station to another—from a scene of peaceful disarming to a blood-stained outbreak, from a brush on the frontier to struggles in the camp before Delhi—wherever rebellion attempted to lift its hydra head, and the arm of Government was needed to crush it; and this, that the thread which ran through the whole coil of administration might be preserved unbroken, and the sequence of events as far as possible maintained. But it must not be supposed that in all these efforts to prevent and punish mutiny—this marching of troops and raising of levies—this disarming of corps that were suspected, or destroying those that broke out—that in this whirl all the other wheels of administration had come to a dead lock—that justice was suspended for war—that ordinary collection of revenue gave way to emergent and summary exaction of supplies. Here was a happy refutation of the old principle *inter arma silent leges*. "Despite a thousand distractions, despite dangers without and within, the judiciary remained unmoved, and the people persisted in litigation,"* and the law was still open to them.

The first shock of the outbreak did perhaps everywhere, more or less, for a few days, throw the machinery out of track: but it was only for the instant. A few days sufficed to set all in order again; and from Peshawur to Kurnal, amid all the excitement and anxiety—in spite of distracting duties on every side—the courts were still at work. The zeal of the magistrate for the safety of the country in the crisis did not override the quieter duties of his own office. As in times of peace, he might be seen in his wonted chair in *kutcheree*, or perhaps more often in his tent, or under a *tope* of trees, administering "baradurree"† justice, with little to mark the change of times, beyond a revolver slung at his side or lying on the table ready at his hand, and a few extra armed guards standing round. At one time he might be seen, with as little appearance of anxiety as might be, chatting over the momentous tidings of the day with some influential native; at another time listening to his *omlah* or *moonshee* drawling through a tedious *misl* of some trifling lawsuit, striving to curb in his thoughts to the dry details, while his mind would range far away in wild anxious conjecture as to

* *Fourth Punjab Report*, p. 1. To this most valuable contribution to the history of the Punjab Government the author is indebted for much important information contained in this chapter.

† This word literally means a house having *twelve doors*, three on each side. This was the general form of the offices of native authorities, as if offering access to all comers from whatever quarter.

the present of some distant scene of action, or the future of this struggle for life or death.

While the fate of the country seemed to be tottering in the scale, and calling upon every one to be "up and doing," what did it not cost many an Englishman to forego the excitement of daring enterprise, or perhaps, in the midst of such excitement, to calm down his mind to investigate some trifling suit about a few yards of ground, or a charge for some petty theft? Yet it was in this never-failing steady work of our kutcherries that men of peace were fighting the fight —shall we say for empire?—rather for our existence.

The energy which was almost ubiquitous, combined with the self-possessed confidence which characterised so many during those weeks of danger, from the Judicial Commissioner himself at Lahore, who set so bright an example, to the isolated Assistant in some remote district, was incalculable in its effects. It kept the machine of government rolling on; and in its steady onward roll over difficulties and dangers, the natives saw proofs of strength and safety, and learned to look hopefully to the result.

The amount of crime throughout the whole Punjab, notwithstanding so many incentives and opportunities, rather lessened than increased on the average of former years. During times of political excitement, such is generally the case with petty crimes, while violent and heinous offences become more common. In the Peshawur district, the land of marauders and thieves, it had remarkably diminished. The new levies had drained off the scum of the population; the more turbulent spirits were diverted from their raids into service in our ranks; and crime lacked its votaries. Not so, however, with *litigation:* notwithstanding the agitation on the whole frontier, and the doubtful tenure of our hold on Peshawur, suitors crowded into our courts in unusual numbers;* and it is more remarkable still that, with all the press of more momentous duties, more suits were decided than in previous years. In Mooltan, too, the district which ranked second for turbulence and theft, it was the same: "Business went on quite as well as usual, the only difference being, that during the year of trouble there were *more* suits decided than in any previous year."† In the other districts of the Punjab there was, in this particular, little difference between this year of blood and former years of peace.

But in the Cis-Sutlej States, especially in the more southern districts, it fared otherwise. They were too near the immediate seat of the rebellion not to suffer from the contagion; the population, too, had so much of the Hindostanee element as to be predisposed to the infection. Here, at the outset, crime tried to throw off the restraint of the law: with the excitement of the outbreak, the road became unsafe, and outrages were committed, without disguise or fear, in open day; but the

* One cause for the unusual number of suits was the issuing a new statute of limitation, reducing the term for recovery of debts from twelve years to six, and thus forcing into court before April 30, 1857, all cases over six years; which flooded the courts with suits.

† *Punjab Report.*

Commissioner, Mr Barnes, at once provided against such a contingency: his effective Assistants were pushed down into the disaffected districts, with absolute powers of life and death in cases of daring and violent crime, which the times called for. Punishment followed rapidly on each crime. Imprisonment would only have increased the difficulty: the lash for petty offences, and the halter for grave ones, were used promptly and freely; and after the first ebullition of feeling thus summarily checked, even these districts settled down into something like their normal state of quietude. And while the ordinary work of the courts went on with so little interruption during those months of danger, the mutiny was, as might be expected, bringing in its train an increase of work peculiar to itself. Martial law, sometimes in all the more dignified and solemn form of a court, but more frequently at a drumhead, dealt summarily with the majority of the rebels; yet there were cases which still found their way into the ordinary criminal courts, and thus swelled the amount of work to be there disposed of.

Moreover, the mutiny led to the introduction of measures bearing on them in no ordinary degree the stamp of bold originality.

Foremost among them must ever stand an order which emanated from Mr Montgomery in his capacity of Judicial Commissioner, one which, for its manly outspoken avowal of Christian sympathy and real toleration, is perhaps without parallel in the archives of India. Striking at the very root of that traditionary policy which, though not avowedly perhaps, yet tacitly and practically, had in Bengal excluded native Christians from service in our ranks, or employment in our Government offices. It was *an invitation to native Christians* to seek our service, and an injunction to all civil officers to admit them when duly qualified, and to advance them equally with Mohammedans and Hindoos.

It ran thus (for such a document demands a place in the history of this mutiny) :—

"The sufferings and trials which the Almighty has permitted to come upon His people in this land during the last few months, though dark and mysterious to us, will assuredly end in His glory. The followers of Christ will now, I believe, be induced to come forward, and advance the interests of His kingdom, and those of His servants.

"The system of caste can no longer be permitted to rule in our services. Soldiers and Government servants of every class must be entertained for their merits, irrespective of creed, class, or caste.

"The native Christians, as a body, have, with rare exceptions, been set aside. I know not one in the Punjab (to our disgrace be it said) in any employment under Government.

"A proposition to employ them in the public service six months ago would assuredly have been received with coldness, and would not have been complied with. But a change has come, and I believe there are few who will not eagerly employ those native Christians competent to fill appointments.

"I understand that, in the ranks of the army at Madras, there are native Christians, and I have heard that some of the guns at Agra are, at this time, manned by native Christians.

"I consider I should be wanting in my duty at this crisis if I did not endeavour to secure a portion of the numerous appointments in the judicial department for native Christians;

and I shall be happy, as far as I can, to advance their interests *equally* with those of Mohammedans and Hindoo candidates. Their future promotion must depend on their own merits.

"I will, therefore, feel obliged by each missionary favouring me with a list of any native Christians belonging to them, who, in their opinion, are fit for the public service.

"It is suggested that no persons be nominated whom the missionaries do not consider, by their character and attainments, to have a good prospect of success. Better wait till a candidate qualifies himself fully than recommend an inferior man.

(Signed) "R. MONTGOMERY."

Such a document needs no comment here.

Another important step was also taken by Mr Montgomery about this time.

The Punjab Government from the first declared that the mutiny was essentially of Hindostanee and Mohammedan origin: the Mohammedans they regarded as the instigators, and the Hindoos as the dupes. Yet the Punjab courts teemed with Hindostanee officials, who hampered them at every step. The Sealkote outbreak fully opened the eyes of the Judicial Commissioner to this state of things, though it had really been felt previously in other parts of the Punjab. He at once called for returns from every district of the number of the native *employés*, and the country from which they came. It then appeared, that although the original Punjab administration had insisted on the employment, as far as possible, of men of the country in the local courts—and the order had been frequently reiterated —yet the men of Hindostan, and especially Mohammedans, had insinuated and wheedled themselves into every post of importance. They were more intelligent and more experienced, and therefore more useful; and the Punjabee was naturally at a discount. In two districts, Sealkote and Gogaira — perhaps the most Mohammedan in population of the whole Punjab south of the Indus—the preponderance of Hindostanees in the courts and the police was preposterous. "The Hindostanee raj," to use Mr Montgomery's own words, "prevailed;" and it was easy to see how this arrangement would, and did, operate most prejudicially: the traitor race were all influential in the only land that remained true. There was only one remedy, and that was at once applied. An order was issued by Mr Montgomery throughout the Punjab, that the number of Hindostanee officials should be forthwith reduced to a fixed, and that in some departments a very low, proportion; but to prevent the whole machinery of justice coming to a dead-lock, it was to be at first gradual, by at once turning out all inefficient Hindostanees, and introducing Punjabees into their place, until the prescribed proportion had been reached.*

* This policy Mr Montgomery vindicates in his calm retrospect of the crisis: "An opinion has gained very general credence that an undue and causeless dislike to Hindostanees has been manifested in the policy of the Punjab Government. It is argued that the revolt was a military one, and that even supposing the Hindostanee army here to be untrustworthy, there was no ground for the universal antipathy to the Hindostanee nation which the Punjab Government has evinced. I would appeal to every officer who has served under it during the memorable 1857, to give his own private experience as to the justice of the measures which have been adopted. I would not ask him to gather inferences from the narrations of any other person: let him mention

On the other hand—for never, perhaps, had the even-handed administration of justice a more fearless champion than Mr Montgomery—the Judicial Commissioner resolved to show, in dealing with natives, that though our hope lay in the antagonism of creed and race, neither race nor creed should avail to insure immunity from punishment for rebellion. Law should claim its victims among high and low, Sikh, Punjabee, and Poorbeah alike.

A few instances of this will suffice :—

At the Sealkote outbreak in July, the jail had been forced, the prisoners released, the darogah and police-guards being at least passive spectators, if not actual abettors.

Now the darogah was a *Sikh.* A few days after the outbreak, when the tide of rebellion had passed on, and order was once more restored, a commission was appointed to punish the captured rebels ; and amongst

the name of the class whom he personally, in his own sphere of labour, mainly feared ; let him say whom he found to be the instigators of plots, the fomenters of sedition, and the prime movers in ill feeling. The answer in almost every separate case would be "the Hindostanees." Were prominent instances of this ill-will necessary, I would quote the conduct of the Hindostanee horse-keepers at Ferozepore, of the Hindostanee servants at Murree, of the Hindostanee native doctors at Murree and Umritsur ; and the fact that the murders of Sealkote were all by Hindostanees—but not all by military Hindostanees, for three persons were killed by one of the jail police. There is no doubt that Hindostanee emissaries to preach a Mohammedan crusade came up from Delhi. It is also to be borne in mind that nearly every office of value was held by Hindostanees, who evinced a strong sympathy with the rebels. That there were loyal and true men I do not doubt, but it was impossible to distinguish them from the bad so truly as to make it safe to trust to any one."—Mr MONTGOMERY'S *Punjab Mutiny Report.*

the first to suffer, under express injunction from Lahore, was the darogah. At that moment the Sikhs were, under Heaven, our main hope: our only trusty force at Sealkote were Punjabee levies, the mass of them Sikhs; yet in the presence of fellow Sikhs did this traitor darogah suffer the extreme sentence of the law.*

Another instance occurred, though at a later period and at a different part of the country. In the Sirsa outbreak and massacre in May, one *Noor Sumund Khan*, the Nawab of Runeea, an influential noble of the district, a hereditary pensioner of the Government—instead of protecting the town and European inhabitants, as he had been called upon to do by Captain Robertson, the Superintendent, by raising from among his retainers a small force of horse and foot—openly took part with the rebels, shared the plunder, and then proclaimed the King of Delhi King of Hindostan, and himself governor of Sirsa! When Sirsa was recovered, this man was seized, tried, and convicted; but there being no proof of his having actually committed murder with his own hands, and it being thought by Major Marsden, who was then Commissioner of Sirsa, that "an example was no longer necessary," the Nawab was recommended by him to mercy. The opinion of Mr Montgomery on such false mercy cannot better be given than in his own words.†

* Nay more, the rope broke by which he was hanged—the still living body fell from the gallows, and was there shot to death by *the Sikh guards* who stood round.

† Letter No. 3873.—From R. Montgomery, Esq., Judicial Commis-

"Of the Nawab's guilt there can be no doubt. He, as also his ancestors, long enjoyed pensions, favour, and consideration from the British Government. Instead of aiding the local authorities, who reposed confidence in him, and whom he professed a desire to serve, he joined the rebels with his adherents, and caused himself to be proclaimed ruler. Although murder is not actually proved to have been committed by himself, yet the city of Sirsa was entirely plundered and destroyed, as were also the Government offices, treasure and property belonging to Government carried off, and the prisoners released from jail. A number of lives are known to have been sacrificed, of which there is no record. I consider it therefore imperative to make examples of such men as the Nawab. The leaders must feel that vengeance will assuredly overtake them. Mercy in this instance would be weakness, and would encourage others to rebel hereafter. I therefore wish the concurrence of the Chief Commissioner to sentence him, *Noor Sumund Khan*, Nawab of Runeea, to be hanged."

The conduct of the Rawab of Runeea had at least been straightforward: he had been open in his treason at Sirsa. But in the neighbouring districts of Hansi and Hissar were traitors who had not the courage to avow their treachery, who, nevertheless, did not escape their richly-deserved fate. *Mooneer Beg*, one of the principal Mohammedans, and *Hookum Chund*, avow-

sioner for the Punjab, to Major F. Marsden, Commissioner of Sirsa, dated Lahore, 17th November 1857 (quoted from the *Lahore Chronicle*).

edly his deadly enemy, the chief banker, and one of the most influential Hindoos of Hansi, with *Fuqeer Chund,* his nephew, a youth of about twenty, had, at the commencement of the outbreak, apparently forgotten their private feud, and conjointly drawn up a petition to the King of Delhi, offering their services, and undertaking to place Hansi and the district around at his disposal. No sooner did General Van Cortland pour down his quickly raised Sikh levies into this district than these men were amongst the foremost to rally round him with professions of loyalty. Van Cortland, only too glad, doubtless, to avail himself of their local influence, received them into favour, and gave them valuable appointments. But when Delhi fell, other spoil than the unknown hidden treasures of that city of gold was sought for: every public document—almost, it may be said, every scrap of paper—found in the palace was caught up and laid by for future examination; among them appeared the traitorous letter from Sirsa! This discovery came like a thunder-clap on these now most faithful and devoted servants of the Company; they were at once arrested and tried, and all three condemned by Mr G. Ricketts, of Loodiana fame, to be hanged. In the case of *Mooneer Beg* and *Hookum Chund,* General Van Cortland, as officiating Commissioner of the district, confirmed the sentence; but on the plea that *Fuqeer Chund,* the youthful scribe, had only written the letter at his uncle's dictation, he mitigated the sentence to imprisonment for five years. Against this Mr Ricketts appealed to the Judicial Commissioner, whose unswerving sense of justice could not discover here, any more than he had done in the case of the Nawab of Runeea, any ground for mercy. "I must confess," he writes to General Van Cortland,* "that I consider the punishment awarded by you to Fuqeer Chund quite inadequate for the offence: I think Fuqeer Chund quite as guilty as Mooneer Beg and Hookum Chund, if anything, more guilty. He deliberately and secretly wrote the petition, Mooneer Beg and another person alone being present. It is absurd to suppose he did not know what he was writing. The petition is clearly and legibly written, well expressed, and evidently by a scholar. He had, in my opinion, everything to gain.

"Had the King of Delhi been successful, his uncle, Hookum Chund, would, in all probability, have been one of the chief officers of the place. On our force reaching Hansi, he presented himself to Mr Ford, and was appointed a Canoongoe of Futtehabad.

"For the above reasons, I concur with Mr Ricketts, and with the sanction of the Chief Commissioner, to whom the proceedings have been submitted, I sentence the prisoner Fuqeer Chund to be hanged by the neck until dead; and I request that you will report to me the day on which the sentence has been carried out.

"It is only by unflinching severity against the lead-

* Letter No. 688.—From R. Montgomery, Judicial Commissioner for the Punjab to the officiating Commissioner at Hissar, dated Hissar, 22d February 1858.—Quoted from the *Lahore Chronicle*.

ers in this rebellion that we can hope to establish faithfulness for the future."*

We now come to instances of a different character. After the fall of Delhi, when quiet was comparatively restored in the Punjab, Sikhs belonging to regiments that had mutinied in the lower provinces began to find their way in some numbers to their own homes in the Punjab (some had even come up before Delhi had actually fallen); having heard, no doubt, of the gentle treatment of the many Sikh recruits who had belonged to the several mutinous corps, and hoping to escape under the general favour in which their body stood during the crisis.

Among the first of such were some Sikhs of the Loodiana regiment. This corps had openly mutinied at Benares, fired at its officers, charged the guns, and endangered the whole city, which was only saved by the opportune arrival of Europeans from below. Of this regiment, some five Sikhs made their appearance at their homes in the Jullundhur district in the beginning of October. They were soon detected, tried, and convicted; and only not condemned to suffer death by the district officer, "on the ground that if all similarly

* This case disclosed another danger, which Mr Montgomery thus points out and meets:—

"The facility with which natives receive appointments, without due inquiry, after the reoccupation of stations, is clearly shown in the case of Fuqeer Chund. I therefore direct that all appointments in the judicial department, held by natives in the Hansi and Hissar district, after the occupation of the stations, be considered only acting ones for a period of one year, and that during this interval, the strictest inquiries be made as to the part the individuals took during the rebellion, and that none of the appointments be confirmed until you are fully satisfied with the conduct of the men."

placed were hanged, the number would be fearful." What says Mr Montgomery to such a plea?

"I cannot concur in the recommendation to mercy in this case, and I regret it the more, as the Sikhs, as a body, have nobly sided with our Government. Doubtless a few Sikhs in a Hindostanee regiment might be carried away, and find it difficult to resist the strong influence brought to bear against them. But in the present case the regiment was composed of Sikhs, and no excuse can be made for them. They mutinied in a body, fired on the European soldiers, and charged them. Their just fate is death, and whoever acts thus—be he Sikh, or be he Hindostanee—deserves to die, and I cannot remit the punishment they justly have incurred." *

Then came some thirty Sikhs of the late 12th N. I., the two wings of which were stationed at Naogunge and Jhansi. Those at Naogunge had turned upon their officers, who, however, escaped, and only the Sergeant-major was killed; but the wing at Jhansi had been guilty of great atrocities: the officers were murdered, and the women and children cruelly butchered. Nor was there any reason to doubt that these men had had their full share in this work of blood; and they were dealt with accordingly. At Loodiana, a city itself teeming with a turbulent population of disaffected Mohammedans, on the very borders of the

* No. 4044.—Letter from R. Montgomery, Esq., Judicial Commissioner for the Punjab, to the officiating Deputy-Commissioner at Jullundhur, dated Lahore, 28th November 1857.—Extract from *Lahore Chronicle*.

fatherland of Sikhism, were twenty-one of these men executed; while the remainder were doomed to the more lenient sentence of transportation for life and imprisonment.

These instances will suffice to show the working of the courts of law. Under such unswerving, uncompromising justice and fearless power, the disaffected trembled, and the well-disposed gathered courage and confidence.

From this glimpse of the judicial officer in his Kucheree, we turn to his myrmidons of the law in his district. During the crisis the Punjab police were, as has been well described, "the right arm of the civil administration." * Native police are generally proverbial for indolence rather than activity, for conniving at rather than preventing crime, for screening rather than detecting offenders, and withal adding to these negative qualities that of cowardice, which stamps almost every native when called on to act *alone*, or beyond the eye of his English master. The population of the Punjab, from which the police are raised, are, in these points, infinitely superior to the inhabitants of the North-West Provinces, or of Bengal. They are more powerful in frame, and more manly in character,† and proportionably more free from these moral defects; yet was it a subject of no little anxiety and fear what course even the Punjab police would adopt when they saw rebellion rampant. But the result exceeded all

* *Fourth Punjab Report*, par. 112.

† One among the many arguments in favour of their being of Scythic origin, the *Juts* descended from the *Getæ*.

hope. It seemed as if the antipathy which a Punjabee almost intuitively bears a Poorbeah had called up all the better qualities of the race: active, energetic, with very few exceptions faithful, they came out with the crisis. Crime was more promptly detected; the ferries watched with faithful jealousy; scarcely an emissary escaped, more rarely still a fugitive mutineer. They had to guard jails, and sometimes to fight for their thanas, and generally acquitted themselves with great credit. From the Mounted Police, who, under Nicholson, so gallantly charged the 55th mutineers at Hotee Murdan, to those who are immortalised by the pen of the Deputy-Commissioner of Umritsur for the capture and destruction of the 26th N. I. on the Ravee, at every point, at Huzara, Loodiana, Jhelum, Sealkote, and other places, they did good service. "Instances these were which will give an idea of the mettle of the Punjab police, and will show that they are men with some pluck about them, and are really fit for something on an emergency."*

What may seem still more remarkable than the almost undisturbed administration of justice during these troublous times, was the regularity with which the revenue was collected in almost every part of the Punjab. Indeed, in some districts, the payments were made *before they were actually due*; a fact which carried with it the cheering assurance that, with the mass of the population, the landholders and cultivators, the continuance of our *raj* was really desired, or at any-

* *Fourth Punjab Report*, par. 112.

rate they were content with the light just system of taxation, and had no wish to change masters, especially with the prospect of the interregnum of anarchy which would be almost inevitable before matters could settle down again. It probably was this feeling as much as, if not more than, that of heartfelt active loyalty, which produced so favourable a result.

Still, as the far-seeing among the Punjab authorities had anticipated from the outset, if the mutiny continued and spread, a financial crisis would, in a few weeks at farthest, be almost inevitable.

As a first step towards meeting this contingency, Mr Barnes had, even in the month of May, opened a loan, to which he invited his right trusty Sikh chiefs to contribute. Puttiala, Jheend, and Nabba, and the lesser rajahs, at once responded, and deposited their money freely. But not so the bankers and merchants—that close-fisted, distrustful, ungrateful class, from whom money can never be obtained but for money's worth.* However, the time was coming when some such course must be adopted on the largest scale. Not only the native chiefs of the Cis-Sutlej States, but those over the whole Punjab, must be called on to co-operate with money, as they had already done with men. And with the month of July the time had come.

The finances had fallen to the lowest ebb. Even here large amounts of treasure had been lost: it was hopeless to look for supplies from the treasuries of the North-west, for they had *all* gone; still less hope from Bengal. The

* *Punjab Mutiny Report*, p. 9.

sums sent up from Bombay,—the revenue, which, considering all circumstances, was in some parts collected with wonderful regularity—and the advances so promptly made by our noble allies—were altogether insufficient to meet the vastly increased demands of the Punjab. Many a Poorbeah regiment, it is true, had wiped its own name off the paymaster's list;* but fresh levies were crowding in by thousands to supply their place, and to draw pay which they had forfeited. At this crisis the master-mind of the Chief Commissioner resolved on giving full effect to the plan originated by Mr Barnes, a step which, to the timid, seemed a desperate one, but which, nevertheless, achieved in the end the success it deserved: a 6-per-cent loan was opened by the Financial Commissioner throughout the Punjab, *to be repaid within a twelvemonth!* Many were there who regarded this step as fatal—an acknowledgment on the part of Government that they were sinking into a state of pecuniary asphyxia; and there is no doubt that on the native mind its first announcement had a prejudicial effect: what did it matter that under the wise and just English Government the petty shopman could accumulate his profits until he became the substantial merchant—that the avowal of increasing wealth now involved no risk—that the many means and false charges, oppression, open robbery, by which under native rule no man was secure of his possessions, had ceased—that now a man's wealth was safe and sacred?

* At Peshawur, too, all the disarmed corps had been reduced to mere "subsistence allowance."

—all this was forgotten. The moneyed class, who owed their all to the justice of the English Government, saw that Government in need, and resolved not to save it from sinking. So far the announcement of the loan seemed to increase the danger of our position, by betraying our weakness. But all this was foreseen ; and full reliance was placed on the local authorities who had to meet the danger.

Among the first called on to face this difficulty and to grapple with it was Colonel Edwardes, as Commissioner of Peshawur ; and as Peshawur was the most inflammatory portion of the Punjab, it may be selected as the best illustration of the raising of the loan. Colonel Edwardes called a meeting of the mercantile class. The *lalas* (bankers), *buneeas* (merchants), attended at the Residency : they listened to Colonel Edwardes's statement, that the money was needed temporarily, and would be repaid within a twelvemonth. They listened, but made no sign ; save perhaps that on each one's face was written the stolid determination not to advance a rupee. From the wealthiest banker to the pettiest merchant, one spirit seemed to pervade all : the Government was insolvent, was sinking, and they were not prepared to save it, much less to sink with it. The Commissioner gave them one day to consider their answer, and appointing them to meet him again at a certain hour the following morning. That hour arrived, but not a man made his appearance. At length, about two hours after the appointed time, they began to assemble ; but, so little like the Asiatic coming into the presence of his superior, they came empty-handed. No *nuzzerana*, no offering of a few rupees, no trays of sweetmeats—the ordinary concomitants of such a meeting: the sullen faces of some, the almost exulting scowl of others, at once showed the Commissioner how little the Government had to hope for from the gratitude of these men, whom it had made what they were. They said they were prepared to advance a few thousand rupees, all they could afford; more they would not, could not do. Colonel Edwardes knew his men: he knew that to yield was to fail—that what an Asiatic will not do of favour, he finds it convenient to do of necessity. With unshaken nerve and peremptory manner, he fined them a heavy sum for having wasted two precious hours of his time, and called upon them at once to give in five lakhs of rupees! Each one more loudly than his neighbour declared his inability: instead of arbitrarily fixing the rate to be paid by each, knowing that a moneyed native is the best gauge of his moneyed neighbour's wealth, he ordered them to assess themselves in any way they chose; but make up the five lakhs they must. In the end one lakh was excused; but upwards of four lakhs were really subscribed by the merchants of this great frontier city; and their leading man (a Kazee, or Mohammedan magistrate) rode up to the Commissioner, and laid his quota in gold coins at his feet. This was the turning-point. Each merchant, as he followed with his several thousand rupees, thus compulsorily embarked in the loan, became possessed of a stake in the welfare of Government, and was converted, from an indifferent spectator of the mutiny, to an interested supporter of the law. The *millionaires*, after depositing their hard cash in the treasury, returned home with their "scrip," greeted by many a jibe and taunt from the city rabble, who revelled in the sight of those obese leeches made to disgorge some of the gains got, perhaps by none of the fairest means, out of their own little stores.

Besides the monetary classes of Peshawur, on whom this loan was thus skilfully brought to bear, there was also another class to some extent affected by it. In that neighbourhood were several petty chiefs and sirdars, who, for services rendered to Government, had been allowed to retain their hereditary property, or had received some small *jageer* in reward for their loyalty. These men were at first keeping aloof; but a hint was conveyed to them that neutrality at such a crisis was as unworthy of them as it was impossible for the Government to submit to; and a warning to each that if he did not at once support and assist Government according to his means, he would forfeit his jageer, had a speedy and salutary effect. The danger that threatened was thus averted; and that bold financial stroke which seemed so hazardous, tended, scarcely less than the military arrangements, to re-establish the prestige of Government at Peshawur, and indeed throughout the Punjab; for the same demand was made elsewhere, and with as complete success, though nowhere was the difficulty so great as at Peshawur.

Among the mercantile classes throughout the Punjab,

the men who, as has been said, were most indebted to the English Government for their wealth and safety, the disinclination to advance money was general. However, so important was it that Government should carry with it this class—as having willingly or unwillingly a stake in its permanency—that it became necessary in some cases to employ arguments more powerful than persuasion. The result was most satisfactory: forty-two* lakhs were contributed altogether; and though only about one-third came out of the coffers of the merchants, still, to that extent at least, Government had a hold, if not on the sympathies, at least on the interests, of this influential, but generally ungrateful malcontent class.

The whole was repaid within the twelvemonth, except the portion contributed by the chiefs, which was transferred into Government securities.†

* The following may be stated as, in rough numbers, the total amounts contributed from the several divisions: Peshawur, rather more than four lakhs; from Mooltan and the Dherajat, about two and a-half lakhs; from Lahore, including that city, Umritsur, and Sealkote, nearly eleven lakhs; from the Jullundhur Doab, about three lakhs; and from the Cis-Sutlej States, involving the interests of cities so important as Umballa, Loodiana, and Ferozepore, about eighteen and a half lakhs.

† See Appendix R.

CHAPTER XXI.

THE MUTINY AND ITS LESSONS.

A REVIEW of all the circumstances of the mutiny, even if confined to those of which the Punjab was the scene, much more so if extended over the rest of India, will establish beyond question the existence of a *conspiracy*. Men there are, no doubt, whose strong sympathies with the Mohammedan will lead them to repudiate most strongly and loudly such an imputation, so far as it affects their own favourites; while others will as vehemently repel the charge when brought against the "mild, faithful Hindoo." But we have to deal with *facts*, and are scarcely called on to speak soft things in behalf of either class merely out of consideration for Islamised or Brahminised prejudices.

Here, however, it may be well, though entailing considerable repetition, to explain more fully the character of the conspiracy, as evolved out of the various circumstances recorded in the preceding pages. It was clearly a *double*, or perhaps, more correctly speaking, a *twofold* conspiracy; the two distinct in origin and in object, but gradually becoming *one* in operation. There was a deep political intrigue, and also a wide military revolt—the one purely Mohammedan, the other mainly Hindoo in character: the former contemplating the annihilation of the Christian power, and the restoration of the Mohammedan rule; the latter probably little more at first than a disaffected struggle to recover fancied lost privileges, and to extort more favourable terms from their masters. Between the two there was no necessary connection, but the infusion of a religious element furnished a connecting link, and thenceforth they became so identical in interest and united in action that their distinctiveness disappeared, and they came to be regarded and dealt with as a joint foe.

First in importance, if not in point of time, was the Mohammedan conspiracy.

The Persian proclamation found in the tent of the Shahzada, at Mohumrah, with its appeal to "the faithful" to exterminate the Feringhees from India—an *Ishtahar* or proclamation of the King of Delhi, announcing that "several princes belonging to the royal house of Delhi had dispersed themselves in the different parts of India, Iran, Turan, and Afghanistan, and had been long since taking measures to compass their favourite end," the extermination of the English—the pilgrimage of Ferozeshah, and the proclamation in which, on his return to India, he openly announced the object of his mission;—these, among other statements, directly point to the existence and the objects of a great Mohammedan conspiracy. And what were the facts elicited at the trial of the King of Delhi?

They are thus summarised by the Judge Advocate General—"A Mohammedan priest with pretended visions and assumed miraculous powers—a Mohammedan king, his dupe and accomplice—a Mohammedan clandestine embassy to the Mohammedan powers of Persia and Turkey—Mohammedan prophecies as to the downfall of our power—Mohammedan rule as the successor of our own—the most cold-blooded murders by Mohammedan assassins—a religious war for Mohammedan ascendancy—a Mohammedan press unscrupulously abetting, and Mohammedan sepoys initiating the mutiny."*

That the Mohammedan should conspire against the Christian, is not to be wondered at—his creed teaches it; the Koran demands it of him: and it would seem that during the last few years this obligation has pressed on his mind with more than wonted force: the mental thermometer of the Mohammedan has been rising to fever-heat of fanaticism. Not only in India, in Borneo too, in Arabia, in Syria—wherever the Mohammedan has come in contact with the Christian—this religious frenzy has burst forth. But in India, more than in other parts, it found its opportunities and its tools; hence the struggle there was more vigor-

* Indeed, the existence of such a conspiracy is assumed by Government itself, for it was one of the most weighty imputations against the chiefs of Jhujjur and Bullubghur, that, knowing what was about to take place, they, though in friendly intercourse with the civil authorities, and professing firm allegiance to Government, had never given any intimation or warning of the coming catastrophe, by which the Government might have been put on its guard.

ous, more desperate in its character and in its issue, and more nearly successful, than elsewhere. Its tools were the Hindostanee army, and it found its opportunity in a spirit of disaffection which was pervading the ranks, and which had become so widespread as already to amount to a *combination.* To give consistency, to consolidate, to organise, and then to make this spirit subservient to their own more ambitious ulterior ends, was comparatively easy. To men fretting under the imagined loss of privileges and brooding over imagined grievances; and at the same time petted and pampered in order to keep them quiet, each concession made to them being regarded as an additional acknowledgment of their value and their power —to men in such a frame of mind, the offer of redress of all grievances, the promise of privileges hitherto unknown, service under princes of their own instead of under foreign invaders and conquerors—above all, the guaranteed sanctity of their caste and the preservation of their creed,—all this was an irresistible *bait.*

This disaffected combination soon ripened into *conspiracy;* and in this conspiracy, though probably more recent in formation and subordinate in character, yet more rapid and prominent in its development, the former one, deeper, wider, and more subtle, was for the time merged and lost sight of.

In the sepoy revolt, the Mohammedan conspiracy was thrown into the background; and even when its true character was disclosed, the more crafty treason of the Mohammedan thrust forward and screened itself behind the more impassioned religious alarm of his Hindoo dupe.

The assertion that such a conspiracy did exist, by no means implies that every soldier in the army was a conspirator; nor is it to be inferred that every one was more or less disaffected. There were in the ranks of that army true men—nobly, heroically true *—and these were contented men; then there was a sprinkling of Sikhs and Punjabees; and there were native Christians in the regimental bands. How is it possible to suppose that in so mixed a body, with different, often conflicting feelings and prejudices, with mutual suspicions and jealousies, a secret of so momentous a character could have been preserved?

Yet there was probably no regiment without its traitors, and they of the most weight and influence, so that the faithful few were too weak in position, as well as in numbers and moral courage, and, still worse, too conscious of a lack of encouragement from their superiors, either to stem the tide of treason, which was daily gaining strength, or to disclose the impending danger. So matters progressed; the grand train of sedition had its branches in every corps. Clever, popular, high-caste, designing men,† of various grades,

* For instance, those of the 13th and 48th regiments N. I., who so devotedly held their posts at the Lucknow Residency during the entire siege.

† How far were the regimental *ukkharrahs* made the nurseries of sedition? Each *calipha* (master), with his sworn band of *chheilas* (pupils) at his back, might easily have been such a centre of treason. That this is no idle conjecture, two out of many instances may be given. When the 14th N. I. were suspected at Jhelum, an old com-

formed so many centres of seditious influence, and thus swayed the whole mass. These were the leaven leavening the whole lump, quietly, gradually disturbing the minds of their comrades; now by an inuendo of the greased cartridge, and the crushed bones in the *otta;* now by an appeal to their national pride and their superstition, that the hundred years of English rule were fast running out, and the defeat of Plassey about to be avenged. Thus, by religious fears and by national hopes, the minds of the mass became more or less shaken in their allegiance; they all more or less became familiarised with the idea that the Badshah was their real *Malik* (master), and were all pledged, in the person of their respective leaders—though probably, beyond a very few in the regiment, ignorant of the nature and real extent of that pledge—to rise at his call, and obey his behest, whatever it might be.*

All, it would seem, were drawn within the vortex of sedition—but not all in one common plot: from the very extent of ground over which they were scattered, this was impossible. There would seem to have been many centres of action—the action of all to be simultaneous, but the character of each to be regulated by circumstances. For instance, at Lahore, Ferozepore,

mandant, who knew the corps well, wrote and warned the officers to watch certain men whom he named, *all caliphas.* When the mutiny broke out there, these very men were proved to be the ringleaders. Again, in the 45th N. I., a *naik,* who was the most popular of the *caliphas,* was the most active of the mutineers.

* The Sealkote troops admitted that their names had been down in the King of Delhi's books since the preceding January, yet they did not break out till the 9th July.

Umritsur, and Philour, the grand object was to seize the forts and arsenals; in the Peshawur Valley, to insure the co-operation of their Mohammedan neighbours.*

But it is also clear that, the special object being achieved in each case, a uniform system was to be then adopted. In every successful outbreak it was adopted: the officers were shot down, the treasury was seized, the jail forced, and then the whole body—not dividing the spoil, and rushing off to their homes—marched off in perfect order, under officers of their own choosing, carried the treasure with them to their appointed rendezvous, and there gave it up intact, and placed themselves under the command of the rebel leaders.† All this, then—the widespread disaffection, the general expectation of a revolt, and the uniform character of the several outbreaks—clearly point to the existence of a preconcerted plan. A conspiracy there was throughout the whole army, though the details, and the ulterior object of it, were probably known only to a chosen few. And this conspiracy was moulded in the hands of the crafty Mohammedan out of the previously existing Hindostanee disaffection.

But whence, it will be asked, arose this spirit of dis-

* The 55th N. I. and 10th Irregular Cavalry, at Nowshera, intrigued with the Swatees; the 51st and 64th N. I., at Peshawur, with the Mohmunds.

† An exception establishes the rule. It was a subject of grievous complaint against the Bareilly Brigade, that when they marched to Delhi, under their wily leader Mohammed Bukht Khan, they refused, despite the taunts and reproaches of the whole rebel army, to give up the treasure and plunder they had brought in.

affection in an army which, as a body of mercenaries who conquered India for the English, and then held their own conquered country for their conquerors, was without its equal in the world's history? What had happened to change the sepoy of old times, whom commanding officers loved, and by whom they were loved again, whom generals were proud of in quarters and in the field—the Hindostanee, sober, cleanly, faithful, docile—into that incarnation of treachery and cruelty and cowardice, for which the Poorbeah mutineer was distinguished in 1857?

Many causes, internal as well as external, had combined to effect this change.

"Old Indians"—men who, in the earlier campaigns of the present century, had led sepoys into action, up to the guns of Bhurtpore, over the snows of Cabul, through the marshes of Burmah,* but whose later years have been spent in peaceful England—still revert in wonderment to the doings of a body of whose faithfulness they never entertained a doubt. What a picture will they not draw of the Jack Sepoy of their day!

But Indian officers of a later date—those who have fought the campaigns of the Sutlej and the Punjab, and who spent the comparatively peaceful years which succeeded in the midst of their regiments—can tell a different tale. They saw, slowly, secretly, yet surely, a change coming over the spirit of their men, from which they augured consequences that they trembled to contemplate.

* Allusion is here made to the first Burmah campaign.

Again and again did they raise the warning voice, but in vain. The more far-seeing of Indian statesmen became alive to the impending danger, and did what in them lay to avert it; *and the irregular force rose up as a counterpoise to the regular army.*

But what *were* the causes thus vaguely hinted at? The author ventures to hope that indulgence will be shown to the unprofessional pen which ventures to answer this question.

Foremost and most important among the causes which produced this change may be regarded that system of centralisation which was being gradually introduced into the Indian army. It weakened, and eventually severed, those links of mutual regard which had formerly bound together the officer and the sepoy—not the secret under-current of *Zenana* influence, so lamentably common fifty years ago—but an open, straightforward, honourable interchange of interest and sympathy. Year by year, little by little, the power and the independence of action which he once enjoyed, was being taken away from the officer, until, beyond the mere manœuvres on a parade-ground, "command" had become little more than a name and an idea. It was no longer in his power to be the friend of his men; the exercise of his own judgment was denied him — he might not promote for good service, he might not supersede or punish for dereliction of duty. Every, the most trivial, act affecting the internal economy of his regiment must be submitted for approval. Then the sepoy had the right of appeal

—not through his commanding officer, but independently of him; and the officer was liable to have his acts called in question and censured on the secret representation of any soldier under his command. Thus, practically, the commanding officer sank down to the position of a commissioned drum-major, whose chief office consisted in carrying out the infliction of punishments as ordered from headquarters; while, on the other hand, the sepoy was virtually a Government spy on the conduct of his European officer. What wonder, then, if the gulf which separated the two became day by day wider? The badly disposed, the idle, the slovenly sepoy might almost laugh at the powerlessness of his commandant to punish; the good, faithful, docile sepoy felt how useless it was to look up to him for praise or reward.*

* A single instance will suffice to corroborate and to furnish an illustration of the above statement:—

On the parade-ground of the 34th N. I., at Barrackpore, on the 29th March, Captain Baugh had been cut down by the fanatic Mungul Pandy, and the guard refused to seize the mutineer; a sepoy, a Mohammedan, Sheik Pultoo, sprang to the rescue of his officer, and saved his life. General Hearsey, who witnessed the whole, on the spot promoted Sheik Pultoo to the rank of havildar, and reported to Government that he had done so. What was the consequence? an official censure from Colonel Birch, the Military Secretary to Government. The General had exceeded his authority; how did he dare to assume such power? The ordinary routine, a court of inquiry—a formal investigation of the circumstances, though performed in open day, in the presence of the General and the whole station—a formal recommendation, was necessary, and, if satisfied, Government would then reward the sepoy! Such a course, at such a moment, could only set up generals and commanding officers as a laughing-stock to the whole sepoy army. However, light began to break in, though very gradually, and still through the medium of native sympathies. On the 14th May, three days after the Delhi massacre, a general order was published, allowing officers commanding stations to appoint courts-martial

It was not, as so often represented, the *paucity* of the officers, it was their *powerlessness*, which destroyed the effectiveness of regiments, and weakened the foundations of the native army. The officer and the sepoy became alienated from one another, and all subordination, maintained in bygone years by regard rather than by fear, came to an end. And as mutual regard passed away, mutual contempt naturally sprang up; the sepoys ceased to be the officer's pride, or the officer the sepoy's friend. An officer learned to regard his regiment no longer as his post of duty and his home; it was a penal settlement, from which staff employ was the only escape.*

When, then, the voice of censure is raised against officers of the old native army for laxness of discipline,

for the summary punishment of offenders. But these courts were to contain "not less than five native commissioned officers." Three weeks later another step was taken; by a general order of the 6th June, the appointment of natives on such courts was left to the discretion of the officer commanding. Still was there no provision for rewarding on the spot any signal act of faithfulness. Happily, to the north of the Jumna, matters had already taken a very different turn. Here the Punjab Government, having established an independence of action, had already asserted and delegated its right to reward or punish.

* It is but justice to mention some few exceptions to this state of things. In the 21st N. I., for instance, officers, in spite of all difficulties and discouragements, retained that kindly feeling for their men which was so nobly repaid in their hour of trial. At the same time, the great outcry about personal influence of officers under this changed state of the army has been proved to be without foundation. A Sam Fisher of the Irregulars, the father of his regiment; a Major Spencer of the 26th N. I., proverbial for his sympathy with his men; poor young Cooper of the 32d N. I., not unworthily called "the model sepoy officer," murdered by the very men among whom, and for whom, they lived—and to these many other instances might be adduced—are the best proof that there was a rottenness in the state which individual zeal, devotion, and tact were utterly unavailing to withstand.

for indifference to their men, for a lack of *esprit de corps*, and innumerable other defects,* justice demands that it should be taken into the account how much this state of things was brought about by successive Commanders-in-Chief endeavouring to engraft English routine on an Indian army. A little more knowledge of the native character, a little more trust in regimental officers, and the Hindostanee army might yet have been the pride and the wonder, instead of proving the 'dread and the curse, of the Indian empire. Such may be regarded the leading internal cause of disaffection.

Other external causes were not wanting. To the Cabul campaign of 1838, that disastrous source of so much national sorrow and shame, may also be traced the origin of a spirit of discontent and mistrust between the Hindostanee army and its rulers. That campaign carried the sepoy, for the first time under the English flag, across the forbidden bounds of the Indus; there it subjected him to personal priva-

* The following statement, made by Sir Charles Napier, will show that the above is no exaggeration—"According to the 'Bombay Officer'" (the name under which Major Jacob addressed a warning to Government), "it is right to place the brave old sepoy at the caprice of prejudiced or ignorant commanding officers, and to protect those glorious veterans is to destroy talent, skill, energy, high principle, and soldier-like pride. . . . I am quite provoked at the silly way in which it is so common to speak of the sepoys in this country. They are admirable soldiers, and only give way when led by brave but idle officers, who let discipline and drill go slack, and do not mix with them."

Sir Charles could not see how the traditional policy of headquarters, which he received from his predecessors, and was so anxious to hand on to his successor, had tended to produce the very evils which he censured.

tions and suffering among the snow-clad mountains of Cabul, which his frame, accustomed to the burning plains of India, was little fitted to bear. It brought also other and graver trials. For days together he marched without meeting with a single well; the frequent, constant desiderata of his Hindoo life, his daily ablutions, so essential a part of his very religion, were necessarily abandoned for months together. Then, in the bazaars of Cabul he sought in vain for a Hindoo Buneeah, from whom to purchase his daily supply of food; in that land of Mohammedans he was compelled to receive his very otta from the impure, defiling hand of Mohammedans. Then, to keep out the biting cold of that inclement region, he was compelled to avail himself of the Afghan *posteen*,* although the very touch of the skin was fatal to his caste.

During the campaign itself, they seemed to bow to circumstances unmurmuringly, and even cheerfully. Nor was it until their return that a sound was heard of discontent. When the 35th Light Infantry, who had formed part of the "illustrious garrison" of Jellalabad, arrived at Ferozepore, a subahdar of the 71st N. I. taunted them with a loss of caste. He was tried, and dismissed the service; but the taunt told. The feeling began to spread in other regiments; and although one or two summary examples were made, the feeling still gained head.

Soon after came another imagined grievance. On the first annexation of the Punjab, all the native

* A jacket of sheepskin.

troops thrown into the newly-conquered province received extra pay, but not so the regiments that relieved them. The 66th N. I., at Umritsur, mutinied in consequence, and were disbanded. The 32d N. I., also, at Wuzeerabad, showed signs of mutiny; but Brigadier Hearsey's firmness and tact restored quiet: still the spirit of disaffection had received an additional stimulus.

In 1856 came another, and, it must be allowed, a more serious cause of complaint. Our newly-annexed provinces of the Punjab containing a manly and martial people, it became very desirable to enlist some of the Sikh and Mohammedan soldiers. When they enlisted, a promise was given that they should never be required to cut their hair or beards, for by both these classes the hair is regarded with great sanctity: unhappily, in 1856, an order was issued by General Anson, directing the Mohammedans to cut their beards after a prescribed fashion. The Punjabees protested against this breach of faith, the commanding officers reported the feeling to the Commander-in-Chief; but General Anson was above all sympathy with such idle prejudices, and directed that the order should be peremptorily carried out, leaving those who refused to submit the option of being dismissed the service.

In the end of that year appeared another order, which, though not only justifiable, but rendered necessary by the refusal of the 38th N. I. to march to Burmah in 1852, required that all enlistments in future should be for general service. This order, striking as it did at the root of the Hindoo's superstitious dread of crossing the water, acted powerfully on the growing discontent of the army.*

Thus it will be seen that various measures, some wise and necessary, others unnecessary and unwise, were tending to spread more widely and more deeply that spirit of disaffection in the army, which, in the hands of the Mohammedan intriguers, proved so nearly fatal to our Indian empire.

It will not be difficult to understand how all these measures, though in themselves merely affecting the military *régime*, were so distorted as to appear so many successive and progressive attacks upon the caste—that is, the religion, for they are practically identical—of the Hindoo.

The being carried beyond the limits of Hindoo land, the loss of his daily ablutions, his food polluted by the touch of the Mohammedan, his body by the touch of a sheepskin, his hair desecrated by the scissors, his liability to be sent on service across the water, all affecting his caste; then, to crown all, the greased cartridge by its touch scattering his caste to the winds, and in its supposed mixture of the fat of the cow and pig attacking Hindoo and Mohammedan alike, and furnishing them with a common object of fear. "Deen!

* The whole of these imagined grievances are very graphically described by a native of evidently considerable intelligence and observation, named Sheik Hedayut Ali, formerly of the 8th N. I., and now in the Bengal Sikh Police Battalion. The paper is translated from the original Oordoo by Captain T. Rattray, Commandant of that force.

Deen!" "for your faith! for your faith!" was the war-cry of the whole army.

Then other collateral influences, too, were unexpectedly tending to the same result, and embracing a still wider range.

Measures had passed the legislature, really prompted by, and indicative of, a large progressive spirit of benevolence, of a Government seeking but the moral and social amelioration of its subjects; yet these were regarded only as more systematic and more authoritative attacks on their religion. The abolition of Suttee, a demoniacal practice under which the more enlightened of the natives themselves groaned;—the endeavour to suppress infanticide, that blight and bane of every Rajpoot home; the re-marriage of Hindoo widows, as an escape from what too often proved a lifelong widowhood of sin and shame; these measures, so disinterested in their object, were regarded by the natives themselves with suspicion—grave suspicion—as unjustifiable interference with caste, with its fancied duties and rights; as so many cautious steps towards the ultimate overthrow of all the creeds of India, and the compulsory conversion of all classes to Christianity.

Now it may seem incredible to an Englishman unacquainted with India, that an idea so vague and so *baseless* should for one moment have entered, much less have so powerfully moved, the mind of a whole nation. Christianity and its civilisation cannot fully appreciate such a form of superstition, with its bigotry and barbarism; but the experience of the last few years has given overwhelming proof that such a state of things *is possible.*

It has left us a complex problem to solve, and many a varied lesson to learn. It has uttered a warning voice to legislators, and to those who have to administer and to carry out the fruits of legislation; to those into whose hands England commits the destinies of her Indian army; to those who have chosen India as the field for private enterprise, and also to those who, regarding Christianity not only as a blessing and a privilege for themselves, but also as a trust committed to them for the good of others.

It speaks to all, to every class of Englishmen in India, in every phase, civil, military, and mercantile; in every station of life, from the council-chamber of the empire to the shop of the tradesman; from the civilian in his kutcherree to the humblest Government clerk in his employ; from the officer in his home to the private soldier in his barrack-room. It reminds him that the Mohammedan regards the Christian as an *unbeliever*, and hates him; the Hindoo looks on him as a man without caste—a *pariah*—and despises him.

The late mutiny establishes this fact, that the active form which it assumed in 1857 it owed entirely to *religious* fears and suspicions; some perhaps, not all, unreasonably, others most causelessly aroused. Those fears and suspicions are not, by any means, yet allayed. Indeed now, perhaps, more than ever, each act of Government is watched with anxiety and mistrust; and, unfortunately, Government protests and assurances have lost much of their weight on the mass of the natives. Moreover, the large influx of Englishmen fresh to India is daily keeping this feeling alive, by heedless, and inconsiderate, often unintentional, offences to that very feeling. It should ever be remembered that the natives, especially the Hindoos, are of a deeply *religious* turn of mind. We may look down with scorn on a mind so constituted as to regard caste as the sum and substance, the beginning and the end, of religion; yet it is a fact, and in our intercourse with such a people the fact should be borne in mind. It need involve no compromise of our own religious principle to have respect to the feelings, while we reprobate the tenets, of other creeds. It need involve no sacrifice of Christian truth to deal cautiously and considerately with superstitious error. It is not necessary, for instance, to recognise in the ranks of the army, in Government offices, or in Government schools, any priority of caste, such as is assumed by natives among themselves. It is enough that we treat all alike; promote worth, reward merit, punish delinquency, in the *Chumar* as well as in the *Kulin Brahmin.* This may be done without wounding their religious sensibilities. And all this is wholly consistent with the efficient action of a Government which a Christian nation exercises over a heathen colony; and it is by such a course alone that India can be well, wisely, and safely ruled.

This warning has the mutiny, in its religious phase, given us. Let the Englishman, by even-handed justice and wise liberality, by truthfulness and probity, by gentleness and courtesy, by sobriety and chastity, in his public and in his private life, show his real superiority, not merely as the result of Western civilisation, but as the fruit of a practical Christianity,—and the warning may not have been sent in vain.

That breach so much to be lamented between the two races may yet be gradually lessened, the mutual antipathy now existing be removed, contempt on the one hand and suspicion on the other be mitigated and allayed, and confidence between the ruler and the ruled, the white and the black, the Christian and the heathen, be restored and blessed.

CHAPTER XXII.

THE MUTINY, AND GOD'S HAND THEREIN.*

A SHORT time after the battle of Waterloo, Alexander Knox, in writing to Mrs Hannah More, commented on that great victory in the following words: "How highly has Britain been honoured! and yet how awfully has all undue exaltation been suppressed by the critical turn which, after all, effected a prosperous conclusion. It was not human wisdom which wrought our deliverance." Nor was it human strength. A single nation on a foreign land combating and overcoming nearly the whole force of Europe, arrayed against her and the cause of freedom which she had made her own, was a glorious sight! Such a sight Waterloo beheld. Yet, with all the glories of that victory—a victory almost without a parallel, in the unequal conflict, the desperate struggle, and the momentous results—there was, in reality, little to feed national pride, or to engender boasting; far more to fill the mind of the conqueror with grateful acknowledgment to the God of Battles.

* The substance of this chapter has already appeared in the pages of a small Indian periodical; but as the author had more right to it than any one else, he has no hesitation in reproducing it here.

On the whole career of Napoleon had been inscribed that Divine assertion regarding one who, in his generation, had been no less the scourge of nations: "Hast thou not heard *how I have done it? Now have I brought it to pass* that thou shouldest be to lay waste fenced cities into ruinous heaps. *Therefore* their inhabitants were of small power, they were dismayed and confounded" (2 Kings, xix. 25, 26). In his downfall at Waterloo was as plainly written the Divine denunciation, "I will turn thee back by the way by which thou camest" (v. 28). Over his defeat the song of exultation rose, like that of Deborah and Barak: "They fought from heaven; the stars in their courses fought against Sisera" (Judges, v. 20).

Turn from Waterloo and its victory to India and its mutiny. "When I look back on the events of the last four months," wrote Sir John Lawrence,* "I am lost in astonishment that any of us are alive. But for the mercy of God we must have been ruined." Thus did he, whom England so justly regards as "the saviour of India" in having held the Punjab, acknowledge the powerlessness of man to effect that great work. He whose iron will, whose wide grasping mind and unwearied energy, carried Englishmen along with him and held down natives, is yet the first to confess it was not human wisdom or human strength that wrought that great deliverance, but the power and will of a

* Extract from a private letter read by Captain Eastwick at the meeting of the East India Company Proprietors, in seconding the resolution that a pension be voted to Sir John Lawrence.

merciful Heaven, whose *fiat* holds the surging minds of nations as it does the billows of the vast deep—"Thus far shalt thou go, and no farther."

How strikingly was this illustrated throughout that eventful period! When the mutiny broke out, the Bengal Presidency contained less than twenty thousand European soldiers, with above ten times that number of native troops; the intruding dominant race were not in all above a quarter of a million, while the races they had conquered and ruled numbered nearly *one hundred millions.** Such were the relative proportions of English and natives.

How far the mutinous spirit in the army extended was not at first known. Mercifully, it affected only a few regiments: but it might have involved the whole army, regular and irregular alike; nay more, it might have carried with it every race from Calcutta to Peshawur—Bengalee, Poorbeah, Punjabee, Afghan—every creed, Mohammedan, Hindoo, Buddhist, Sikh—and then, not an Englishman, not a Christian, could have escaped!

Look again at the state of the world, and of the political relations of England, at that time. Had the alliance with France been then tottering in the scale, England would not have dared to weaken herself at home even to rescue her noblest colony. Had the Russian war been still raging, she could have ill spared any troops for India, when already compelled to fall back on her militia in order to throw every available soldier into the Crimea. Had the Persian expedition

* This calculation refers to the Bengal Presidency only.

been still fighting its way to rescue Herat, Bombay, denuded as it was of troops, would have been powerless to succour the Punjab, or perhaps even to hold her own. Whereas we were at peace with our nearest and most formidable neighbour, and the two momentous wars had been brought to a close. The alliance with France gave confidence and liberty of action; the peace with Russia sent back to England an army trained and tried, and still eager for service; the treaty with Persia, only just ratified, set free the large force which a few weeks before were engaged in the Gulf; and although a third war with China had begun, this, instead of crippling us, proved our readiest strength and stand-by. The exigencies of India far exceeded the demands of China. To maintain our existence in the one was more important than to vindicate our character, supposed to have been insulted, in the other. The fleet, despatched, as it was then thought, to punish and humble China, was stopped in its course to save India.

And lastly, the formidable Dost Mahomed at Cabul had only a few weeks before entered into treaty with us at Jumrood—a treaty, the terms of which were too favourable to him for even his "Afghan faith" (Latinè, *Punica fides*) to violate.

Turn from these more public facts in the world's history to minor incidents in the Mutiny itself. The only Mohammedan of influence north of the Sutlej, Sheik Imam-oo-deen, of Lahore and Cashmere notoriety, had died a few weeks before, and with him passed away the only possible hope of Islam combination in the Punjab.

On our northern frontier, in the Swat Valley, the laboratory of Mohammedan intrigue, the right hand of the alchemist was paralysed at the very moment when he had seemed to have attained the grand *eureka* of his life. The *Badshah*, whom the wily Akhoond of Swat had raised, in order to gather under the green banner of the prophet every Mohammedan fanatic, and to recover Peshawur over the corpses of the unbelievers —this creature-king *died on the very day** that the tocsin of rebellion was sounded forth from Delhi; and the fanatic fury which was to have overwhelmed Peshawur spent itself in civil war in the Swat Valley.

Nor were the English left without warning. In many quarters the alarm was being sounded. At Umballa an Afghan trooper of the 4th Light Cavalry charged the whole regiment with a mutinous spirit; and a Sikh sepoy of the 5th N. I. disclosed the origin of the fires which were breaking out there every night, and the existence of a conspiracy in all the native corps.† At Philour the Commissary of Ordnance was told in mysterious language that blood would soon flow. At Mooltan the missionary was openly taunted with the fruitlessness of his labours, and told that in a very few weeks not a Christian would remain in India. In other places the same; but all these warnings were

* See vol. i. p. 292. † See vol. i. p. 49.

alike unheeded. In the sense of security they were laughed at.* Providentially not so at Lahore.† Here was a plot for placing every fort and arsenal of the Punjab in the hands of mutinous sepoys on the morning of the 15th May. On the 12th it was discovered by a Sikh policeman, disclosed to the authorities, and acted on; and Lahore, Umritsur, Philour, and Ferozepore were saved.

The mention of the 15th of May also suggests another point. The statement of the Sikh, and the disclosures of intercepted letters, led to the belief that this was the day originally fixed on for a general rise from Delhi to Peshawur. Why was not it delayed till then, when by a simultaneous and fatal combination every Christian in Upper India would have been at the mercy of the traitors? The 3d Light Cavalry at Meerut had on the morning of the 9th witnessed the degradation and imprisonment of their comrades; maddened, thirst-

* The following extract from Thornton's *Chapters of Indian History* will show that this has ever been the case with Englishmen in India:—

"Looking at the events which preceded the unhappy affair [at Vellore], it seems impossible to avoid feeling surprise at the unconsciousness and serenity displayed by the European authorities up to the moment of the frightful explosion. No apprehension appears to have been entertained, although the massacre was preceded by circumstances abundantly sufficient to justify it, and though the approaching danger was not left to be inferred from circumstances. Positive testimony as to the treacherous intentions of the native troops was tendered, but, unfortunately, treated with disregard and contempt."—(Pp. 9, 10.) Nearly a month before, a man named Mustapha Beg reported the conspiracy, but was pronounced *mad*, and no notice was taken of his warning.

Every word of this was as true of the state of things in the beginning of 1857 as in 1806, to which period it referred.

† See vol. i. pp. 93, 94.

ing for revenge, impatient of a delay of even a few days, which might have insured their success, they rose the next night, released their comrades, murdered their officers, instigated the *budmashes* of the bazaar to plunder and massacre, and themselves joined by the infantry made for Delhi. The die was cast; the *Jahad* was begun!

Nor was this all. It has been often said, and justly, "The telegraph saved the Punjab." But what gave the telegraph its value? In vain would it have flashed forth its warning on the morning of the 15th May, with every station in mutiny, every fort in the hands of its traitor guard; each would have had to struggle for its own existence, and unable to help its neighbour. It was the premature outburst at Meerut that gave the priority of intelligence, which proved above all value. The punishment of the troopers, condemned by some as unwisely severe and desperate, at any rate effected this good; calling up the vengeance of the traitors, it accelerated the explosion, it hastened the catastrophe; and thus disconcerting the traitors in their very treason, and throwing out all the plans at other stations, it sounded forth the warning note to the English. They heard it, and, "forewarned," were "forearmed."

Many minor incidents also there were in the progress of the mutiny not unworthy of note. A so-called accidental change of plans regarding the parade church-service at Umballa, on the morning of the 10th May, disconcerted a deeply-laid plot, and averted a massacre which would probably have been as appalling as that of which Meerut was the scene a few hours later.*

Take another incident—the siege-train crossing the Sutlej on the 21st May. Weary and anxious was the task of keeping the bridge of boats together during the six hours the train was passing over. Within two hours after the last carriage was clear, the bridge broke away before the force of the swollen river; but the train was safe! †

Pass we on towards Delhi. The very delays and difficulties at which the energy and impatience of man fretted, were not without ultimate good; they permitted the fuller development of the foul conspiracy, and disclosed the real vastness of the surrounding danger, of which all were so unconscious.

Then disasters were turned to account. The partial failure at Ferozepore set free one regiment, and the mismanagement at Jullundhur another, and a battery; while the disasters at Jhelum and Sealkote gave the entire Moveable Column and the heroic Nicholson,—all to strengthen the siege.

Again, before Delhi itself, a mere handful of men besieging a city so vast that they could not compass one-tenth part of its fortifications, or number a tenth part of the enemy opposed to them, were enabled to hold on against daily attacks, formidable in numbers and plan, against treachery within as well as rebellion without — against dangers innumerable which were

* See vol. i. pp. 187, 188. † See vol. i. p. 206.

known, and perhaps even more unknown, there to hold on during three months of an Indian scorching pestilential season—the very fierceness of the sun apparently tempered to their need—the season itself more than usually favourable, and free from sickness—there to hold on still, and in the end succeed! Yet withal how weak, how powerless, how really at the mercy of the rebels had they only known their own strength, was that little band of heroes!

Why did not the rebels, as they so easily might, cut off the army from its supports in the Punjab? To have done so would have stopped all the supplies, and the whole force must have perished with hunger. Why did not the native servants, who had the lives of their masters in their hands, join in one vast conspiracy, and in a single night poison every Englishman in that camp? Why, again, when the whole force had, on the 14th September, been thrown into the assault, did they not make the rear-attack upon the camp, and then turn a triumph into a massacre? Why, on the following morning, when they who survived the assault were powerless from drink, the too-ready prey to the snare so craftily laid for them, did not the rebels rush back and recover the city in an almost resistless slaughter? Why not? He in whose hands are the hearts of men, willed it otherwise.

Their most formidable plans were frustrated, their deepest counsels and most deadly machinations defeated, by internal jealousies and feuds — their very numbers proved their weakness.

Once more: had Delhi been the *only* focus of rebellion, humanly speaking, it must have been successful. Providentially, a second was formed at Lucknow, and so each weakened the other. Had the thousands of mutineers who rallied to Lucknow and wasted their fury on that heroic garrison been added to those thousands who concentrated on Delhi, Delhi could never have been taken by the handful of men the Punjab could spare. With a double siege, a divided army, the one weakened the other, and both failed.

It may be said that half the siege of Delhi was carried on at Lucknow, and the relief of Lucknow half effected before Delhi!

Our tale is told—our task is done. We have seen how the storm rose and the hurricane swept over our vast Indian possessions, as they lay wrapt in fancied security (if we may be allowed the metaphor), like a fleet of richly-laden argosies riding at anchor in a peaceful haven.

Those that lay beyond the fury of the storm felt only the roll of the ground-swell and escaped; others were stranded and their freight abandoned, and the surviving crews hardly rescued as they clung to the shattered wrecks; one wholly perished. ONE—with her has lain our tale—saw the danger, ran out to sea, and weathered the storm. Such was the course of the Punjab.

Our tale has told how she bore on like a gallant bark in a seething sea; how billow after billow gathered up to overwhelm her; how she wore round to meet each as it came—now struggling in the trough, now rising with the wave—how there were master-minds at the helm, and a Protecting Power above; and how she was saved!

We who are alive, and remember the perils of 1857, shall we not say with the Psalmist, "*It is of the Lord's mercy that we were not consumed*"?

APPENDIX.

NOTE K, page 26.

GENERAL ORDERS BY MAJOR-GENERAL REED, PROVINCIAL COMMANDER-IN-CHIEF.

HEADQUARTERS, CAMP BEFORE DELHI,
July 17, 1857.

LIEUTENANT-GENERAL SIR P. GRANT, K.C.B., having, in a general order dated the 17th June, at Calcutta, announced his having assumed command of the Bengal army from that date, Major-General Reed has ceased to exercise the duties of Provincial Commander-in-Chief.

Major-General Reed, having been recommended by his medical advisers to avail himself of a sick certificate to repair to the hills, as the only chance of his recovering his shattered health, which has latterly prevented him from taking an active part in the field operations, has made over the command and charge of this force to Brigadier-General A. Wilson.

It is with the greatest reluctance the Major-General has come to the determination to take this step, but his duty to his country must be paramount to any selfish consideration; and being incapacitated himself for the post by disease and weakness, he has no alternative than to devolve his arduous duties upon another.

Of Brigadier-General Wilson's merits it is unnecessary for Major-General Reed to speak: his judgment, gallantry, and conduct have been conspicuous since he led his small but victorious band from Meerut up to this day.

It only remains for the Major-General to congratulate the forces before Delhi on being placed under so able a commander as Brigadier-General Wilson.

Major-General Reed takes this opportunity of requesting the headquarters and divisional Staff to accept his thanks for the great assistance received by him, and by his lamented predecessor, Major-General Sir H. Barnard, K.C.B., not only in the exercise of their departmental duties, but also in the operations in the field.

To Brigadier-General Chamberlain, Acting Adjutant-General of the army; Colonel Congreve, C.B., Acting Adjutant-General, her Majesty's forces; Colonel Beecher, Quartermaster-General of the army; Lieutenant-Colonel the Honourable R. W. P. Curzon, Acting Quartermaster-General of her Majesty's forces; Lieutenant-Colonel Young, Judge - Advocate General: Captain Norman, Assistant Adjutant - General of the army; Captains Garstin and Hodson, Officiating Deputy-Assistant Quartermasters-General of the army; Major Ewart, Deputy-Assistant Adjutant-General, and Captain Stewart, Officiating Deputy - Assistant Adjutant - General; Captain Maisey, Deputy Judge-Advocate General; and Captain Shute, Deputy-Assistant Quartermaster - General of Division,—his acknowledgments are eminently due.

The Major-General's warmest thanks are due to the whole artillery of the force, who have on all occasions behaved with conspicuous gallantry, and have ever maintained the reputation of their distinguished corps.

To Lieutenant-Colonel Baird Smith, and the Engineer department, Major-General Reed offers his most sincere acknowledgments for the valuable services they have rendered.

To Lieutenant-Colonel Thomson, Deputy Commissary-General, and his assistants, to Superintending Surgeon Tritton, and all the officers of the medical department, the Major-General's best thanks are due for their indefatigable and successful exertions.

To Brigadiers Grant, Longfield, Jones, and Showers, and to the gallant officers and troops, European and native, under their orders, the Major-General begs to award his tribute of admiration for their brilliant and distinguished conduct in a succession of attacks, in which the enemy have on every occasion been repulsed. The behaviour of the troops has been beyond all praise.

Major-General Reed cannot forbear from recording the name of Major Reid, as having commanded the post which has been subject to the most frequent and constant attacks of the enemy, from which they have always been driven with great loss by the able dispositions of that officer, so admirably seconded by the troops under his command, comprising parties of her Majesty's 60th Royal Rifles and other corps, with the gallant Sirmoor Battalion and corps of Guides.

In conclusion, the Major-General desires to express his thanks to the officers of his personal Staff for the uniform assistance he has received from them upon every occasion, and he only regrets he has not had more frequent opportunities of witnessing their distinguished conduct in the field; to Captains Lowe, Reid, and Turnbull, Aides-de-camp; to Assistant-Surgeon W. F. Mactier; and to Lieutenant R. C. Low, Orderly Officer; as well as to Lieutenant W. H. Greathed, of Engineers, who acted as Aide-de-camp to the General commanding from the 7th ultimo, besides performing the duty of Field Engineer, when his services where needed in that capacity.

Note L, page 80.

Brigadier-General Nicholson to the Adjutant-General of the Army.

Goordaspore, *July* 19, 1857.

Sir,—I have the honour herewith to forward, for the information of his Excellency the Commander-in-Chief, an account of my proceedings, and of the column under my command, since the date of my last letter* (the 27th ultimo).

* The author regrets he has not been able to meet with a copy of the letter here referred to.

2. In it I reported the disarming of the 33d and 35th Regiments Native Infantry, and the reasons which had induced me to have recourse to that measure.

3. On the same date I commenced retracing my steps from Philour, and on the 5th July encamped with the column at Umritsur.

4. I selected this station for an encampment mainly on account of its centricality, my position there enabling me to afford speedy aid, if required, either to Lahore or the Jullundhur Doab, while, at the same time, it overawed the Manjha, and rendered hopeless any attempt to mutiny on the part of the 59th Regiment Native Infantry.

5. On the morning of the 7th I received intelligence of the mutiny of the 14th Native Infantry at Jhelum, and that it was successfully holding against the force sent to disarm it under Colonel Ellice. I waited throughout the day and following night in the hope of hearing of the defeat of the 14th, but this expectation not having been realised, and unfavourable accounts continuing to arrive, I reluctantly felt myself obliged to disarm the 59th Native Infantry at sunrise on the 8th.

6. I feel bound, however, to place on record my belief that, both in conduct and feeling, this regiment was quite an exceptional one at the present crisis. It had neither committed itself in any way, nor do I believe that, up to the day it was disarmed, it had any intention of committing itself; and I may deeply regret that, even as a precautionary measure, it should have become my duty to disarm it. I beg very strongly to recommend this corps, both as regards officers and men, to the favourable consideration of Government.

7. Early on the morning of the 10th I received intelligence by telegraph that the troops at Sealkote, consisting of the 46th Native Infantry and the right wing 9th Light Cavalry, had broken out into open mutiny the previous morning. This intelligence was confirmed half an hour later by a musician of the 46th Native Infantry, who rode in, express, with the news. I immediately disarmed the left wing 9th Cavalry with the column, a step I had refrained from when disarming the 33d and 35th Regiments, lest it should prematurely excite the wing at Sealkote.

8. In the course of the day information reached me from

various quarters that the Sealkote troops had marched in an easterly direction the previous evening. Their object was evidently to plunder the station of Goordaspore, and get the 2d Irregular Cavalry there to join them. They would then, no doubt, have proceeded, *viâ* Noorpore and Hosheyarpore, to Jullundhur, whence they would have made the best of their way to Delhi. At Noorpore they expected to be joined by the 4th Regiment Native Infantry, and at Hosheyarpore by the 16th Irregular Cavalry.

9. It was evident that, as the mutineers had two days' start, and as Goordaspore was something over forty-one miles from my encampment, no time was to be lost; I therefore decided on reaching that station in a single forced march; and this, with the aid of ekkas and ponies for the infantry, was successfully accomplished in less than twenty hours.

10. The mutineers were at this date (the 11th) at Noorkobe, about fifteen miles on the right bank of the Ravee. Fearing that if I opposed their passage of the river they might break away southwards, and so escape me, I decided on allowing them to cross without molestation, and accordingly remained at Goordaspore until 9 A.M. the following morning; when, hearing they had commenced crossing by a ford at the Trimmoo ferry, about nine miles distant, I moved out against them with a force as per margin.*

11. I came upon them at noon about a mile on this side the river. Their infantry was drawn up in a line, its right resting on a serai and dismantled ghurree (small fort), its left on a small village and a clump of trees. Their cavalry appeared to be pretty equally distributed on the flanks.

12. I advanced to the attack in the following order—viz., three guns light field-battery in the centre; the troop of horse-artillery, equally divided, 100 yards on either side; 300 of H. M.'s 52d Light Infantry, with Enfield rifles, in extended order, at one pace between and on the flanks of the artillery. The remainder of H. M.'s 52d, with the Punjab infantry, were in rear as supports and reserve. The new police res-

* 3d Troop, 1st Brigade, Horse Artillery; three guns No. 17 Light Field-battery; H. M.'s 52d Light Infantry; detachment from the 3d and 6th Punjab infantry (184 men); one company 2d Police battalion; two newly-raised ressallahs.

sallahs I employed to mask the artillery until, at about 600 yards, a threatened charge of a party of the mutineer cavalry induced me to unmask and unlimber the three guns on the left to check it. The sight of the guns had the desired effect, and we resumed our advance, except that the police, being now no longer useful as maskers, and seeming undesirous of engaging, were ordered to the rear.

13. My intention was to advance within 300 yards of the mutineers' position, and then open fire simultaneously from the artillery and Enfield rifles, the latter weapons being known to be thoroughly effective at that distance, while the smooth-bore musket, with which alone the mutineers were armed, is comparatively useless.

14. The action commenced by the mutineer infantry opening upon us with file-firing at, as nearly as possible, the above distance. We lost no time in replying, and for about ten minutes they stood up very well indeed against the great odds opposed to them, many of them advancing boldly up to the very guns; meanwhile the cavalry had made several rushes in detached parties on our flanks and rear, but had always been repulsed by the file-firing of our infantry.

15. The new police ressallahs fled when threatened with a charge; but considering their want of discipline, and how very recently they had been raised, I cannot say that I consider them very culpable; there were, however, some honourable exceptions.

16. The mutineers were followed up to the bank of the river by the artillery, which occasioned them some little loss both in crossing and after they had gained an island in the centre, on which they had a 12-pounder iron gun. A few rounds were fired at us from this piece, but without effect.

17. The enemy left dead upon the ground on which they fought 120 men; many were swept away by the river. Their wounded were probably not less than double the above number. All their camp-equipage, &c., on this side of the river fell into our hands.

18. The want of cavalry (which crippled us sadly during the action), the depth of the water in the ford, and the fatigue the troops had undergone on the previous day, all conspired to prevent me from attempting to pursue the enemy across the

river. I therefore left the Punjab infantry with Lieutenant Boswell in the serai, and brought back the European infantry and artillery to their encampment at Goordaspore, there to await news of the further movements of the mutineers.

19. On the 13th I appointed Captain Adams Assistant Commissioner (kindly placed at my disposal by Mr Roberts, the Commissioner), to command the detachment at the ghaut, with a view to his watching and furnishing intelligence of the remnant of the mutineers on the island. From this officer's information, corroborated as it was from other quarters, I ascertained that the discomfiture of the mutineers in the action of the 12th had been much more complete than I had at first supposed, and that not more than 300 men remained with the gun on the island; also, that all, or very nearly all, of those who had dispersed, had first divested themselves of their arms and accoutrements.

20. I accordingly at once decided on attacking the remnant on the island, and with this view, on the evening of the 15th, got down two boats from ferries high up the river; all the boats in our immediate neighbourhood having been sunk by the civil authorities on the first news of the approach of the mutineers. At daybreak on the morning of the 16th, H. M. 52d Light Infantry, and one company of the Punjab infantry, with one company of police battalion,* crossed one mile and a quarter below the enemy's position; our guns placed higher up the stream keeping the enemy's gun in play. When the whole of the infantry had crossed, the advance commenced, the 52d leading in skirmishing order. The affair was over in a few minutes, without any check, and with a loss to us of only six men wounded. A few resolute men among the mutineers died manfully at the gun; the rest fled, and were either slain on the bank or driven into the river.

21. I do not need to dwell upon the services which the Column has rendered the State in these operations; his Excellency will himself thoroughly comprehend and appreciate them.

My best thanks are due to officers and men of all grades,

* Lieutenant Boswell, with another company, was employed in watching a ford higher up the river.

and both arms, for the cordial and valuable assistance I have throughout received from them, more particularly to Colonel Campbell, commanding H. M.'s 52d Light Infantry; Lieut.-Colonel Dawes, commanding the Artillery; Captain Bourchier, commanding No. 17 Light Field-battery; Captain Blane, H. M. 52d, my Brigade-Major; and Captain Grindlay, 6th Light Cavalry, Deputy-Assistant Quartermaster-General to the column.

Lieutenant Angelo, 59th Native Infantry; Lieutenant Dixon, 9th Light Cavalry; and Lieut. Baillie, 35th Native Infantry, also made themselves extremely useful in reconnoitring and otherwise, and I much regret that a severe wound received by the latter officer will temporarily deprive me of his services.

22. I cannot conclude without expressing my obligations to Mr Roberts, the Commissioner and Superintendent of the Division, and to Captain Adams, the Assistant Commissioner of Goordaspore. Both officers were present in the affair of the 12th and 16th, and afforded me much valuable assistance throughout in the way of information. Captain Adams also commanded the Punjab infantry and police detachment at the ghaut from the 13th to the 16th instant, and the detachment which crossed the river on the latter date.

Lieutenant Perkins, Assistant Commissioner, Umritsur, was present in the action of the 12th, and had his horse wounded.

J. Nicholson, Brigadier-General,
Commanding Punjab Moveable Column.

Note M, page 110.

Memorandum, showing the Position of Troops, &c. &c., on the Alarm-Bugle sounding, and other Arrangements for the Defence of the Station of Peshawur.

Alarm-Posts.

1. The alarm-posts of H. M. regiments are at the guns stationed in their respective lines, that of the Artillery in the

park; that for the Peshawur Light Horse in front of its own lines. The European infantry stationed in the artillery barracks will proceed to the rear of the park.

The armed native infantry and cavalry corps will be drawn up in front of their respective quarter or standard guards —the cavalry in close column of squadrons, the infantry in quarter-distance columns, right in front, all facing towards the lines.

The disarmed native regiments will fall in in rear of their quarter or standard guards, drawn up in the same way as the others, but facing outwards.

2. Corps will remain at their respective alarm-posts until they receive orders to move; and an officer from each regiment will be immediately despatched to the Residency for orders (having first obtained the countersign from their own regimental quarter or standard guards).

Residency the Headquarters of Staff.

3. The Residency will be considered the headquarters of the staff; and on the "alarm" sounding either by day or night, officers will attend there for orders.

Ladies.

4. In the event of an alarm, ladies will proceed to the Residency; but should it so happen that those residing at the western end of cantonments are unable to reach it, they will take refuge in the nearest European hospital.

Women and Children.

5. Women and children will take refuge in the hospitals of their respective regiments, except in the Artillery, where the canteen will be the place for refuge; and the guard there will be increased to twenty men from the European infantry stationed in the lines, and also a party of twelve infantry will be sent to strengthen the hospital guards.

The European infantry hospitals will, on the "alarm" sounding, be at once reinforced by twenty men; and all sick men able to use arms will invariably be provided with them at all times.

Field and Subaltern Officers of the Day.

6. The field and subaltern officers of the day will proceed immediately to the spot where the danger or attack is, calling first at the nearest European regiment for an inlying picquet, to take with him.

To sleep at night near inlying Picquet, 87th.

7. The field and subaltern officers of the day will sleep at night near the place where the inlying picquet of H. M. 87th Regiment is located. A government tent will be pitched for their accommodation, and the field-officer will direct a mounted orderly to remain there during the day, in order to convey any message to the field-officer, whose own quarters there might be a difficulty in finding out, and a delay, in consequence, ensue.

Field-Officer's Requisition for Troops to be complied with.

8. The field-officer's requisition for troops, from any corps, is to be immediately complied with.

9. The field or subaltern officer of the day (not drawing horse allowance) will be supplied with a horse from the Peshawur Light Horse during his tour of duty, on a requisition being made to the officer commanding that corps.

10. The native mounted orderlies detailed for duty for the field and subaltern officers, will remain in attendance on them all day, as well as all night.

Protection of Magazines.

11. Commanding officers are to make arrangements for the protection of their own magazines, by reinforcing the guard on the "alarm" sounding.

Officers of European and Native Regiments to live near, and sleep in, their Lines.

12. Officers of European and native corps will invariably sleep in their own regimental lines at night—that is, within the precincts of the lines or barracks occupied by their own men. In the daytime, too, they will absent themselves as little as possible from their lines.

Patrolling of Lines.

13. Commanding officers are responsible that their lines are properly patrolled at night. Officers commanding European regiments will be particularly careful in posting sentries for the due protection of their flanks.

Natives found going about after Gunfire at night to be confined.

All natives found moving about the roads after gunfire at night to be confined, and made over the following morning to the cantonment joint magistrate for punishment.

Alarm-Signals.—Duty of Officers commanding.—Mackeson Post, on hearing Alarm-Signal from Fort.—Duty of Field-Officer of the day, ditto.

14. On the "alarm" signal being fired from the fort, the officer commanding the Mackeson Post will immediately proceed with a party of (50) fifty Europeans, fifty natives, and some cavalry, to the fort, to render assistance. In the mean time, the field-officer of the day, with the inlying picquet of H. M. 87th Regiment, will reinforce the Mackeson Post.

Fort Signals.

15. The following are the fort signals:—In the daytime (2) two guns from the fort, at an interval of a minute, and at night (1) one gun, followed by a rocket, will indicate that there

is a disturbance in the city. Three guns in the daytime, and at night two guns, followed by a rocket, will indicate that the fort is attacked.

Station Cavalry Patrols at Night.

16. Cavalry patrols will continue to proceed, as usual, along the centre and circular roads of cantonments; viz., a party from each cavalry picquet patrolling to the picquet on its right at uncertain hours. The left cavalry picquet, furnished by the 18th Irregular Cavalry, will patrol the centre road, as far as the mess-house of H. M. 87th Regiment, and the right picquet of the 7th Irregular Cavalry the remainder of the Pukka road, on the eastern side of the 87th mess.

Reinforcement of the Residency Guard is, on Sundays, to take place at the hour appointed for Evening Service.

17. As a protection to the families of officers and others attending divine service on Sunday evening, the reinforcement of the Residency guard will take place on Sundays at the hour appointed for evening service. Troops marched to church will invariably be armed and accoutred.

Attention of Officer of Guard at Residency to be particularly directed to the Church.

The attention of the officer on guard at the Residency is, during the hours of divine service, to be particularly directed to the safety of the church.

Duties of Officers commanding Wings of Brigade.

18. The officers commanding the wings of the brigade will be struck off the roster for garrison duties, with a view to their seeing that the above orders are rigidly enforced; and they will each report to the Brigadier commanding, on Monday mornings, that all the provisions of the above orders have been attended to during the week.

These officers will, at night, sleep as near the centre of their respective wings as practicable.

They will be provided each with two mounted orderlies, who will always be in attendance.

Bugler for the Brigade-Major.

19. A bugler will be detailed to remain at the quarters of the Major of brigade; and on the "alarm" being sounded, whether from the Residency or from any corps in cantonments, it will be taken up by all regiments.

Rules to be made known to every Officer.

20. These rules are to be made known to every officer, and commanding officers will report to the Major of brigade, for the Brigadier's information, whenever this has been effected.

By order.

(Signed) A. H. D. Campbell, Captain,
Officiating Major of Brigade.

Note N, page 123.

Kuppoorthulla Rajah.

Jursa Singh, the founder of the Alloowallea *Misal,* had been among the most adventurous and successful of the Sikh sirdars who established themselves on the ruins of the Mohammedan power in the Punjab. He first called forth the zeal of the *Khalsa,* and by its means rose to power. Starting from his own native village of Alloo, near Lahore (which gave its title to the Misal), Jursa Singh began by absorbing many adjacent villages and considerable tracts of land north of the Ravee; he then crossed that river into the Jullundhur Doab, and conquering several of the petty chiefs, became master of a princely domain in that fertile district; then, passing farther south, possessed himself of extensive tracts across the Sutlej.

In 1758 he occupied Lahore itself, and from the mint of the Moghul coined money that proclaimed the triumph of "Jursa the Kalâl," at the head of the Khalsa, over the Punjab territories of Ahmeed Shah. Dying childless, his estates passed to his brother Bhag Singh, from whom they descended in all their entirety to his son Futteh Singh. So great was the influence of this chief, that even the crafty ambitious Runjeet Singh dared not compete with him for the supremacy of the Sikhs, and, preferring to regard him as an equal than a rival, was content to secure his favour and connivance by the interchange of turbans, the bond of eternal friendship. This accounts for the fact that, in the treaty with the English in 1808, the two appear together as *joint sirdars.* A very few years after, however, Futteh Singh began to fear the rapacity of his *turban-brother.* In 1826 he fled across the Sutlej, and threw himself on the protection of the English; but the following year, on the promises and entreaties of Runjeet Singh, he returned to Lahore, and was left in peaceful possession of his lands; which, on his death, descended to his son Nehal Singh—their aggregate revenue then amounting to about twelve lakhs. When the Sikh war broke out, Nehal Singh played the traitor to the English, whom he was bound by treaty to support, and in consequence all his estates south of the Sutlej were confiscated, and in those in the Baree Doab he was allowed only a life interest. Thus, what with forfeitures and lapses, the income of the present Rajah Rundheer Singh was greatly reduced. At the time of the mutiny it scarcely amounted to more than one lakh of rupees, out of which he had to support his dignity, and to maintain a large body of hereditary retainers and clansmen. When this is taken into consideration, a better estimate may be formed of his services.

NOTE N, page 155.

BRIGADIER-GENERAL NICHOLSON TO THE DEPUTY ASSISTANT ADJUTANT-GENERAL, DELHI FIELD-FORCE.

CAMP, 4TH INFANTRY BRIGADE, BEFORE DELHI,
Aug. 28, 1857.

SIR,—I have the honour to report, for the information of Major-General Wilson, commanding before Delhi, that agreeably to his orders I marched from this at daybreak on the 25th, with the troops noted in the margin,* to intercept a force of the enemy, said to be moving from Delhi towards Bahadoorghur, with the intention of attacking us in rear.

On my arrival at the village of Nangloor, about nine miles from this (and to reach which I had to cross two difficult swamps), I learned that the enemy had been at Talmu the previous day, and would probably reach Nujufghur in the course of the afternoon; I therefore decided on leaving the Bahadoorghur road, and, if possible, coming up with and routing the enemy at Nujufghur before nightfall.

I crossed a tolerably deep and broad ford over a branch of the Nujufghur jheel, near the village of Bassrowla, at about 4 P.M., and found the enemy in position on my left and front, extending from the bridge over the Nujufghur canal to the town of Nujufghur itself, a distance of a mile and three-quarters or two miles. Their strongest point was an old serai on their left-centre, in which they had four guns; nine more guns were between this and the bridge.

It was five o'clock before the troops were across the ford and parallel with the position. As the enemy was so far advanced, and I had no guides, I laboured under the disadvantage of being compelled to make a very hasty reconnaissance.

The plan which I determined on was to force the left-centre

* One squadron H.M. 9th Lancers, sixteen guns Horse Artillery, 120 Guide Cavalry, 80 of 2d Punjab Cavalry, wing of H.M. 61st Regiment, 420 bayonets; 1st European Bengal Fusiliers, 380 bayonets; 1st Punjab Infantry, 400 bayonets; 2d Punjab Infantry, 400 bayonets; detachment of Sappers and Miners, 30; 200 Mooltanee Horse.

(which, as I have said, was the strongest part of the position), and then, changing front to the left, to sweep down their line of guns towards the bridge.

I accordingly formed up her Majesty's 61st Regiment, the 1st Fusiliers, and the 2d Punjab Infantry (with the exception of 100 men of each corps, whom I had told off on the march as a rearguard and reserve), with four guns on the right and ten on the left flank, supported by the squadron of 9th Lancers and Guide Cavalry; and after the artillery had fired in a few rounds, I advanced and charged with the infantry.

The enemy was driven out with scarcely any numerical loss to us (though her Majesty's 61st had a most gallant and promising officer, Lieutenant Gabbett, mortally wounded), and I then changed front to left, and so turned the position in which their guns were. The enemy made little resistance as we advanced, and were soon in full retreat across the bridge, with our guns playing upon them, thirteen of their field-pieces having fallen into our hands.

At the same time that I attacked the serai I directed Lieutenant Lumsden, officiating commandant of Major Coke's corps, the 1st Punjab Infantry, to advance and clear the town of Nujufghur, on our right. This service was well performed by Lieutenant Lumsden, who, after passing through the town, brought his right shoulders forward, and followed in rear of the main line.

The enemy's guns were now all in our possession, and I supposed the conflict at an end, when it was reported to me that a few men had concealed themselves in the little village of Nuglee, which was at this time a few hundred yards in rear of our line. I immediately sent orders to Lieutenant Lumsden, who was then nearly abreast of the village, to drive them out; but, though few in number, they had remained so long that our troops were on all sides of them, and seeing no line of retreat open, they fought with extreme desperation.

Lieutenant Lumsden was, I regret to say, killed with eleven of his men; twenty-six more were wounded, and I was obliged to send back the 61st Regiment to reinforce the 1st Punjab Infantry. This corps also suffered the loss of another gallant officer, Lieutenant Elkington, dangerously wounded, and five men killed; and several more were wounded before the village was in our possession.

The enemy's cavalry, apparently not less than 1000 strong, more than once made a show of charging during the action, but were on each occasion driven back by the fire of our artillery. Our own cavalry I regretted much my inability to employ against them; but I had been obliged to leave the squadron, 2d Punjab Cavalry, under Lieutenant Nicholson, and 120 of the Mooltanees, to look after the baggage; and I had of Lancers, Guides, and Mooltanees, not more than 300 left to escort the guns and form a reserve.

I passed the night at the bridge, with the 1st Fusiliers and 2d Punjab Infantry, and a detachment of Artillery and Lancers. I had the bridge mined and blown up by the Sappers, and all the waggons and tumbrils which I had not the means of bringing away were also blown up by Major Tombs; shortly after daybreak I started on my return to camp, and fearing lest more rain should render the ground (already sufficiently difficult) quite impracticable, I brought the Column in the same evening.

It only now remains for me to fulfil the pleasing duty of expressing my extreme satisfaction with the conduct of the troops in these operations. No soldiers ever advanced to the attack of a position with greater gallantry and steadiness than her Majesty's 61st Regiment, the 1st Fusiliers, and the 2d Punjab Infantry. No infantry was ever more ably assisted by artillery. Major Coke's regiment, under its gallant and lamented officiating commandant, Lieutenant Lumsden, sustained its high reputation.

The troops are likewise entitled to great credit for the cheerfulness with which they bore the hardships they were exposed to; they marched at daybreak, and had to cross two difficult swamps before their arrival at Nangloor, and as it would not have been prudent to take the baggage across the ford at Bassrowla, they were obliged, after fourteen hours' marching and fighting, to bivouac on the field without food or covering of any kind.

The officers to whom I am most indebted for their services on this occasion, and whom I would beg to bring prominently to the favourable notice of the Major-General, are Major Tombs, commanding the artillery (this officer's merits are so well known to the Major-General that it is unnecessary for me to dwell upon them); Major Jacob, commanding 1st Fusiliers; Captain Green, commanding 2d Punjab Infantry; and Captains Remington and Blunt, and Lieutenants Wilson and Sankey, of the Artillery. I also received every assistance from my staff and orderly officers, Captain Blane, her Majesty's 52d, my Brigade-Major; Captain Shute, Deputy Assistant Quartermaster-General; Captain French, 35th Native Infantry, and Lieutenant Dixon, late 9th Light Cavalry, my orderly officers; and Lieutenant R. C. Low, on the staff of the Major-General commanding.

Lieutenant Sorell, Her Majesty's 9th Lancers, to whom I intrusted the command of the cavalry, with the guns during the action, and of the rearguard on the 26th, performed these duties very much to my satisfaction. The same remarks apply to Captain Gordon, Her Majesty's 61st, who commanded the reserve during the action and night of the 25th.

Sir Theophilas Metcalfe was good enough to accompany and give me the benefit of his local knowledge; he was also present and very forward on the attack on the serai.

Lieutenant Generte, of the Engineers, deserves credit for the very complete and successful manner in which he blew up the bridge.

I enclose a return of captured guns and ordnance stores, a casualty roll, and a sketch of the ground, prepared by Captain Shute, of the Quartermaster-General's department.

I have, &c.,

J. Nicholson, Brigadier-General,
Commanding 4th Infantry Brigade.

Note O, page 183.

General Wilson thus officially records his opinion of the services of Major Reid and his Goorkhas:—

"I cannot refrain from bringing to the notice of Major-General Gowan, with a view to the same being submitted to his Excellency the Commander-in-Chief, and through him to the Supreme Government, the admiration with which I, as well as the whole force, have viewed the gallantry with which this noble officer, with the gallant band under him, has held the important post intrusted to his command.

"With the aid of her Majesty's 60th Royal Rifles, his own regiment, the Sirmoor Battalion, assisted by reliefs from the Guide Corps of infantry, the 4th Sikh Regiment, and the 1st Punjab Infantry, this officer has from the 8th of June, the date of the arrival of this force at Delhi, sustained and defeated twenty-four separate attacks upon his position up to the 6th instant; and from that date to the present, constant worrying attacks, day and night, by both infantry and cavalry.*

"I have no words to express my admiration of the endurance and gallantry displayed throughout this long period by Major Reid and the officers and men who have served under him; but I now thus briefly record my opinion of their merits, in the certain hope that Major-General Cowan, C.B., will recommend them to higher authority for the greatest honours that can be bestowed upon them." . . .

Major-General A. Wilson's Official Report of the Assault of Delhi.

Note P, page 198.

To Captain H. W. Norman, Assistant Adjutant-General of the Army.

Headquarters, Field-Force, Delhi, *Sept.* 15.

Sir,—I have the high satisfaction of reporting, for the information of the Major-General commanding in the upper

* Mr Charles Raikes, in his *Notes on the Revolt, &c.*, thus graphically describes a visit to this little garrison:—"I walked over the ruins of Hindoo Rao's house with astonishment. How men could have held a building so battered and riddled with shot and shell, the very target of the enemy, is a marvel; yet as the siege progressed, when it was proposed to remove even the sick and wounded in hospital, they violently protested against being carried away from their comrades, even to a place of safety. In this hospital, Major Reid pointed out the mark where a patient had been cut in two by a round-shot."—P. 79.

provinces, and through him of his Excellency the Commander-in-Chief and of Government, that on the morning of the 14th inst. the force under my command successfully assaulted the city of Delhi.

Under the present circumstances, Major-General Gowan will, I trust, allow me to withhold for a time a full and complete detail of the operations from their commencement to their close, and to limit myself to a summary of events.

After six days of open trenches, during which the Artillery and Engineers, under their respective commanding officers, Major Gaitskell and Lieutenant-Colonel Baird Smith, vied with each other in pressing forward the work, two excellent and most practicable breaches were formed in the walls of the place, one in the curtain to the right of the Cashmere Bastion, the other to the left of the Water Bastion, the defences of those bastions and the parapets giving musketry cover to the enemy commanding the breaches having also been destroyed by the artillery.

The assault was delivered on four points. The 1st column under Brigadier J. Nicholson, consisting of her Majesty's 75th Regiment (300 men), the 1st European Bengal Fusiliers (200 men), and the 2d Punjab Infantry (450 men), assaulted the main breach, their advance being admirably covered by the 1st battalion of her Majesty's 60th Rifles, under Colonel J. Jones. The operation was crowned with brilliant success, the enemy, after severe resistance, being driven from the Cashmere Bastion, the Main Guard, and its vicinity, in complete rout.

The 2d column, under Brigadier Jones, of her Majesty's 61st Regiment, consisting of her Majesty's 8th Regiment (250 men), the 2d European Bengal Fusiliers (250 men), and the 4th Regiment of Sikhs (350 men), similarly covered by the 60th Rifles, advanced on the Water Bastion, carried the breach, and drove the enemy from his guns and position, with a determination and spirit which gave me the highest satisfaction.

"The 3d column, under Colonel Campbell, of Her Majesty's 52d Light Infantry, consisting of 250 of his own regiment, the Kumaoon Battalion (250 men), and the 1st Punjab Infantry (500 men), was directed against the Cashmere gateway. This column was preceded by an explosion-party, under Lieutenants Home and Salkeld, of the Engineers, covered by the 60th Rifles. The demolition of the gate having been accomplished, the column forced an entrance, overcoming a strenuous opposition from the enemy's infantry and heavy artillery, which had been brought to bear on the position. I cannot express too warmly my admiration of the gallantry of all concerned in this difficult operation.

The reserve, under Brigadier Longfield, Her Majesty's 8th Regiment, composed of Her Majesty's 61st Regiment (250 men), the 4th Regiment, Rifles (450 men), the Belooch Battalion (300 men), the Jheend Rajah's Auxiliaries (300 men), and 200 of Her Majesty's 60th Rifles, who joined after the assault had been made, awaited the result of the attack, and on the columns entering the place, took possession of the posts I had previously assigned to it. This duty was ultimately performed to my entire satisfaction.

The firm establishment of the reserve rendering the assaulting columns free to act in advance, Brigadier-General Nicholson, supported by Brigadier Jones, swept the ramparts of the place from the Cashmere to the Cabul gates, occupying the bastions and defences, capturing the guns, and driving the enemy before him.

During the advance, Brigadier-General Nicholson was, to the grief of myself and the whole army, dangerously wounded; the command consequently devolved on Brigadier Jones, who, finding the enemy in great force, occupying and pouring a destructive fire from the roofs of strong and commanding houses in the city on all sides, the ramparts themselves being enfiladed by guns, prudently resolved on retaining possession of the Cabul Gate, which his troops had so gallantly won, in which he firmly established himself, awaiting the result of the operations of the other columns of occupation.

Colonel Campbell, with the column under his command, advanced successfully from the Cashmere Gate by one of the main streets beyond the "Chandnee Chouk," the central and principal street of the city, towards the Jumna Musjid, with the intention of occupying that important post. The opposition, however, which he met from the great concentration of the enemy at the Jumna Musjid and the houses in the neighbourhood—he himself, I regret to state, being wounded—satisfied him that his most prudent course was not to maintain so advanced a position with the comparatively limited force at his disposal, and he accordingly withdrew the head of his column and placed himself in communication with the reserve, a measure which had my entire approval; I having previously determined that, in the event of serious opposition being encountered in the town itself, it would be most inexpedient to commit my small force to a succession of street-fights, in which their gallantry, discipline, and organisation could avail them so little.

My present position, therefore, is that which, under such a contingency, I had resolved to occupy and establish myself in firmly, as the base of my systematic operations for the complete possession of the city. This embraces the magazine on one side, and the Cabul Gate on the other, with the Moree, Cashmere, and Water bastions and strong intermediate posts, with secure communication along the front and to the rear.

From this base I am now cautiously pressing the enemy on all points, with a view to establishing myself in a second advanced position, and I trust before many days to have it in my power to announce to the Supreme Government that the enemy have been driven from their last stronghold in the palace, fort, and streets of the city of Delhi.

Simultaneously with the operations above detailed, an attack was made on the enemy's strong position outside the city, in the suburbs of Kissengunge and Pahareepoore, with a view of driving in the rebels and supporting the main attack, by effecting an entrance at the Cabul Gate after it should be taken.

The force employed on this difficult duty I intrusted to that admirable officer Major C. Reid, commanding the Sirmoor Battalion, whose distinguished conduct I have already had occasion to bring prominently to the notice of superior authority, and who was, I much regret, severely wounded on this occasion. His column consisted of his own battalion, the Guides, and the men on duty at Hindoo Rao's (the main picquet), numbering in all about 1000, supported by the auxiliary troops of his Highness the Maharajah Rumbeer Singh, under Captain R. Lawrence.

The strength of the positions, however, and the desperate resistance offered by the enemy, withstood for a time the efforts of our troops, gallant though they were, and the combination was unable to be effected. The delay, I am happy to say, has been only temporary, for the enemy have subsequently abandoned their positions, leaving their guns in our hands.

In this attack I found it necessary to support Major Reid with cavalry and horse-artillery, both of which arms were admirably handled respectively by Brigadier Hope Grant, of Her Majesty's 9th Lancers, commanding the Cavalry Brigade, and Major H. Tombs, of the Horse Artillery, who inflicted severe punishment on the enemy, though I regret their own loss was very heavy.

The resistance of the rebels up to this time has been that of desperate men, and to this must be attributed the severe loss we have sustained, amounting proximately, so far as I am able to judge, in the absence of casualty returns, to 46 officers killed and wounded, and about 800 men. Among those of whose services the State has been deprived are many officers of distinction and merit, holding superior commands, whose places cannot be supplied; and I have specially to lament the loss which has been sustained by that splendid corps the Engineers, nine officers of that arm having fallen in the gallant performance of their duty.

Until I am in possession of reports from brigadiers and other commanding officers I shall be unable to enter more fully into the details of these operations, and I trust the circumstances under which I write will excuse any slight inaccuracies or imperfections which my despatch may exhibit.

The absence of such reports also prevents my bringing to notice the names of those officers and men who have specially distinguished themselves. This will be my grateful duty hereafter. But I cannot defer the expression of my admiration for the intrepidity, coolness, and determination of all engaged, Europeans and natives, of all arms of the service. I have, &c.,

A. Wilson, Major-General,
Commanding Field-Force.

From Major-General A. Wilson, Commanding Delhi Field-Force, to the Adjutant-General of the Army.

DELHI, *Sept*. 22.

Sir,—In continuation of my despatch of the 16th inst. I now have the honour to forward a report for the information of the Major-General commanding in the upper provinces, his Excellency the Commander-in-Chief, and the Government, of the further operations of the force under my command since that date.

During the 17th and 18th we continued to take up advanced posts in the face of considerable opposition on the part of the rebels, and not without loss to ourselves, three officers being killed, and a number of men killed and wounded. On the evening of the 19th the Burn Bastion, which had given us considerable annoyance, was surprised and captured.

On the morning of the 20th our troops pushed on and occupied the Lahore Gate, from which an unopposed advance was made on the other bastions and gateways until the whole of the defences of the city were in our hands.

From the time of our first entering the city an uninterrupted and vigorous fire from our guns and mortars was kept up on the palace, Jumna Musjid, and other important posts in possession of the rebels; and as we took up our various positions in advance, our light guns and mortars were brought forward and used with effect on the streets and houses in their neighbourhood.

The result of this heavy and unceasing bombardment, and of the steady and persevering advance of our troops, has been the evacuation of the palace by the King, the entire desertion of the city by the inhabitants, and the precipitate flight of the rebel troops—who, abandoning their camp property, many of their sick and wounded, and the greater part of their field-artillery, have fled in utter disorganisation—some 4000 or 5000 across the bridge of boats into the Doab, the remainder down the right bank of the Jumna.

The gates of the palace having been blown in, it was occupied by our troops at about noon on the 20th, and my headquarters established in it the same day.

The great diminution of our strength by losses in action during the last few days, added to the severe sickness prevailing among the troops, has prevented my immediately organising and sending a column in pursuit; but a force, under command of Lieutenant-Colonel Greathed, will march to-morrow morning towards Bolundshuhur and Allyghur to intercept the rebels, whose intentions are said to be to cross the Jumna at Muttra. My intelligence, however, I regret to say, is very defective.

The King, who accompanied the troops, it is believed, for some short distance, last night gave himself up to a party of Irregular Cavalry, whom I had sent out in the direction of the fugitives, and he is now a prisoner under a guard of European soldiers. Three of the shahzadas, who are known to have taken a prominent part in the atrocities attending the insurrection, have been this day captured by Captain Hodson, and shot on the spot.

Thus has the important duty committed to this force been accomplished, and its object attained. Delhi, the focus of rebellion and insurrection, and the scene of so much horrible cruelty, taken and made desolate; the King a prisoner in our hands; and the mutineers, notwithstanding their great numerical superiority and their vast resources in ordnance, and all the munitions and appliances of war, defeated on every occasion of engagement with our troops, are now driven with slaughter, in confusion and dismay, from their boasted stronghold.

The details of the operations have been so fully entered into in my previous despatch, and annexed reports and returns from the various commanding officers, that little remains for me to say, but to again express my unqualified approbation of the conduct and spirit of the whole of the troops, not only on this occasion, but during the entire period they have been in the field.

For four months of the most trying season of the year this force, originally very weak in number, has been exposed to the repeated and determined attacks of an enemy far outnumbering it, and supported by a numerous and powerful artillery. The duties imposed upon all have been laborious, harassing, and incessant, and notwithstanding heavy losses, both in action and from disease, have been at all times zealously and cheerfully performed.

I beg to add my most cordial concurrence in the commendations bestowed by officers commanding brigades, columns, and detachments on the officers and men named in their several reports, and I have to express my own deep obligations to those officers themselves for the valuable assistance I have at all times received from them.

To Major F. Gaitskell, who recently assumed command of the artillery in the field, consequent on Brigadier Garbett having been disabled by a wound, and to the officers and men of that distinguished arm, to whose energy and untiring zeal the successful issue of the operations is so largely attributable, I have to offer my hearty thanks. And particularly am I indebted to that excellent officer, Lieutenant-Colonel Hogge, Director of the Artillery Depôt, who volunteered his services as Commissary of Ordnance with the siege-train, through whose able superintendence of the park, and arrangements for the supply of ammunition to the batteries, our artillery was enabled to deal out the destruction which was effected; as also to Captain J. Young, Deputy Commissary, and Mr J. Stolesbury, Assistant-Commissary of Ordnance, for their exertions during the whole siege.

To Lieutenant-Colonel Baird Smith, Chief Engineer, who, in ill health and while suffering from the effects of a painful wound, devoted himself with the greatest ability and assiduity to the conduct of the difficult and important operations of the siege; to his gallant and eminently talented second, Captain A. Taylor; and to the whole of the officers and men of the Engineer Brigade, my thanks and acknowledgments are especially due for having planned and successfully carried out, in the face of extreme and unusual difficulties, an attack almost without parallel in the annals of siege operations.

To that most brilliant officer, Brigadier-General J. Nicholson, whose professional character and qualifications are so well known and appreciated, I am under the greatest obligations for the daring manner in which he led his column to the assault; and I deeply deplore that his services are for the present lost to the State.

To Brigadier Hope Grant, C. B., Commanding the Cavalry

Brigade, and to Brigadiers J. Longfield and W. Jones, C.B., commanding infantry brigades, I am deeply indebted; and I have to offer my best thanks to Colonel G. Campbell, commanding Her Majesty's 52d Light Infantry, and to that intrepid and excellent officer, Major C. Reid, of the Sirmoor Battalion, both wounded while gallantly leading columns of attack; as also to Colonel J. Jones, commanding the 1st battalion 60th Royal Rifles—a regiment which has shown a glorious example, both in its daring gallantry and its perfect discipline, to the whole force—for the ability with which he covered the advance of the assaulting columns.

I have pleasure also in bringing favourably to notice the services rendered by Lieutenant-Colonel H. P. Burn, attached as field-officer to the 1st brigade of infantry, and by Captain Seymour Blane, Her Majesty's 52d Light Infantry, major of brigade to Brigadier-General Nicholson.

Colonel J. L. Denniss, of Her Majesty's 52d Light Infantry, whom I placed in charge of the camp during the operations, is entitled to my thanks and acknowledgments for the able dispositions he made with the troops under his command for the due protection of his important charge.

To the officers of the general staff of the army, and to those of the staff of the Field-Force, my cordial acknowledgments are due for the admirable manner in which they have performed their responsible duties.

To that very distinguished officer, Brigadier-General N. B. Chamberlain, Adjutant-General of the Army, who, though still incapacitated by a severe wound previously received, proceeded to the ridge at Hindoo Rao's, and performed essential service after Major Reid had been wounded, and it became necessary to resume that position.

To Captain H. W. Norman, Assistant Adjutant-General of the Army, who on this, as on each and every occasion, has been distinguished by his gallantry, zeal, and professional ability.

To that experienced officer, Major R. S. Ewart, Deputy-Assistant-Adjutant-General, and his gallant and energetic coadjutor, Captain D. M. Stewart, Deputy Assistant Adjutant-General, who have conducted the duties of this important department with the force much to my satisfaction; and to

Captain E. B. Johnson, Assistant-Adjutant of Artillery, who volunteered to command the 24-pounder breaching battery, most ably and effectually carried out the duty assigned to him, and who rejoined my personal staff on the morning of the assault, and who has throughout these operations given me the most zealous and efficient support, I am greatly indebted for the assistance they have afforded me.

I beg also to bring very favourably to notice the officers of the Quartermaster-General's department, Captain D. C. Shute, Captain H. M. Garstin, and Captain W. S. R. Hodson, who has performed such good and gallant service with his newly-raised regiment of Irregular Horse, and at the same time conducted the duties of the Intelligence Department under the orders of the Quartermaster-General with rare ability and success; also that active and gallant officer, Lieutenant F. S. Roberts, attached to the Artillery Brigade in the capacity of Deputy Assistant Quartermaster-General.

Lieutenant-Colonel Keith Young, Judge-Advocate General, also, and his deputies, Captain T. C. Maisey and Captain H. W. Wilson, most zealously assisted me in carrying my orders.

To the officers of my personal staff—Captain C. H. Barchard, who has served with me, first as my orderly officer and subsequently as aide-de-camp, and to whose zealous and untiring exertions I am deeply indebted; to Captain J. R. Turnbull, 2d aide-de-camp, Captain R. H. D. Lowe, and Lieutenant R. C. Lowe, extra aides-de-camp, I am under great obligations for the zeal and readiness with which they on this and all other occasions have performed their duties. My thanks are also due to Major H. A. Ouvry, who attended me on the day of the assault.

For the valuable aid at all times rendered by the officers of the civil service who have been attached to the force I have to record my warm acknowledgments. Mr Hervey Greathed, agent to the Deputy-Governor, North-Western Provinces (whose subsequent sudden death I deeply lament), and Mr C. B. Saunders, both of whom attended me in action, and made themselves most useful; Sir T. Metcalfe, whose gallantry in conducting General Campbell's assaulting column through the city was conspicuous; and Mr R. W. Clifford, who was also in attendance on me, are all entitled to my thanks.

While, however, in acknowledging the services of those officers whose good fortune it was to be present at the assault, and in the action of the 14th, I have only performed a grateful duty, I should be greatly wanting if I failed to record the names of those who have previously distinguished themselves, but who, incapacitated by wounds or sickness, were unable to join in the operations of that day.

Among these I have specially to notice Brigadier St. G. D. Showers, whose cool gallantry on the numerous occasions in which he has been engaged has been conspicuous.

Also Colonel A. M. Becher, Quartermaster-General of the Army, who, though prevented by a severe wound, received in June last, from taking an active part in the field, has at all times rendered me zealous assistance.

Lieutenant-Colonel T. Seaton, C.B., of the 35th Native Infantry, attached to the force, a most valuable and experienced officer, of whose services I have been deprived owing to a wound received by him on the 23d of July.

That admirable officer, Lieutenant-Colonel Murray Mackenzie, commanding the 1st Brigade of Horse-Artillery, of whose services I have also been deprived by a wound which he received when in charge of the heavy batteries at an early stage of our operations.

That officer so distinguished in our frontier warfare, Major J. Coke, commanding the 1st Punjab Rifles, severely wounded at the head of his regiment on the 12th of August; and the gallant commander of the Guides, Captain H. D. Daly, who was very severely wounded leading a most daring charge on the enemy's guns in the action of the 19th of June.

I need not observe how largely the success and efficiency of an army depends on the regularity of its supplies. Under circumstances of peculiar difficulty, in a district the population of which has been inimical, and in which civil authority has ceased to exist, this force has, from the commencement, been kept well and sufficiently provisioned with supplies of every description, the issue of rations to the soldiers having been as regular, both in quantity and quality, as in cantonments. My warmest thanks are therefore due to Lieutenant-

Colonel W. B. Thompson, Deputy-Commissary-General, the admirable and indefatigable head of that department in the field; as also to Lieutenant T. H. Sibley, principal executive officer; to Lieutenant Waterfield, and to the other officers serving in that department.

With the medical arrangements of Superintending Surgeon E. Tritton I have every reason to be satisfied, and he is entitled to my cordial acknowledgments. At such a trying season of the year, and in a notoriously unhealthy locality, the sickness and mortality have, of course, been heavy. In addition to those sufferings from disease, the hospitals have received almost daily accessions of wounded men. The labours, therefore, of the medical department have been unceasing, notwithstanding there has not been at any time the slightest failure in the arrangements for the care and comfort of the very numerous patients.

Among those medical officers whose unwearied zeal and superior ability have come prominently before me, are—Officiating Superintendent Surgeon C. M'Kinnon, M.D., who has been in the medical charge of the 1st Brigade Horse Artillery; Surgeon J. H. Kerr Innes, 60th Royal Rifles; Surgeon J. P. Brougham, 1st Fusiliers; Surgeon E. Hare, of the 2d Fusiliers; Assistant-Surgeon J. J. Clifford, M.D., of the 9th Lancers; and Assistant-Surgeon W. F. Mactire, M.D., on the personal staff of the late Commander-in-Chief.

Credit is also due to Surgeon D. Scott, M.D., medical storekeeper.

The duties and offices of Provost-Marshal to the force have been conducted by a very deserving old non-commissioned officer, Sergeant-Major Stoud, 3d Brigade Horse Artillery, whom I recommend to favourable consideration for a commission.

The names of other non-commissioned officers deserving of a similar reward I shall have the pleasure of submitting hereafter.

I should neither be fulfilling the repeatedly-expressed wishes of the Artillery officers attached to this force, nor following the dictates of my own inclination, if I failed to acknowledge the valuable assistance which has, throughout the operations before Delhi, been most cheerfully given by the non-commissioned officers and men of her Majesty's 9th Lancers and the 6th Dragoon Guards in working the batteries. Without it, owing to the comparatively small number of artillerymen, I should have been quite unable to man the batteries efficiently, or to keep up the heavy fire which, aided by these men, I have happily been able to do. To these regiments, therefore, and to Brigadier Grant, who so readily placed a certain number of his men at my disposal for such purpose, I tender my best thanks.

It would be an omission on my part were I to pass over in silence the good services and loyal conduct of one who has already been rewarded by the Government for the friendly assistance he rendered to our army in Afghanistan—I allude to the Nawab Jan Fishan Khan, who, with his brave nephew, Sirdar Bahadoor Meer Khan, and their retainers, accompanied me from Meerut, was present at the actions on the Hindon, and has since taken part in nearly every action in which this force has been engaged.

Of the loyal services rendered to the State by the Rajah of Puttiala, which must be so well known to the Government, it may not be considered necessary for me to speak; but it is incumbent on me, in my capacity as commander of this force, to acknowledge officially the great assistance the Rajah's troops have afforded me in enabling the numerous convoys of ammunition and stores to travel in security and safety to my camp under their escort and protection.

Equally is it my duty to bring prominently to the notice of Government the admirable service performed by the Jheend Rajah and his troops, under command of Lieutenant-Colonel H. F. Dunsford. They have not only had very harassing duties to carry out in the constant escort of convoys of sick and wounded men, ammunition, &c., but they have also aided me in the field on more than one occasion, and finally participated in the assault of the city.

Lastly, I trust I may be excused if I thus publicly acknowledge the all-important and invaluable aid for which I am indebted to the Chief Commissioner of the Punjab, Sir John Lawrence, K.C.B., to whose indefatigable exertions in reinforcing me with every available soldier in the Punjab, the successful result of our operations is, I unhesitatingly pronounce, attributable, and I take this opportunity of recognising the advantage derived from the presence of the troops of his Highness the Maharajah Runbeer Sing, in alliance with the British force, the moral effect of which has been great. And although unsuccessful, I regret to say, in the actual accomplishment of that part of the operations in which the Jummoo Contingent was engaged on the 14th, I can attach no particle of blame to those troops, as I consider, under the circumstances in which they were placed, the very strong position which they had to attack, and the prolonged and determined resistance which they encountered from an enemy superior to them in number, arms, training, and experience, that they behaved, under their gallant commander, Captain R. C. Lawrence, and the other British officers serving with them, to whom my best thanks are due, as well as they could have been expected to do.—I have &c.,

A. WILSON, Major-General,
Commanding Delhi Field-Force.

NOTE Q, page 262.

THE FORMATION OF THE WUFFADAR PULTUN WAS AUTHORISED IN THE FOLLOWING EXCELLENT DEMI-OFFICIAL CIRCULAR.

About the end of April, the Chief Commissioner of the Punjab proposed that the faithful remnants of the 61st and 36th N.I., who mutinied at Jullundhur, and the 3d who mutinied at Philour, should be re-armed

This proposal has now been sanctioned by the Governor-General.

The fidelity of these men was not a matter of supposition, but of actual proof; when their corps mutinied, they remained firm.

Afterwards it was thought necessary to disarm them; since then, however, they have behaved perfectly well. Up to the moment of the mutiny at Jullundhur, some of the men protected their officers, and some guarded a portion of the treasure. Such men as these do seem now to be worthy of receiving back their arms. As yet there has been no confidence shown them, and none but nominal duties required of them ; it is now a duty we owe to these men to reward them for their fidelity.

The detachments number 255 sepoys, 26 native commissioned, and 63 non-commissioned officers.

They will be formed into a special corps, to be styled "The Wuffadar Pultun, or faithful corps," in memory of their signal fidelity at a moment of almost universal treachery. This new corps will be on the same footing as the Punjab Irregular Corps, with a commandant, second in command—adjutant, and medical officer. There will be four companies. The numbers will not be augmented. At present they will be stationed at Philour, where there are no Punjabee troops with whom they might come in collision.

The feeling between Hindostanees and Punjabees is bitter, and the Punjabees would be sure to taunt the Poorbeahs.

The commandant will be Major Innes of the 61st, and Captain Marquis of the 3d will be second in command. The commanding officer will be under the Chief Commissioner; he will have the same magisterial powers as the commanding officers of the Punjab Irregular Regiments.

When he convicts a man of offences requiring imprisonment, he inflicts the punishment and dismisses the man. If the offence is one only demanding dismissal, then the commanding officer, as a rule, will report to the Chief Commissioner beforehand. If, however, the case be emergent, he may dismiss at once, reporting afterwards ; so that there will be no lack of power in the regimental officers to enforce discipline.

The grounds on which the arms are restored, and the condition of service, will be explained to the men. Any man who may not like to join the new corps will have the option of taking his discharge.

The present experiment is an interesting and important one.

The success will much depend on the discretion of the

European officers, and upon their determination to treat the men with firmness and consideration, and to give them a fair trial. If the scheme succeeds, an effect will be produced upon the disarmed regiments, of whom there are so many in the Punjab, and who still believe that the British are bent upon their entire destruction sooner or later. It may also have some influence on the mind of Hindostanees generally, and show them that we do not wish to make the present contest a war to the death between the *White* and the *Black*, and so long as we undertake to govern Hindostan, we do not wish to proscribe Hindostanees, nor to deprive them of all chance of retrieving their reputations.

NOTE R.

Note R, page 287.

Statement of the 6 per cent. Punjab Loan.

Divisions.	Districts.	Amount of 1857-58.	Total Rupees.
Cis Sutlej States,	Umballa,	* 10.77.193 0 0	
	Ferozepore,	1.88.000 0 0	
	Loodianah,	2.43.800 0 0	
	Simla,	1.10.906 0 0	
	Thanessur,	2.38.700 0 0	18.58.599 0 0
Trans Sutlej States,	Hosheyarpore,	1.00.200 0 0	
	Jullundhur,	1.00.500 0 0	
	Kangra,	1.05.900 0 0	3.06.600 0 0
Lahore,	Umritsur,	2.12.119 0 0	
	Goojranwalla,	92.600 0 0	
	Goordaspore,	30.700 0 0	
	Lahore,	1.80.600 0 0	
	Sealkote,	† 5.78.800 0 0	10.94.819 0 0
Jhelum,	Jhelum,	48.400 0 0	
	Rawul Pindee,	27.800 0 0	
	Shahpore,	6.000 0 0	
	Goojrat,	66.700 0 0	1.48.900 0 0
Leia,	Dehra Ismail Khan,	56.866 4 0	
	Dehra Ghazee Khan,	2.500 0 0	
	Khanghur,	88.550 0 0	1.47.916 4 0
Mooltan,	Jhung,	19.480 0 0	
	Gogaira,	98.829 0 0	
	Mooltan,	1.22.683 3 6	2.40.992 3 6
Peshawur,	Peshawur,	4.19.300 0 0	4.19.300 0 0
Hissar,	Hissar,	15.917 0 0	
	Bhuttee,	35.413 0 3	51.330 0 3
		Grand Total Rs.	42.68.456 7 9

* Of this the chiefs of Puttiala, Jheend, and Nabba contributed Rs. 8.35.000.
Of this the Maharaja of Cashmere contributed Rs. 5.71.000.

Return of Killed, Wounded, and Missing, of the Delhi Field-Force, from the commencement of operations in the neighbourhood of Delhi on 30th May 1857, up to the capture of the city on the 20th September.

CORPS.	Effective Strength, Sept. 11th.	Killed.		Wounded.		Missing.	Total.
		Officers.	Men.	Officers.	Men.		
Staff,	—	4	—	9	—	—	13
Artillery,	—	4	43	23	216	—	286
Engineers,	—	3	4	19	6	—	32
H. M. 6th Dragoon Guards,	123	1	18	2	9	—	30
H. M. 9th Lancers,	391	1	26	2	64	—	93
H. M. 8th Regiment,	322	3	24	7	129	—	163
H. M. 52d Light Infantry,	302	1	18	4	73	5	101
H. M. 60th Rifles, 1st Battalion,	390	4	109	10	266	—	389
H. M. 61st Regiment,	402	2	30	7	112	4	155
H. M. 75th Regiment,	459	5	79	14	184	3	285
H. C. 1st Bengal Fusiliers,	427	3	95	11	210	—	319
H. C. 2d Bengal Fusiliers,	370	4	79	6	156	—	245
Attached to Native Corps,	—	12	—	28	—	—	—
Total,	3186	47	525	142	1425	12	2151

Abstract

Abstract of Killed, Wounded, and Missing, of the Delhi Field-Force, from 30th May to 20th September.

	Officers.	Native Officers.	Non-Commissioned Officers.	Drummers.	Rank and File.	Total.	Horses.
Killed,	47	14	80	7	865	1012	139
Wounded,	142	49	207	10	2389	2795	186
Missing,	—	—	1	—	29	30	53
Total killed, wounded, and missing,	189	63	288	17	3283	3837	378

	Europeans.	Natives.	Total.
Killed,	572	440	1012
Wounded,	1566	1229	2795
Missing,	13	17	30
Total,	2151	1686	3837

Memorandum.—Those officers who died of wounds during the siege, are included as killed, but those returned as killed of other ranks, were all killed at the time, there being no documents available to show what number of wounded soldiers died in consequence of their injuries:—

2163 officers and men were killed, wounded, and missing, prior to September 8th, on which date the batteries for the reduction of the place were opened.
327 ditto ditto from above date until morning of assault.
1170 ditto ditto in the assault on September 14th.
177 ditto ditto from September 15th, until final capture of the city on the 20th idem.

3837 Total.

LIST OF OFFICERS KILLED, DIED OF WOUNDS, OR WOUNDED, in the operations near and before Delhi, including the actions on the Hindon and at Badlee-Serai, from the 30th May 1857 to the final capture of the place on the 20th September 1857.

KILLED, OR DIED OF WOUNDS.

Brigadier-General Nicholson, commanding 4th Infantry Brigade, wounded in the assault, September 14; died of his wound, September 23.

Colonel C. Chester, Adjutant-General of the army, killed at Badlee-Serai, June 8.

Captain E. W. Russell, 54th N. I., Orderly Officer to Brigadier Wilson, at Badlee-Serai, June 8.

Captain J. W. Delamain, 56th N. I., Orderly Officer to Brigadier Wilson, at Badlee-Serai, June 8.

Captain R. C. H. B. Fagan, Artillery (wounded June 30), killed in a breaching battery, September 12.

Lieut. E. H. Hildebrand, Artillery (wounded June 30), killed in a breaching battery, September 7.

Lieut. H. G. Perkins, Artillery, in action at the Hindon, May 31.

Lieut. T. E. Dickins, Artillery, wounded July 20; died of wound, July 27.

Second Lieut. F. L. Tandy, Engineers, in the assault at the Cashmere Gate, September 14.

Second Lieut. E. R. Jones, Engineers, wounded July 18; died of wounds, July 24.

Captain T. M. Greensill, 24th Foot, Assisting Field-Engineer, accidentally shot, July 20.

Assistant-Surgeon S. Moore, 6th Dragoon Guards, wounded at the Hindon, May 31; died of wound, June 2.

Brigadier Lieut.-Colonel R. A. Yule, 9th Lancers, in the rear attack, June 19.

Lieut. W. W. Pogson, H.M. 8th Regiment, wounded July 23; mortally wounded in the breach, and died September 17.

Lieut. W. R. Webb, H.M. 8th Regiment, mortally wounded in the assault, and died September 15.

Lieut. W. H. Mountsteven, H.M. 8th Regiment (previously slightly wounded), July 9.

Lieut. J. H. Bradshaw, H.M. 52d L. I., in the assault.

Capt. F. Andrews, H.M. 60th Rifles, at the Hindon, May 30.

Ensign W. H. Napier, H.M. 60th Rifles, wounded in action at the Hindon, May 30; died of wound, June 4.

Lieut. M. A. Humphrys, 20th Regiment N. I., attached to H.M. 60th Rifles, wounded June 19; died of wound, June 20.

Ensign E. A. L. Phillips, 11th N. I., attached to H.M. 60th Rifles, slightly wounded, June 12; killed at the Bank House, September 16.

Lieut. T. Gabbett, H.M. 61st Regiment, at Nujjufghur, August 25.

Ensign S. B. Elkington, H.M. 61st Regiment, mortally wounded at Nujjufghur, August 25, and died a few days after.

Captain E. W. J. Knox, H.M. 75th Regiment, at the Flag Staff Battery, June 12.

Lieut. J. R. S. Fitzgerald, H.M. 75th Regiment, wounded slightly, June 8, at Badlee-Serai; killed in the breach, September 14.

Lieut. A. Harrison, H.M. 75th Regiment, at Badlee-Serai, June 8.

Lieut. E. V. Briscoe, H.M. 75th Regiment, in the attack on the Lahore Gate, September 18.

Lieut. W. Crozier, H.M. 75th Regiment, in the Subzee Mundee, July 18.

Major G. O. Jacob, 1st European Fusiliers, slightly wounded at Nujjufghur, August 25; killed in the assault, September 14.

Captain G. G. M'Barnet, 55th N. I., attached to 1st Fusiliers, in Kissengunge, September 14.

Lieut. E. Speke, 65th N. I., attached to 1st Fusiliers, in the assault, September 14.

Lieut. S. H. Jackson, 2d Fusiliers, in the right flank attack, June 23.

Second Lieut. D. F. Shirreff, 2d Fusiliers, mortally wounded at the capture of the Ludlow Castle Battery, August 12; died of wound, August 14.

Lieut. C. F. Gambier, 38th Light Infantry, attached to the 2d Fusiliers.

Ensign O. C. Walter, 45th N. I., attached to the 2d Fusiliers, died of sun-stroke while in action, July 18.

Ensign E. C. Wheatley, 54th N. I., attached to Sirmoor Battalion, at the main picquet, June 17.

Lieut. J. H. Browne, 33d N. I., attached to the Kumaon Battalion, August 6.

Lieut. J. Yorke, 3d N. I., attached to 4th Sikh Infantry, wounded June 30 ; died of wound, July 1.

Brevet Captain W. G. Law, 10th N. I., attached to 1st Punjab Infantry, killed July 23.

Lieut. E. J. Travers, 2d in command, 1st Coke's Rifles, slightly wounded, July 21 ; killed, August 2.

Lieut. W. H. Lumsden, Adjutant, 1st Coke's Rifles, at Nujjufghur, August 25.

Ensign J. S. Davidson, 26th N. I., attached to 2d Punjab Infantry, in the assault, September 14.

Lieut. R. P. Homfray (17th N. I.), attached to 4th Punjab Infantry, in Delhi, September 16.

Lieut. Quintin Battye, Commandant of Cavalry, Guide Corps, mortally wounded under the walls, June 9 ; died the next day.

Lieut. A. W. Murray, 42d N. I., attached to Guide Corps (previously severely wounded), in the assault, September 14.

Lieut. C. B. Bannerman (1st Bombay N. I.), attached to Beeloch Battalion, September 7.

Lieut. R. W. Alexander, 3d Regiment N. I., in the rear attack, June 19.

WOUNDED.

Brigadier-General N. B. Chamberlain, Adjutant-General of the army, July 14, severely.

Colonel A. M. Becher, Quartermaster-General of the army, June 19, severely.

Lieut. F. S. Roberts, officiating Deputy-Assistant Quartermaster-General, July 14, slightly.

Brigadier H. Garbett, C.B., Artillery, August 8, slightly.

Brigadier H. G. D. Showers, commanding 1st Infantry Brigade, August 12, severely.

Captain H. E. H. Burnside, H.M. 61st, Brigade Major, 3d Infantry Brigade, July 9 and September 14.

Lieut. F. C. Innes, 60th N. I., July 12, slightly.

Lieut.-Colonel T. Seaton, C.B., 35th N. L. I., July 23, severely.

Lieut.-Colonel R. Drought, 60th N. I., July 23, severely.

Major J. H. Campbell, Artillery, September 11, severely.

Brevet Lieut.-Colonel M. Mackenzie, Artillery, July 2, severely.
Captain E. K. Money, Artillery, July 23, severely.
Captain J. Young, Artillery, June 18, slightly.
Brevet Major H. Tombs, Artillery, June 17 and September 14.
Captain T. E. Kennion, Artillery, August 6, severely.
Captain A. Light, Artillery, June 8, slightly.
First-Lieut. A. Bunny, Artillery, July 23, slightly.
First-Lieut. H. Bishop, Artillery, June 19, slightly.
First-Lieut. G. Baillie, Artillery, August 10, slightly.
First-Lieut. A. Gillespie, Artillery, September 11, slightly.
First-Lieut. E. L. Earle, Artillery, September 11, slightly.
First-Lieut. A. H. Lindsay, Artillery, August 12, slightly.
Lieut. C. Hunter, Artillery, June 8, slightly.
Second-Lieut. J. Hills, Artillery, July 9, severely.
Second-Lieut. M. Elliott, Artillery, July 9, severely.
Second-Lieut. P. Thompson, Artillery, July 14, severely.
Second-Lieut. A. H. Davidson, Artillery, June 8, severely.
Captain E. B. Johnson, Artillery, at the Hindon, May 31, slightly.
Second-Lieut. E. Frazer, Artillery, Aug. 7, slightly.
Second-Lieut. R. F. Hare, Artillery, June 8, slightly.
Second-Lieut. H. Chichester, Artillery, July 18, slightly.
Lieut. and Riding-Master S. Budd, Artillery, Sept. 8, slightly.
Assistant-Surgeon W. W. Ireland, Artillery, August 25, at Nujjufghur, dangerously.
Lieut.-Colonel R. Baird Smith, Engineers (Chief Engineer), September 12, slightly.
Lieut. W. W. H. Greathed, Engineers, September 14, in the assault, very severely.
Lieut. J. T. Walker, Bombay Engineers, July 14, severely.
Lieut. F. R. Maunsell, Engineers, August 12 and September 14.
Lieut. J. G. Medley, Engineers, September 14, severely.
Lieut. P. Salkeld, Engineers, September 14, dangerously.
Lieut. E. Walker, Engineers, September 14, slightly.
Lieut. G. T Chesney, Engineers (Brigade Major), September 14, severely.
Lieut. W. E. Warrand, Engineers, September 14, dangerously.
Lieut. H. A. Brownlow, Engineers, September 14, dangerously.
Lieut. M. G. Geneste, Engineers, July 18, slightly.
Lieut. J. St J. Hovenden, Engineers, September 14, severely.
Lieut. Pemberton, Engineers, September 14, severely.
Lieut. A. E. Perkins, Engineers, June 17, slightly.
Second-Lieut. J. N. Champlain, Engineers, June 17, slightly.

Second-Lieut. R. B. C. Pemberton, Engineers, September 14, slightly.

Second-Lieut. P. Murray, Engineers, September 10, slightly.

Second-Lieut. H. A. L. Carnegie, Engineers, July 14, slightly.

Ensign (local) L. Gustavinski, Punjab Sappers, September 14, severely.

Ensign (local) C. Anderson, Punjab Sappers, September 14, slightly.

Captain C. P. Rosser, H.M. 6th Dragoon Guards, September 14, dangerously.

Lieut. A. A. de Bourbel, H.M. 6th Dragoon Guards, at the Hindon, May 30, severely.

Captain the Hon. A. H. A. Anson, H.M. 84th Regiment, attached to H.M. 9th Lancers, September 14, slightly.

Lieut. B. Cuppage, 6th Light Cavalry, attached to H.M. 9th Lancers, September 14, slightly.

Lieut. J. Watson, 1st Punjab Cavalry, September 14, slightly.

Lieut. H. H. Gough, 3d Light Cavalry, attached to Hodson's Horse, September 14, slightly.

Brevet Lieut.-Colonel J. C. Brooke, H.M. 8th Regiment, September 14, severely.

Captain E. G. Daniel, H.M. 8th Regiment, July 9, severely.

Brevet Major R. Baynes, H.M. 8th Regiment, September 14, dangerously.

Brevet Captain D. Beere, H.M. 8th Regiment, September 14, severely.

Brevet Captain E. N. Sandilands, H.M. 8th Regiment, August 10 and September 14, slightly.

Lieut. G. F. Walker, H.M. 8th Regiment, September 14, in the assault, severely.

Lieut. W. F. Metze, H.M. 8th Regiment, September 14, slightly.

Colonel G. Campbell, H.M. 52d Light Infantry, September 14, in the assault, slightly.

Captain J. A. Bayley, H.M. 52d Light Infantry, September 14, in the assault, severely.

Lieut. W. Atkinson, H.M. 52d Light Infantry, September 14, in the assault, slightly.

Ensign T. Simpson, H.M. 52d Light Infantry, August 16, slightly.

Captain H. F. Williams, H.M. 60th Rifles, June 19, severely.

Captain C. Jones, H.M. 60th Rifles, June 23, severely.

Captain G. C. H. Waters, H.M. 60th Rifles, August 7, slightly; September 14, severely.

Lieut. H. P. Eaton, H.M. 60th Rifles, September 10, dangerously.

Lieut. J. D. Dundas, H.M. 60th Rifles, June 19, slightly.
Lieut. H. G. Deedes, H.M. 60th Rifles, June 12, slightly.
Lieut. P. J. Curtis, H.M. 60th Rifles, June 12, slightly; September 14, severely.
Lieut. M'Gill, H.M. 60th Rifles, June 19, slightly.
Ensign W. G. Furle, H.M. 60th Rifles, August 10, severely.
Ensign A. C. Heathcote, H.M. 60th Rifles, June 17, slightly.
Surgeon J. H. K. Innes, H.M. 60th Rifles, May 30, slightly.
Captain W. E. D. Deacon, H.M. 61st Regiment, September 14, severely.
Lieut. T. M. Moore, H.M. 61st Regiment, September 14, slightly.
Lieut. W. H. W. Pattoun, H.M. 61st Regiment, July 18, severely; died of dysentery at Simla in November.
Lieut. A. C. Young, H.M. 61st Regiment, September 14, severely.
Lieut. C. J. Griffiths, H.M. 61st Regiment, July 9, severely.
Lieut. T. B. Hutton, H.M. 61st Regiment, July 9, slightly.
Lieut. R. Hutton, H.M. 61st Regiment, August 10, severely.
Ensign E. B. Andros, H.M. 61st Regiment, July 9, slightly.
Lieut.-Colonel C. Herbert, H.M. 75th Regiment, June 8 and September 14, slightly.
Captain T. C. Dunbar, H.M. 75th Regiment, June 8, slightly.
Captain A. Chancellor, H.M. 75th Regiment, June 8, slightly; died of wound at Kussowlie.
Captain R. Dawson, H.M. 75th Regiment, June 8, dangerously.
Captain R. Freer, H.M. 27th Regiment, attached to H.M. 75th Regiment, September 14, in the assault, slightly.
Lieut. and Adjutant R. Barter, H.M. 75th Regiment, June 8, severely.
Lieut. C. R. Rivers, H.M. 75th Regiment, June 8 and July 14, slightly; since dead of cholera.
Lieut. E. Armstrong, H.M. 75th Regiment, Sept. 14, slightly.
Lieut. G. C. N. Faithfull, H.M. 75th Regiment, July 14, slightly.
Lieut. C. M. Pym, H.M. 75th Regiment, June 8, slightly.
Ensign R. Wadeson, H.M. 75th Regiment, Sept. 14, severely.
Ensign Dayrell, 58th N. I., attached to H.M. 75th Regiment, September 14, severely.
Paymaster D. F. Chambers, H.M. 75th Regiment, September 14, slightly.
Assistant-Surgeon S. A. Lightgow, H.M. 75th Regiment, June 8, slightly.
Colonel J. Welchman, 1st Fusiliers, June 23, dangerously.
Captain S. Greville, 1st Fusiliers, June 8, at Badlee-Serai, slightly; August 12, before Delhi; September 14, in the assault.

Captain E. Brown, 1st Fusiliers, June 17, dangerously.
Lieut. H. M. Wemyss, 1st Fusiliers, September 14, severely.
Lieut. J. W. Daniell, 1st Fusiliers, July 14, severely.
Lieut. Butter, 1st Fusiliers, September 14, in the assault, slightly.
Lieut. E. A. C. Lambert, 1st Fusiliers, September 14, slightly.
Lieut. A. G. Owen, 1st Fusiliers, August 12, slightly; September 14, severely.
Second-Lieut. N. Ellis, June 8, at Badlee-Serai, slightly.
Captain J. P. Caulfield, 3d Regiment N. I., attached to 1st Fusiliers, September 14, slightly.
Captain W. Graydon, 16th Grenadiers, attached to 1st Fusiliers, September 14, severely.
Lieut. E. H. Woodcock, 55th N. I., attached to 1st Fusiliers, September 14, severely.
Lieut. A. Elderton, 2d Fusiliers, September 14, severely.
Lieut. C. R. Blair, 2d Fusiliers, June 30, dangerously.
Lieut. J. T. Harris, 2d Fusiliers, June 27, severely.
Captain J. C. Hay, 60th N. I., attached to 2d Fusiliers, September 14, dangerously.
Captain D. Kemp, 5th Regiment N. I., attached to 2d Fusiliers, July 9, severely.
Lieut. F. N. Walker, 60th N. I., attached to 2d Fusiliers, July 18 and September 14.
Major C. Reid, 10th N. I., Commandant Sirmoor Battalion, September 14, in Kissengunge, severely.
Lieut. D. B. Lockhart, 7th N. I., attached to Sirmoor Battalion, severely.
Lieut. S. Ross, 9th N. I., attached to Sirmoor Battalion, July 14, slightly; since dead of cholera.
Lieut. A. Tulloch, 20th N. I., attached to Sirmoor Battalion, July 14.
Lieut. H. D. E. W. Chester, 36th N. I., attached to Sirmoor Battalion, July 14, slightly.
Lieut. A. H. Eckford, 69th N. I., attached to Sirmoor Battalion, July 9, slightly.
Captain H. F. M. Boisragon, second in command Kumaon Battalion, severely.
Lieut. A. B. Temple, 49th N. I., attached to Kumaon Battalion, August 6, slightly.
Lieut. C. F. Packe, 4th Regiment N. I., attached to 4th Sikh Infantry, June 30, severely.
Lieut. F. H. Jenkins, 57th N. I., attached to 4th Sikh Infantry, September 14, severely.

Lieut. A. Pullan, 36th N. I., attached to 4th Sikh Infantry, July 9, severely.

Major J. Coke, 10th N. I., commanding 1st Punjab Infantry, "Coke's Rifles," August 12, severely.

Lieut. C. J. Nicholson, 31st N. I., acting Commandant 1st Punjab Infantry, September 14, severely.

Lieut. H. T. Pollock, 35th Light Infantry, attached to 1st Punjab Infantry, July 14, very severely.

Lieut. T. M. Shelley, 11th N. I., attached to 1st Punjab Infantry, September 14, slightly.

Ensign (local) C. Prior, attached to 11th N. I., September 14, slightly.

Captain G. W. G. Green, Commandant 2d Punjab Infantry, September 14, slightly.

Lieut. Frankland, second in command, September 14, severely.

Captain H. D. Daly, 1st Bombay Fusiliers, Commandant Guide Corps, June 19, severely.

Lieut. T. G. Kennedy, officiating Commandant Guide Cavalry, June 12, severely.

Lieut. R. H. Shebbeare, 60th N. I., attached to Guide Corps, July 14, twice slightly.

Lieut. C. W. Hawes, Adjutant, attached to Guide Corps, July 14, slightly.

Lieut. E. E. B. Bond, 57th N. I., attached to Guide Corps, September 14, severely.

Lieut. A. W. Murray, 42d Light Infantry, attached to Guide Corps, June 23, slightly; July 9, severely.

Ensign O. J. Chalmers, 3d N. I., attached to Guide Corps, July 5, severely.

Lieut. H. de Brett, 57th N. I., attached to Guide Corps, July 14, slightly.

LIST OF OFFICERS AND OTHERS KILLED OR WOUNDED in other parts of the Punjab and the Meerut Division.

AT MEERUT, *May* 10, 1860.

Lieut.-Colonel J. Finnis, 11th N. I., killed.

Captain Macdonald, 20th N. I., killed.

Captain Taylor, 20th N. I., killed.
Lieut. Henderson, 20th N. I., killed.
Lieut. Pattle, 20th N. I., killed.
Mrs Macdonald, 20th N. I., killed.
Mrs Chambers, 11th N. I., killed.
Veterinary Surgeon Phillips, 3d Light Cavalry, killed.

At DELHI, *May* 11.

Simon Fraser, Esq., C. S. Commissioner, killed in the Palace.
—— Hutchinson, Esq., C. S. Magistrate, killed in the Palace.
Captain Douglas, Commandant of Palace Guards, killed in the Palace.
Rev. M. J. Jennings, Chaplain, killed in the Palace.
Miss Jennings, killed in the Palace.
Miss Clifford, killed in the Palace.
Mr Nixon, Chief Clerk to the Commissioner, killed at the Calcutta Gate.
Lieut.-Colonel Ripley, 54th N. I., mortally wounded at the Cashmere Gate, died in Cantonments.
Captain R. M. Smith, 54th N. I., killed at the Cashmere Gate.
Captain C. Barrowes, 54th N. I., killed at the Cashmere Gate.
Lieut. Edwards, 54th N. I., killed at the Cashmere Gate.
Lieut. Waterfield, 54th N. I., killed at the Cashmere Gate.
Surgeon Dopping, 54th N. I., killed at the Cashmere Gate.
Lieut. Butler, 54th N. I., wounded at the Cashmere Gate, and murdered in a Goojur village.
Lieut. Osborne, 54th N. I., wounded at the Cashmere Gate; escaped to Meerut.
Captain Gordon, 74th N. I., killed at the Cashmere Gate.
Lieut. Reveley, 74th N. I., killed at the Cashmere Gate.
Lieut. J. D. Smith, 74th N. I., killed at the Cashmere Gate.
Lieut. G. D. Willoughby, killed in a Goojur village.
Conductor Scully, killed in the magazine.
Conductor Crow, killed in the magazine.
Sergeant Edwards, killed in the magazine.

At JULLUNDHUR, *June* 6.

Major Macmullen, 6th Light Cavalry, wounded slightly.
Lieut. F. J. S. Bagshawe, 36th N. I., mortally wounded.
Ensign Bates, 36th N. I., severely.
Captain Basden, 61st N. I., severely.

Ensign Hawkins, 61st N. I., severely.
Ensign Durnford, 61st N. I., subsequently died.

AT JHELUM, *July* 7.

Captain Spring, H. M. 24th, killed.
Colonel Ellice, H. M. 24th, severely wounded.
Lieut. Streatfield, H. M. 24th, wounded.
Lieut. Chichester, H. M. 24th, wounded.
Mr Scott, C. E., a volunteer, wounded.

AT SEALKOTE, *July 9th.*

Brigadier F. Brind, C.B., killed.
Superintending Surgeon Graham, killed.
Dr J. Graham, Medical Storekeeper, killed.
Captain Bishop, 46th N. I., killed.
Rev. J. Hunter and family, killed.
Lieut. Prinsep, 4th Cavalry, wounded.

And besides these,—
Ens. Chalmers, attached to Mooltanee Horse, September 25.
Mr Thompson, extra Assistant-Commissioner, a volunteer with 17th Irregular Cavalry, severely, September 25.
Major Redmond, H. M. 61st Regiment, wounded at Ferozepore, May 14.
Veterinary Surgeon Nelson, killed at Ferozepore, August 19.
Major Spencer, 26th N. I., at Mean Meer, July 30.
Mr L. Berkeley, extra Assistant-Commissioner at Gogaira, September 23.

GLOSSARY

OF

WORDS USED IN THE COURSE OF THE NARRATIVE.

Bagh ....a garden; *Ram Bagh,* a sacred garden at Umritzur; *Koodseea Bagh,* a garden outside the walls of Delhi.

Bang ....an intoxicating decoction from hemp.

Bazaar ....a market-place; *Sudder Bazaar,* the chief market of a town or station.

Bearer ....a native servant; also a carrier of a palanquin or doolee.

Bhai ....a brother; *Bhai-bund,* a kinsman, a comrade.

Bhistee............a water-carrier.

Budm'ash ....a man with a questionable mode of living; a scoundrel; from *bud,* bad; and *m'ash,* livelihood.

Bukree-eed......a very important Mohammedan festival, commemorating the offering of a *calf* by Abraham in the place of his son *Ishmael,* and evidently an Ishmaelite corruption of the Scriptural narrative of the offering of the ram in the stead of Isaac; from *Bukree,* calf; and *eed,* festival.

Burkandaz ......an armed policeman; a matchlock-man; from *burk,* lightning; and *andaz,* throwing.

Charpoy ....a bed; from *char,* four; and *pai,* feet.

Chit or Chitti...a letter or note.

Chup'attee ......a thin pancake, made of unleavened meal, the ordinary food of natives.

Chuprassee ......a messenger—from wearing a badge, *chuprass.*

Coolee... ....a labourer, an inferior carrier.

Cutch'erry ......a court of justice; a civilian's office.

D'AK ....the post; mode of conveying letters; also a relay of horses, or bearers on a journey.
DEEN ....religion.
DOAB ....a country lying between two rivers; from *do*, two, and *ab*, water.
DOOLEE ....a litter for carrying sick or travellers.
DURWAZAH ......a gate of a house or city.
FERINGHEE........a European; apparently a corruption of "Frank," the distinctive name for Europeans among Mohammedans during the Crusades.
FAQEER ....a religious mendicant—a class of rogues.
GHAZEE ....a Mohammedan martyr for his faith.
GOLANDAZ.........a native artilleryman; from *gol*, a ball; and *andaz*, throwing.
GOOJUR ....a race of Hindoos of very low caste, professedly cattle-feeders (from *gao*, a cow); but practically thieves and robbers.
GAREE ....a native cart.
HAVILDAR.........a native non-commissioned officer, corresponding to our sergeant.
HOOKAH............a native pipe.
JAGEERDAR ......a landholder on feudal tenure.
JEMADAR ....a native commissioned officer, corresponding to our lieutenant.
JHEEL...............a marsh, or shallow lake.
JUNGLE ....a dense wilderness.
KHAN ....a chief, or head of a clan.
KOTWAL............the head of the police in a town or city.
KOTWALLEE ......the office of the Kotwal, the chief police court.
LOOT ....plunder.
LOTAH ....a drinking vessel.
MAHARAJAH ......"Great Rajah," the highest Hindoo title.
MOHURRUN ......one of the greatest Mohammedan feasts.
MUNDEE............a market; *Subzee Mundee*, the vegetable market.
MUND OR MAUND } ......an Indian weight, equivalent to about 80 lb. English.
MUSJID ....a mosque; *Jumma Musjid*, the chief mosque.
NAIK ....a native non-commissioned officer, corresponding to our corporal.
NUDDEE............a river, or brook.
NULLAH ....a water-course, a dry bed of a river, a drain.
NAWAB ....a Mohammedan title.
PANDEES ....the distinctive title of a particular caste of Brahmins. From the circumstances of the first two sepoys who were hanged at Barrackpore, both belonging to this class, the term began to be generally used as designating a "mutineer."

Poorbeah.........literally means a man from the East (from *Poorub,* "East") *i. e.* from the east of the holy river, the Ganges, including Oude and Behar, from whence the mass of our Hindostanee troops came.

Punjab............the land containing five rivers; *Panj* or *Panch,* five, and *ab,* water.

Rajah............a Hindoo title.

Ressala............a troop of horse.

Salaam............health; a form of salutation.

Shah-zada......son of a King, a prince.

Sepoys............native infantry soldiers.

Sowar............a trooper of irregular cavalry, or police.

Subahdar.........the highest native commissioned officer, corresponding with our captain.

Syce..............a native groom.

Thana............a district police station.

Thanadar......the chief police officer of a district.

Zamindar.........a landholder, a farmer.

INDEX.

INDEX.

THE END.